Yoga inVision 10

I0140373

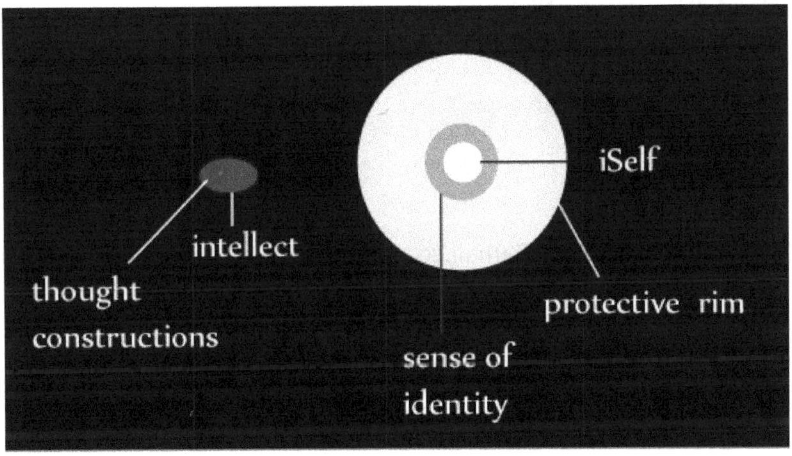
iSelf
intellect
thought
constructions
protective rim
sense of
identity

iSelf and sense of identity escaped from influence of intellect, which shrinks due to lack of energy supply from sense of identity. The identity is centralized on iSelf. It has an expanded protective rim. It is focused on iSelf.

Michael Beloved

Shiva Art:	Sir Paul Castagna
Illustrations:	Author

Correspondence:
Michael Beloved
19311 SW 30th Street
Miramar FL 33029
USA

Email: axisnexus@gmail.com
              michaelbelovedbooks@gmail.com

Paperback ISBN: 9781942887263
eBook ISBN: 9781942887270
LCCN: 2020903729

Cover:
- Rishi Singh Gherwal, teacher of Arthur Beverford, who was the first teacher to instruct the author in postures and third eye meditation. Rishi demonstrates a subtle body agnisara abdomen elimination practice.

Table of Contents

INTRODUCTION

This is the tenth of the Yoga inVision series. It relates experiences and practices done from September to October, 2011. These give beginners ideas of the physical, psychological and spiritual experiences one may have when doing asana postures, pranayama breath-infusion and *pratyahar* sensual energy withdrawal. Beyond that is higher yoga, which Patañjali named the *samyama* procedures. He defined *samyama* as a combination of *dharana* deliberate focus, *dhyana* spontaneous focus and *samadhi* continuous spontaneous focus. During practice, these progress one into the other. If one is expert at *pratyahar* sensual energy withdrawal, one may graduate to *dharana* which is deliberate focus of the attention to a higher concentration force or person. As soon as one masters *dharana* one may slip into *dhyana* which is an effortless focus on a higher concentration force or person. Once you practice *dhyana*, *samadhi* happens as the continuous effortless focus on a higher concentration force or person.

Many persons on a spiritual path feel that they can construct a process as they advance. This idea denotes failure. After all, if the supernatural and spiritual environment, is not already there, no one can create it now. It is either there or it is not. For instance, if one intends to moves to a different country, then of course one will fail if the country intended does not exist. It has to be there prior. Similarly, what you aim for as spiritual life, must be there already, or one will find that the aspiration is incorrect. This is why I speak of a concentration force or person. I could have said concentration person or divine person, or God. I did not because I do not know how anyone's spiritual path will develop.

One may leave an island in the safest boat and still the vessel may sink. One should keep one's mind open and be willing to work with fate. In spiritual development, there is providence too. What one desires to have one may not achieve. What one wishes to see may never appear.

These Yoga inVision journals show how sporadic my course of yoga was. This is after years of practice. It gives some idea of what to expect. Once you get through the lower yoga practice, you will see advancement in a more stable way but it may be incremental, accruing little by little, with bright flashes here and there.

Part 1

***Nadis* Cleared**

During exercises, kundalini did not rise as frequently as before, instead it remained anchored at the base chakra. The *nadis* were infused with breath energy but they lacked the shock energy from kundalini.

However, this is a good development in the sense that it proves that the *nadis* are cleared and are staying cleared and do not require the shock charge from kundalini to be cleared. Initially in kundalini yoga, the energy moves up the spine, through the central channel which is called the *sushumna nadi*.

After regular practice for years, one can induce kundalini to go into the tiny *nadis* which are throughout the subtle body. After this is done for some time, those channels may remain cleared so that when there is breath infusion, the energy goes into the *nadis* promptly even without taking help from the power of kundalini.

Kundalini rose from the base chakra to the navel. This is different to the navel chakra which is on the spine. It is different to the navel chakra which spreads from the spine frontwards into the body. This is the navel itself.

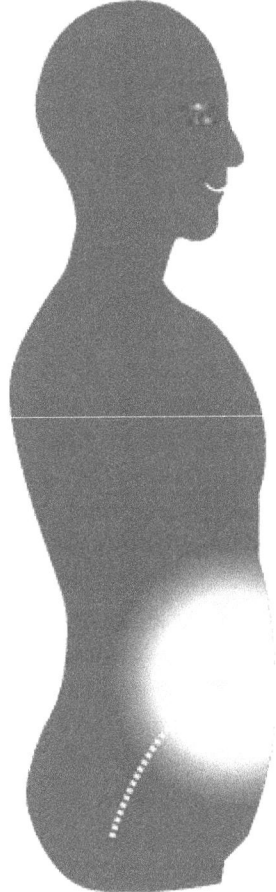

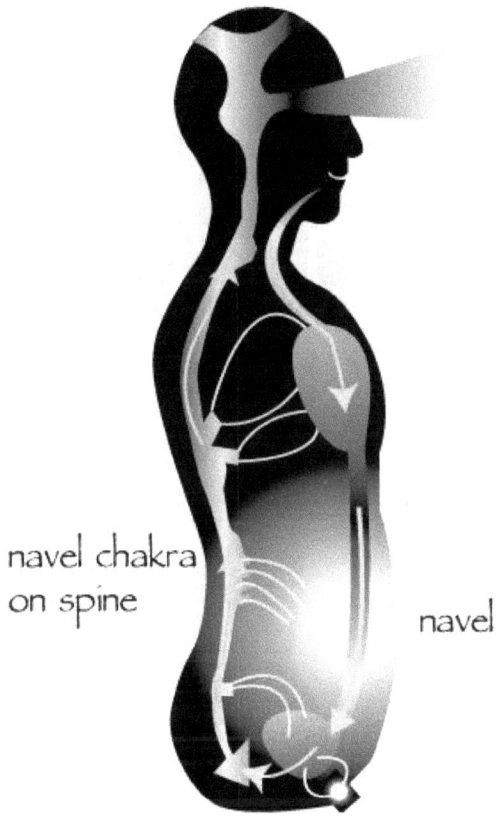

navel chakra
on spine

navel

When kundalini spread from the base to the navel, it took the shape of a yellow-white flame which had a cooling feeling but which looked like a fire.

After doing the breathing for some time, kundalini aroused again but it rose with full distribution because of the *nadi* clearance which was present. It traveled evenly upwards and moved into the forearms and hands.

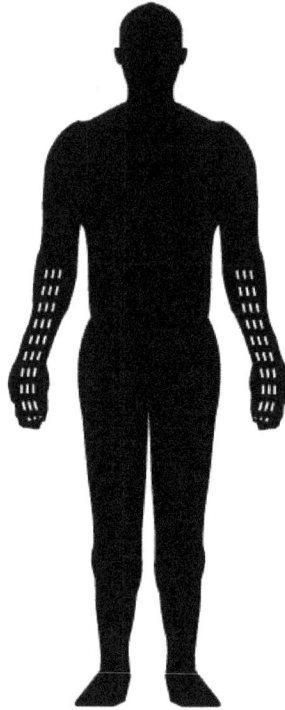

Buying a Few Seconds of Life

Last night I got in touch with a few persons whom I knew while I was in the Hare Krishna temple system. These persons were married early on. They separated because the man acquired another woman. His wife did not agree to their being in a polygamist situation.

As we conversed the lady turned to me and asked if I had additional children. I told her I did not. She smiled and looked at her husband who started a second batch of children with his second wife, for whom he separated from this lady.

I remarked, "It is okay to begin families, even on one's dying bed but if one has to use the time for spiritual practice, then as an economic move, one cannot do so because there will not be sufficient time to maintain a family and complete the practice. Most of all there is the issue of obligation to the yoga guru or spiritual master."

In this life, as soon as one is born one becomes obligated to the family from which the body was derived. That is the first obligation which no one can bypass. That presses every baby from the first breath. In addition, other obligations are formed. For instance, when one attends school one forms friendships. There is obligation to friends which may develop into life-long commitments. For me I was lucky. From about 14 years of age, I travelled much. I did not have much obligations to friends because I always had to move to another location. But then another thing happens which is that one develops obligations because of sexual needs. One associates just to get sexual proximity and without knowing it at the time, one signs an invisible document with fate, to be responsible for whatever sexual engagement one participates in.

In adult years, one can look back and laugh at the whole thing, about how stupid and naive one was in youth and how one thought that sex was enjoyment; that it was free and pleasant. It is like when one takes a large loan for a palatial house but for some reason one did not read the mortgage. When one is unable to pay, one is evicted. They confiscate whatever money and assets one has. They sent one away penniless.

Suppose I was to get a young lady to be a wife and begin a family all over again. What will happen? How will the obligation to my yoga gurus be serviced? How will I prepare for death of my body?

This body is beyond sixty years of age? How long will it last? Ten years? Ten days? Who knows? Cruel Fate does not care. It will take this body when it is convenient for it to do so. Even to kill this body one needs assistance from fate. Sometimes someone wants the body to die and fate objects. Sometimes a man wants to buy a few seconds of life and fate willfully kills the body any way. What will fate gain by not allowing an old man to live for say another five minutes. But fate does not care. It runs the concourse of life with no regard for anybody.

I taught yoga for some years. One difference I find between me and others is that I feel obligated to yoga gurus. Other people do not care about a guru, what to speak of respecting or feeling obligated. I feel obligated. I feel that I must reserve whatever time I can for yoga techniques.

Sense of Identity Reform

In inSelf Yoga™ there is no facility for destroying the sense of identity or eliminating it as there is in other systems. The reason for this is simple. In this yoga a fact is faced, which is that one cannot destroy something which was antecedent to one's objective consciousness.

In our position we can destroy a log of wood by burning it. We may destroy a liquid by evaporating it but in all cases, such destructions are partial only since really what we do is to displace a substance from one location into another.

As soon as I sat to meditate this morning, I noticed naad sound. This happened without having to look for it or remind myself to locate and fuse into it. That is good. In meditation you begin many parts of the practice by making efforts but eventually if you progress, some aspects happen spontaneously. This is due to change of habit and the psyche cooperating for the achievement.

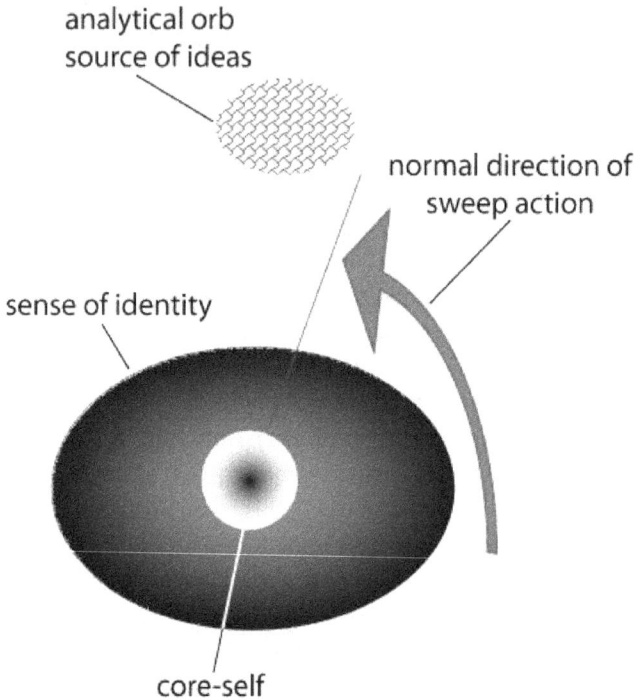

As I attuned to naad, I noticed a sweeping action in a counterclockwise direction in the sense of identity psychic organ. I realized that this action was a check to see if the intellect had information in the form of memories, sensual ideas or images. I immediately arrested the sweep and brought it to the naad. I moved the sweep about 90 degrees back to the right side of the head where naad sound was heard.

After this for about three minutes there was no action in the sense of identity. Then another sweeping action began. I arrested that and brought it to naad.

This meant that the sense of identity which surrounds the coreSelf, has an automatic function to check with the intellect for information. Once the information is procured, ideas are forcibly presented to the core which in turn becomes occupied with the information. Hence if this tendency of the sense of identity is checked, the coreSelf would be freed to comply with Patanjali's instruction for a vrittis-less mind space.

Kundalini Curl

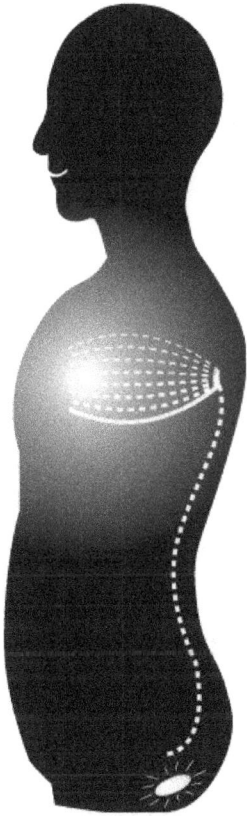

During exercises, kundalini rose many times. In one arousal it went into the heart chakra on the spine. It burst on the chest side of the spine going to the left and right in a flat configuration. During another arousal kundalini electrified the center of the body. It went into the throat. I applied the neck lock which constricted the throat. The kundalini energy formed into a bubble which enlarged into the throat since the neck lock prevented it from going any further through the neck.

When I sat to meditate, I noticed naad. I did not forget it. I did not remind myself to look and be attentive to it. This happens in some meditations where one is immediately aware of naad even without thinking of it. In other meditations, one may forget naad for five, ten or fifteen minutes even after one sits to meditate. Then suddenly one realizes that one did not connect with it. One wasted time. Or one was distracted by a thought energy which one observed in the mental chamber.

After hearing naad, I looked to see its location, if it was on the left or right, up or down. I noticed it on the right but it was not in its usual position which is near the right ear. It was not sourced from the same place which is outside the right ear, outside the psyche. It was instead inside the psyche. It was high up in the back-right side of the subtle head. When I tried to reach the source point, I realized that I could not because naad was in another dimension. To double check its location, I listened on the left side and noticed that naad was absent there.

It was projected into my psyche from a place which I could not access, like if someone can be located and not be located, like a shadow which is alive, which is real but which one cannot touch or handle in any way. Observing that this was the situation of naad, I decided to keep in touch with it, and continue the meditation.

I looked into the frontal part of the subtle head. Kundalini pushed itself into the head as an energy flow which came through the front of the neck and which flowed through the front of the head, around the intellect (intellect) and then curled backwards. I moved above the intellect and remained there but I was particular to keep in touch with naad.

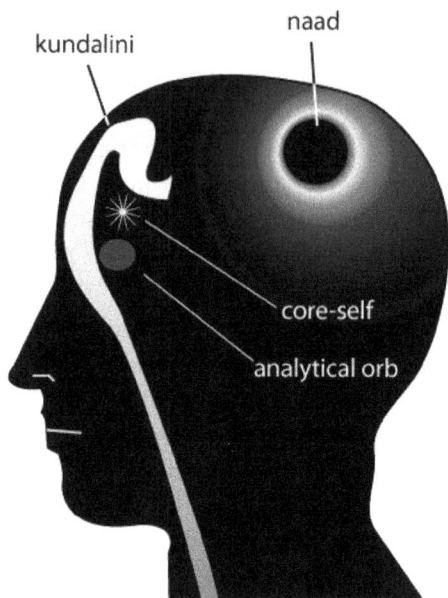

kundalini

naad

core-self

analytical orb

Balance in Kundalini

During meditation kundalini rose as usual. It ascended evenly on both sides of the trunk, on the right and left. Usually kundalini rises with more intensity on one side than the other. Sometimes it ascends on one side only and does not rise on the other. This is quite natural because perfect balance does not mean that one aspect equally matches the other.

For instance, one lung, the right one, is larger than the other. One side of the body is usually more adept at making certain actions than the other. One eye may have a vision ability which is different to the other.

When kundalini rises more on one side than on the other, the yogi should take note of it. For that matter any movement of kundalini should be observed. Psychic sensitivity is a must in yoga practice. A person who does yoga and who is not aware of the movements and operations of the subtle body during sleep for instance, really has a task before him. He must develop the required sensitivity. If one is insensitive so many things will happen which one will be unaware of.

There is nothing more mysterious than confidence in ignorance, in not knowing, in not being sensitive. If one is not aware of something which is evident, one will be confident only in the fact that whatever it is, it is not there. One's confidence will be applied to ignorance.

Yoga requires high psychic sensitivity so that the slightest movement in consciousness, the slightest shift, is noted. When I sat to meditate, I realized that Rishi Singh Gherwal left a message in the psyche. It read this:

"Why are the diagrams not presented?"

That was in reference to two diagrams which he drew in thin air yesterday in my head. He said I should publish these for the benefit of others. These are of the difference between the energy flow in the thighs and groin areas in an ordinary subtle body and in a yoga siddha subtle body.

Normal Psyche   yoga siddha psyche

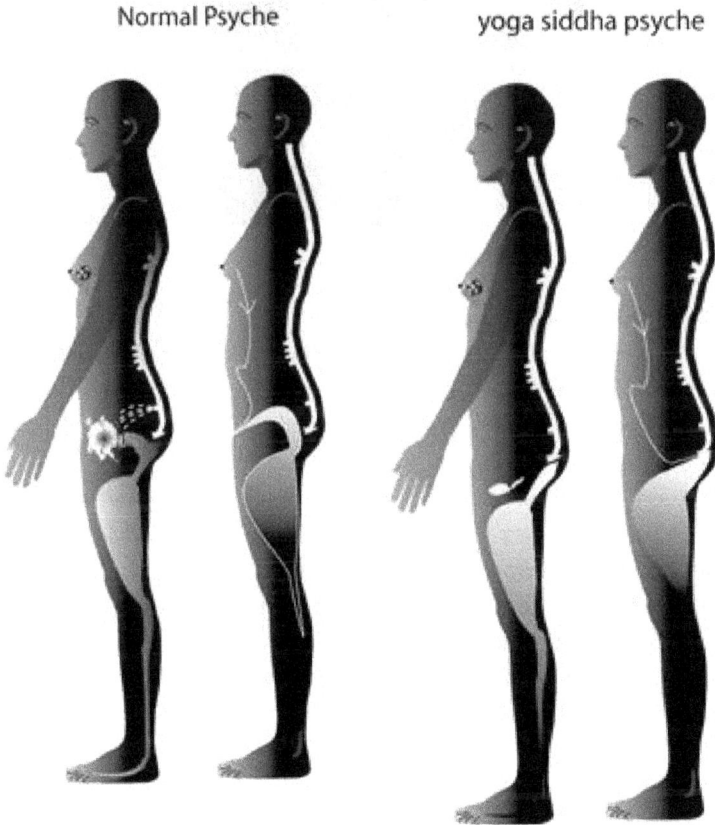

When I sat to meditate, naad sound was in the back top of the head. I went towards it but it was not located in a way where I could enter it. I went to the chakra at the back top of the head. I stayed there listening to naad which was like it was there and not there, like something which has a location and still cannot be targeted.

Kundalini punched through the back top of the head during the exercises. As soon as I sat to meditate, I perceived a shaft of kundalini energy going through that chakra. I entered the shaft and listened to naad from there. After fifteen minutes, I looked forward towards the third eye. I saw hazy orange-colored light in a rectangular cloud shape.

What was of interest though was that there was a bead energy, like a tiny orb, in the sense of identity. It had an interest in getting ideas and images from the intellect which was nowhere to be seen.

I realized then and there that this little orb was the switch which takes a yogi out of blank meditation and which invokes the intellect to produce images. I will have to identify this orb at another time. It should be controlled. When I saw it, it was like a polished stone about half inch in one direction and about quarter inch in the other direction in the form of an oval. Soon after I saw it, it disappeared.

Two Psychic Organs for Control

Patañjali system of meditation culminates in various types of *samadhi* or transcendence consciousness which he described in the *Yoga Sutras*. However, to experience these states, one must bring the mind into a blank condition by some means.

After that one must remain in that blankness consciously by some means. *Patañjali* listed five disturbances which are hostile to the blank condition.

- correct perception
- flawed perception
- imagination
- sleep
- memory

There are two organs which process these negative aspects. These are:

- intellect
- kundalini lifeForce

Hence, if one can change the way these organs function, one would comply with Patanjali's request for a meditative state which is free of those five aspects.

Kundalini controls sleep. It is the only psychic organ which has total control over sleep. The intellect controls correct and flawed perception, in addition to imagination and memory.

Memory is a special aspect but it cannot reach the coreSelf directly. Its only access to the core is through the intellect. If the intellect is controlled, memory is automatically made powerless according to the degree of control exhibited by the yogi.

Patañjali described the blank state of mind as being the same condition which one experiences when an idea vanishes in the mind and just before another idea emerges. There is a momentary blank spot at that time. *Patañjali* referred students to that blank condition as a sample of the required state.

There is however a problem with this idea in that usually the mind operates at such a speed that one cannot observe the blank pause which occurs between a vanishing idea and a newly-emerging one.

Imagine a rapid wheel which suddenly rotates in the opposite direction. If its movement is fast, one will not see when it stops rotating in one direction to switch to the other. There must be a zero-acceleration moment but unless one uses a time-motion video, one cannot see the zero condition.

It is the same with the mind. The yogi must develop a way of either increasing the rate of perception or slowing the movement of the mind when it creates ideas. Then he perceives the blank spot between the termination of an old idea and initiation of a new one.

Patanjali's idea is that the mind should remain in the blank condition for extended periods, for more than a moment. When the yogi masters that, there will be various types of *samadhi* perceptions and insights. Some are described in the *Yoga Sutras*.

Thinking-Energy Response Switch

There is a thinking-energy response mechanism in the subtle body. It operates in an impulsive way which is difficult to control. It takes years of meditation to get this switch to operate favorably. Its default function is to operate involuntarily. A yogi must work in meditation to influence it.

Nature endowed us with an automatic thought response mechanism which is set to the *"on"* position for our convenience but as soon as one desires to curtail social involvement and increase spiritual progress, this kind act of nature becomes an unwanted feature in the psyche.

A yogi must notice how the mind responds to thoughts which penetrate it from the outside and how the iSelf is influenced by these thoughts and how its energy is arrested and used to create further thinking. A yogi should study the design of the thought reception mechanism and then find a way to set this switch to *"off"* as its default condition.

If one fails to do this, Patanjali's idea of *samyama* which is the three higher states of meditation will hardly be experienced.

No yogi, no limited being, can abolish or permanently get rid of the iSelf, the self-identity. It will not happen. One should not waste time trying to achieve that. What one should do is to find a way to monitor the association of the iSelf so that it does not imperil itself psychologically. Get it into isolation. Check to see how it releases itself from that or how something else releases it from that. Gain mastery of its interaction with the other parts of the psyche.

Process of Learning Yoga

Breathing was very good this morning with both nostrils remaining clear. Kundalini did not rise in a big way but the various *nadi*s were not clogged.

Kundalini did rise into the chest. It went under the tongue and spread there in the throat as a simmering slightly heated energy. The breath infusion cleared the head of the subtle body.

When I sat to meditate, naad sound was absent as a sound energy. It was there by the right ear in the distance but only as a beam pipe force which was crystal clear and jell-like coming in and hitting the coreSelf.

After about fifteen minutes of meditation, that naad force appeared to change into the usual sound energy. This was not a change in the force but only a change in the level of existence I was on in relation to the force. The frontal part of the head was blank. Patanjali's instruction for there to be no operations of the mento-emotional force *(chittavritti)* was honored.

During the exercises, just before I sat to meditate, Rishi Singh Gherwal appeared in the distance but he did not come near. He was there for about three minutes.

In dealing with yoga gurus, one should act as advised. Relationship with these persons improves if one complies with instructions. As in every learning process, the student must complete lessons to advance.

There is no sense in badgering the teacher if one fails to do the lessons. One must be confident that by doing the lessons one will advance. By attending school during toddler and teenaged years, one learns, even if one does not understand the education process. Such is learning. It applies to yoga as well.

Slight Shifts in Consciousness

Over the years teaching kundalini yoga and meditation, I asked students to keep notes but it seems that this is one of the most difficult practices to complete. It is however beneficial to the student if he or she makes notations. The main benefit is that the mind becomes trained to notice the slightest alteration in consciousness. Eventually what is subjective, subliminal and subconscious comes within the purview of the conscious mind.

This is important especially for helping a person to develop perception of very slight movements in consciousness. When doing kundalini yoga exercises and when meditating, some slight adjustments and slight shifts in consciousness may carry with them profound insight which otherwise would go unnoticed if the mind is not sensitive enough to observe them. Taking notes about the practice causes the mind to require of itself, the ability to observe the most minute shifts.

The mind has a tendency to focus on the physical reality, on the vulgar aspects of existence and on what is blatant but that tendency discourages spiritual advancement. We should make effort to improve the mind's psychic sensitivity. That is done by requiring that the mind should make sensitive observations.

Kundalini and Sex Experience

In some instances, kundalini may rise and remind one of sex experience. In sexual sensation however kundalini takes a natural route which is sponsored by nature for reproduction. It is interpreted as pleasure but it is the means of reproducing life forms.

Our pleasure interpretation comes because of where we are located when observing the movements of energies during sex experience. Those who are part of the reproductive energy and who are about to get a body from the reproductive force do not regard it as pleasure because they are not located in the energies in an observational stance.

To turn away from the sex experience and go in the direction of spiritual perception, one must cause kundalini to abandon the quest for reproductive intentions. That is not an easy feat because it is unnatural. Kundalini will not willingly depart from the reproductive aims. No amount of daydreaming or philosophizing will cause kundalini to divert from reproduction. It has to be disciplined and induced from that natural procedure.

Last night in the astral world I explained this to a deceased person. Kundalini uses the reproductive route life after life. It has full confidence in that system. When one tries to adjust that, kundalini is resistant.

Is anyone willing to abandon all of his or her cultural credits? Until we reach a stage of maturity where cultural credits mean little to us, we cannot embark on the spiritual journey in real terms. No one stands in anyone's way. No one prevents anyone from making spiritual progress. It is someone's tendencies which prevent him.

Popularity is the Curse

This morning's exercises went well except for constant bombardment from thoughts from numerous individuals. In some sessions, thoughts come in a barrage. They besiege a yogi. Kundalini rose on occasion. Once it rose through the trunk into the neck on either front side of the neck, where it felt like little needles and pins with a bliss feeling. The energy was compressed. It did not scatter.

Once it rose all the way into the head into the nostrils where it felt like little lightning bolts firing tiny bliss energies like micro-pins.

When I sat to meditate another group of thoughts attacked. It took fifteen minutes to locate naad sound in the back of the head. After being stationed in naad I noticed a golden energy at the third eye area.

Knowing many people is the bane of yoga practice. The least number of persons one knows, the better off one will be at the time of final departure from the body. Popularity is a curse which negatively impacts yoga progress.

Nityananda Baba's Comments

During exercises this morning, kundalini was agreeable to rising. It rose through the chest region and went into the neck on the right and left sides separately. In the neck it felt like tiny bubbles with bliss energy compressed.

After exercises I sat to meditate. Nityananda Baba came. He is the person who inspired the *Brahma Yoga Bhagavad Gita* book. Most of the information in that book, is based on his system of brahma yoga practice. He touched my head. He said this, "A long way to go here. Keep practicing."

He remarked that generally the energy of kundalini spreads through the trunk of the body but it did not spread enough through the subtle head. He directed me to be in the top back part of the head where there is a special chakra. Naad sound followed me there.

Time Stood Still

This morning meditation resulted in more kundalini rises. Some were small rises and half-hearted attempts to rise. The little ones were noted but will not be reported.

While doing exercises one should note the small rises and the attempts to rise by kundalini. This is important for developing objectivity in a subjective energy. One's psychic perception is greatly improved if one develops this kind of sensitivity whereby one can note incremental adjustments or shifts in the energies.

During the session kundalini rose through the left and right side of the trunk. It jumped from one side at the base to another side up in the trunk of the body. These actions cause those parts of the psyche to be released from having to feed on lower energies. This in turn sets the stage for advanced meditation.

When I sat to meditate, naad sound was heard immediately. Based on an instruction from Swami Rama, I went to the intellect in the frontal part of the head. When I got there, naad sound seemed to follow me. It was clearly heard.

In that area where thoughts usually appear, there were no ideas. It felt like being in a hollowed dark space. The lack of thoughts, images or impressions was stunning.

After meditation, I sat in the same position and then slipped into a parallel world. There were three people in that place. One befriended me and made efforts to integrate me Into their situation.

These persons had no physical bodies. Somehow, they slipped into that parallel world and existed there without knowledge of anything elsewhere.

They had no idea of a past life, nor of the past history of their world. They lived like trees do in this world, where there is no sense of time or place, no assessment of history and no understanding about how the future could be molded by the present. It was as if one went to a place where time stood still.

Calling Naad

Exercises this morning went well. Kundalini did a lightning strike from the left side of the base chakra to the right side of the body up under the arm pit and into the arm. That felt like a mint strike of bliss energy.

I worked for some time to get kundalini into the thigh bones and knees (left then right side). I switched to getting the head of the subtle body infused. It took some time to do this but the head was blank which is ideal for *Patañjali* meditation practice. It felt like being in a hollow coconut. There were no thought disturbances. This is an example of a favor by fate, a great opportunity for a yogi to make progress.

When I sat to meditate, there were no yoga teachers in the astral vicinity, but there was a message energy which was left in my psyche by Swami Rama. It said this.

> *If the frontal part of the head is hollow, if it has no thoughts and will produce none, stay in the front but bring naad forward. Remain fused in naad.*

To bring naad to the front, call it. it will come forward and remain near you. If you call and it does not come that means that the frontal part is resistant to naad in which case, abandon the front area, go to the back. Fuse into naad there.

Using this instruction, I called naad and it came near. I kept fused to it but it kept a space between the coreSelf and itself, a space of one inch.

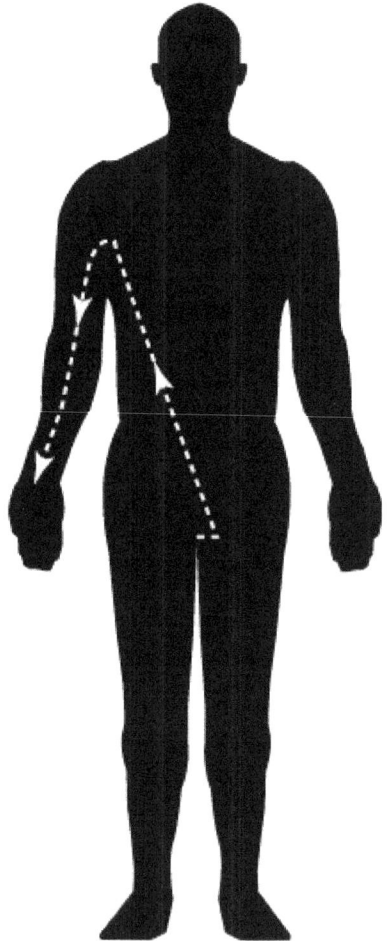

I situated myself as coreSelf where the intellect usually is with images and ideas. The intellect was just as if it did not exist.

After some time, there was a flash vision from the third eye which was from life in another dimension. There was a fox running to catch another creature. This lasted for a split second. I resumed the meditation on naad in that hollow intellect space.

Yogi who was a Bull

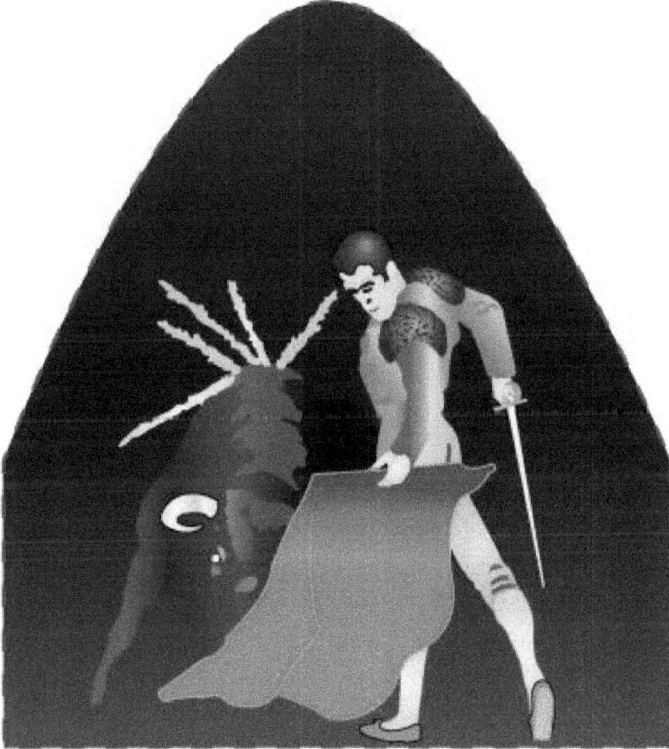

In the diagram of a matador, I depicted the general whereabouts and situation of the coreSelf. Who is the coreSelf in this illustration? It is not the matador. It certainly is not the cape nor sword, nor pikes which are stuck in the bull.

That leaves only the bull.

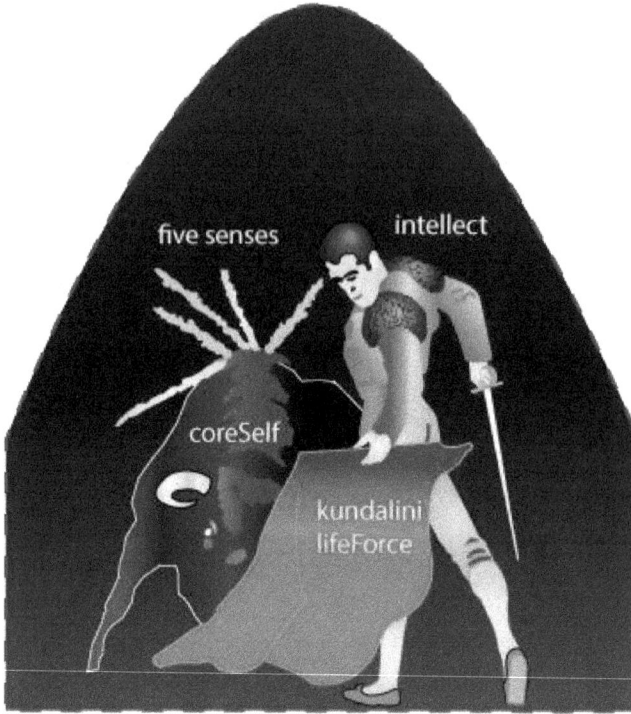

The coreSelf as the bull is lured into the moving action of the cape which is manipulated by the matador. The cape is the kundalini energy. The matador is the intellect. The five pikes are the five senses. When the bull ignores the waving red cape, the matador takes action to stimulate the bull. He throws the five senses into action. They pierce the body of the bull, thereby getting its attention and irritating it sufficiently for it to charge the cape. Using the five senses, the intellect aggravates the bull, thereby attracting the bull's interest to the cape, which is the kundalini energy, the lifeForce.

The real enemy of the bull is the matador or intellect but the bull does not know this. It is bewildered by the random movement of the cape. Instead of goring the matador to death, the bull charges the cape and attempts to push its horn through it, but to no avail since the cape is designed to deflect from the horns of the bull.

A question arises as to why the matador or intellect has more intelligence than the coreSelf which is represented by the bull which is an inferior species with a rudimentary brain?

Another question concerns the possibility of the bull realizing that its enemy is the matador. Can the bull ever evolve sufficient intelligence to know that?

Regarding the sword. What is it? Why does the intellect carry a hidden weapon which is intended to kill the bull by piercing its heart?

What a great illustration! I see this as the self (bull) struggling with the mind (the matador) which controls the direction of emotions with the cape. The cape is symbolic of the emotions. Unless the self can recognize the connection between emotions and the thoughts which are provoked by the senses (the five pikes), it has little power over the intellect (mind). If the self (bull) can see that the intellect is the cause of all suffering it can subdue the intellect and become at peace with itself as well as the intellect. Emotions flash like the cape of the matador. The self is attracted to those emotions. It is bewildered by them.

As far as the illustration is concerned, I was in Spain some years ago. I found a post card with a matador. Seeing that post card, I was simultaneously inspired by Krishna to see that the situation of the selves in the physical world is exactly as depicted in the scene.

I bought the post card and forgot it, until a few days ago when I located it with some papers. Then again that inspiration from Krishna was realized. I got the urge to describe it.

It is so beautiful when you are outside of it, looking in on the scene. The matador is elegant and attentive. Keeping the bull focused and occupied the cape plays its part perfectly. The hand and the sword are alert. They patiently wait for the opportunity to strike the bull. The poor animal has little understanding of the danger. The senses as the pikes play their part in motivating the bull. They hang after delivering their impulsions into the body of the confused helpless animal.

The matador has very little intention of using the sword. If he kills the bull, his fun will cease. His glory will be short-lived. Spectators will rise to their feet either to approve or condemn his action.

If the spectators disapprove the matador will be depressed. If they approve, he will have to bring another bull into the arena. The animal will have to be trained beforehand to recognize the cape and be excited as the matador flickers it.

Once the matador is familiar with a particular bull, he does not want to kill it. He becomes attached to the animal but he wants the animal to get curious or angry and charge because otherwise there is no excitement to thrill the audience.

The self cannot die. The death of the self in this case means the discouragement of the self, to the point where it becomes inactive when it is overwhelmed by negative energies. But it does not stay in those conditions forever. The matador does not want the self to remain in those states for long, because then the matador has no game to play in the arena.

What is the sword?

We can consider that the matador has the sword to protect himself from the bull, not to kill the creature. It is his ultimate means of protection. He does not want to use it to kill the bull. His means of controlling the bull is the cape.

The real problem for the bull is the cape not the sword. It is dangerous but still the real threat is the cape. On occasion the bull is scared of the hidden object and the hand which holds it. It does not know the object. It wants to get behind the matador to see what is held in that hand but the matador skillfully does not allow the bull to see it. The matador only wants the bull to be attentive to the cape.

There is no point in the bull charging the flickering cape. The sword has no significance, if the bull would not charge. The matador does not chase the bull. We have never seen a matador run after a bull in a Spanish arena. It always was a bull which charged. In other words, if the matador really intended to use the sword, he would charge the bull and do the needful.

We still have to understand exactly what the sword is and why it is used at any time by the matador. Since it has the upper hand as designed by nature, why does the intellect have to carry a weapon?

We took birth with bodies which have weapons. Check the teeth, nails and muscles. Siblings may fight. One may go into an animal rage and bite the other. Teeth are not there for eating only. They are weapons. What is the necessity for these in the human species? Why the need for security and protection from the environment and from other creatures of the same or different species?

Because the intellect carries the weapon of analysis, it can blackmail and intimidate the self into cooperating with the plan of the inquisitive and blind lifeForce and shortsighted senses. When the yogin silences the weapon of analysis, he is for the time being, freed from its harassments.

At that time the senses are powerless to influence him. They lose the protective support of their powerful ally, the intellect. The yogin no longer has to fight the memory to stop it from whimsically and impulsively showing unwanted ideas in visual and auditory forms. With such distractions reduced to nil, one progresses quickly and can move the attention into the realm of the chit akasha, the sky of consciousness.

Cast of Fate (June 4, 2011)

This morning breath infusion went well for about three-fourths of the way through it. Then everything crashed as some persons arrived astrally and demanded attention. The situation was such that I directed the infused energy into the bodies of those persons. I spent twenty minutes of the exercise session doing that.

When I sat to meditate immediately after, I spent most of the session sending more energy to those persons. I heard naad sound but due the pressing need of these persons I could not keep my attention to that.

Sometimes, as fate would have it, something like this happens at the time of death of the physical body. To service the social needs of others, a yogi gets thrown here or there by providence. Thus, he loses the bid to reach a siddhaloka place where the yoga gurus reside.

Subsequently when his luck is negative, he becomes a condemned being having to take another body haphazardly in the social milieu of the conditioned beings in this world.

No one is greater than fate. In fact, everyone is in the cast of fate. A yogi should hope for the best, feeling that perhaps providence will facilitate him.

Failed Meditation

According to *Patañjali* meditation means *samyama*, but during some sessions one does not attain the desired states. *Samyama* is the three higher states of yoga as one sequential practice.

The other five out of a total of eight stages are not considered to be meditation but they are preliminary. They should be used when one fails to attain *samyama*. A yogi should be honest and not pretend that he can always do *samyama*. The yogi is not absolute. A pretense of absolute control will hurt. One should be practical. One should recognize failure.

This morning kundalini did not rise in the usual way where one can track its upward or downward movement by sensations. Instead the rising of kundalini was through its spreading influence such that its energy moved without sensation.

I did a full session and sat to meditate. During the breath infusion energies from other persons reached me. I mentally barricaded myself from those intrusions. Eventually I decided to confront the energy of those foreign thoughts. I directed the infused breath to the thoughts. It took five minutes of constant bombardment to dissipate the thought force.

However, when I sat to meditate more thoughts came from three sources. It was such that I did not hear naad sound. Instead, the thoughts presented themselves. I sent back response energies to those persons who sent the thoughts. This took fifteen minutes of the meditation time.

After that I meditated but mentally, I was exhausted. Those thoughts absorbed the infused energy. Because of destined interferences which are successful at thwarting a yogi, meditation is not always successful, but that is all the more reason to continue the practice.

Long-Distance Astral Travel

Just after meditation, someone whose physical body is located in Guyana, reached me. My physical and astral bodies were in South Korea. The distance that person's subtle body traveled was 9500 miles.

Reason for the travel?

There was a past life energy in the person's subtle body which required fulfillment for association. It forced the subtle body to make that long journey.

A similar thing can happen after one is departed from a physical body and lives only in a subtle form, where one may take a new embryo to meet a certain person in the physical world. In other words, on the mere whim of an urge, one may haphazardly without any sensible reason, take another body some place somehow.

Images not Uploaded in the Mind

In meditation the naad sound was detected fifteen seconds after the meditation began. However, naad was not at its usual location. It was up high in a remote place above the top back curve of the head. I tried to reach the source point but it was too remote, like something coming from a distant galaxy which a yogi can never reach but can perceive it as a faint signal coming from somewhere.

Even though I infused the body for an hour, still some images from a movie I saw yesterday flashed in the mind. They flashed partially and did not load into full blown images. I watched and noticed that due to the presence of the infusion energy, the images loaded partially and not fully. It was as if there was a tidal wave rising over a person on a beach and then suddenly the wave retrogressed and disappeared by some compelling force.

Soon after as I listened to naad there was an illuminated cloud-like energy ahead in the center of the eyebrows. It was like a bright cloud which is illuminated by moonlight at night.

Yogi on his Knees

This morning during breath infusion, kundalini rose with intensity and concentration of the infusing subtle force. It rose on either side of the trunk and went into the shoulders and collar bones. The feeling was one of compacted bliss energy with microscopic light entering tiny energy molecules of the subtle body.

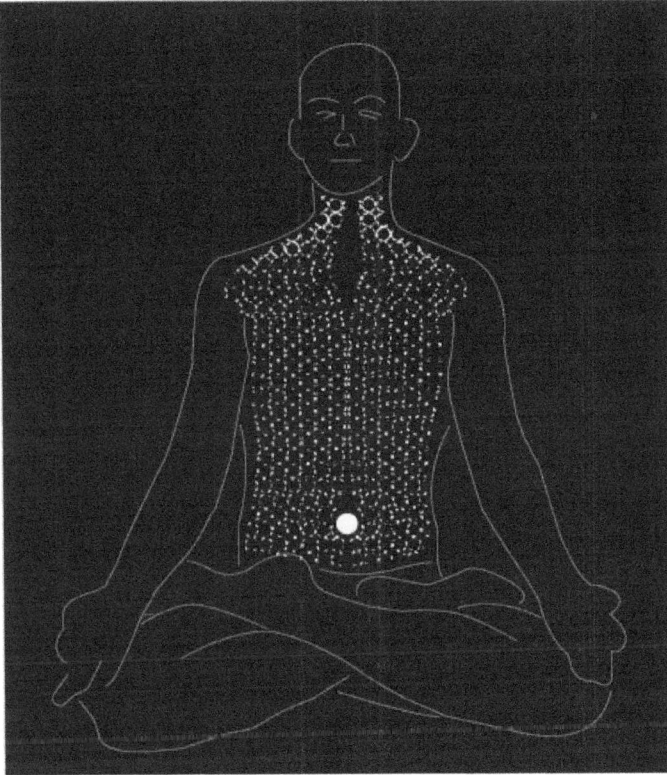

I worked on getting the infused energy to pass through the navel center without obstruction. After about fifty minutes of exercises, I shifted focus to the head and began working with the infused energy to strike various parts, like the frontal part, the mid-section, the back of the head, the lower back of head and the top of neck.

When I sat to meditate, I reached naad immediately. It came from the right ear vicinity. Swami Rama appeared in my head. He explained how advanced yogis put Patanjali's instruction into practice. He said.

There is no argument about methods in yoga. Methods are not the issue. The issue is results. Suppose you can blow a whistle and enter samadhi, then what is the argument?

Provided the results are factual and not imaginary use whatever works for you. Get to the place where the mind chamber is cleared of thoughts and images. Remain in that state for a time, say for at least ten minutes.

Once you achieve that you can practice Patanjali yoga which consist of staying in the clarified mental chamber for long periods of time, waiting there in silence.

The real problem is to cause the mind to be in that state without having to sit there and compel the mind, or without struggling to produce that condition.

If in meditation you must struggle with the mind, that is not samyama. *If the psyche is not infused, one should infuse it by a valid method. Infuse the system so that when you sit to meditate, the mind is blank because of the quality of energy within it.*

Patanjali meditation begins from the point of having a mind which of its own accord does not have images and thoughts. There is no question of observing thoughts or letting thoughts come and go in Patanjali system. That is not samyama. *That is the stage of practice before* samyama.

Part 2

Third Eye Images

While doing the exercises this morning, kundalini arose in various parts of the body, specifically in the arms, under the cheek bones, and in the lower lip. When it went into the lower lip, that area of the body felt like little bliss energies tingling.

During the meditation session which followed, the third eye had an in and out diminishing round energy, which began behind me and then receded in the distance through the center of the third eye.

At one time for ten minutes, there were images at the third eye. Each image scene lasted about five seconds and then immediately another one was manifested. These were like looking through transparent prints in the dark using moonlight as a source of illumination.

Beverford's Subtle Visit

During the morning session which took place using the air in South Korea, I aroused kundalini many times. There was one unusual arousal which was with kundalini moving up each half of the trunk of the body, coming up in a compressed way and infusing all cells. It felt like a crammed bunch of tiny cells, all with frosty bliss energy.

When I sat for meditation naad was heard but it was below the left ear.

After about twenty minutes, Arthur Beverford appeared in the subtle head. He began a conversation about taking a new body. He left his old body somewhere supposedly in the Philippines some years ago. He is in the process of getting a new body. We discussed the old system in Tibet where students went and found their teacher in his new body and try to convince the new set of parents to allow for spiritual practice to begin in childhood.

He then shifted to his third eye practice and said that he reached a stage where his coreSelf would remain in the central position in the subtle head. It focused from there on the center of the eyebrows with a non-grasping attitude. Beverford thinks that for success in this method there should be stress on non-grasping in the focus energy.

Discussion about Death

I took a flight yesterday. This lasted fourteen hours. While on the aircraft, Swami Rama came. He mentioned the fact that people avoid death, even great yogis and spiritually-aware people. He said that once the body reaches fifty-five years of age, one should regard every day as one's last. He said this.

If you confront the issue of death on a daily basis, it can become a source of life for you.

Why avoid considering it? If you are to migrate to another country you prepare for it. You secure money. You acquire passport and visa. You make contact with relatives or friends abroad. You pack a suitcase carefully considering what you will and will not need in the new place.

Why do this and then avoid the great migration which will happen when the body dies? Why not prepare for that as well?

Patanjali brought it our attention, that death is such an undesirable thing, that even the wise men who practiced yoga in his time, tried their best to avoid considering it. Why is that?

It may be because there was no definite information about the hereafter. I was in India. I got an Indian body in the past life. We got information about Great Britain from books, news reports and countrymen who went there and came back with descriptions. We wanted to go because it was a much-desired place.

But death, who goes there and returns? Who writes a travel guide about what to expect and what to do there? Where is the travel agent who arranges passage there?

Do not say that you avoid thinking of death because it is irrelevant. Do not say that you do not regard it because you are eternal. Do not say that you are not a person who worries about the future.

Relationship with the Yoga Teacher

Regularity in yoga practice is connected to one's personal motive for practice as well as to one's relationship with the yoga teacher. There is a big attempt to deny human relationship and its obligations but no matter where one will go, one must form relationships and take care in maintaining these. In yoga, accountability for practice is vital if one is to be consistent.

Sometimes, someone calls inquiring as to the reason for not practicing consistently. This problem is solved by developing a relationship with a teacher for being obligated to that person for practice. Trouble with this is that students sometimes find it hard to respect a teacher to that extent. Some other students are not in the mood to be accountable to anyone.

Wonderful Naad

During practice this morning Swami Rama gave instructions about stopping the navel chakra from interfering with the energy which comes to it from the lungs and intestines. One has to look down in the body during breath infusion practice and be sure that the energy travels through the navel region and is not being constrained there. If one finds that there is a burning sensation when one does intense breath infusion, it means that the navel will hoard the energy. One should do one's best to force the energy through the navel and down into the pelvic region.

As I did practice, kundalini rose many times. One strange arousal was through each half of the trunk of the body and then spread down the arms into the fingers, such that the back of the palm of the hand felt as if there were tiny cramp energies, except that these feelings were bliss saturated. I stretched the arms to allow the energy to be unhindered.

When I sat for meditation naad sound was heard. It was by the right ear but after ten seconds, it switched to a place at the upper right side of the head. It was distant but audible. It had tiny treble sounds blended even though one frequency was predominant.

Swami Rama entered my subtle head after about ten minutes. He discussed the frontal part of the brain and the disturbing intellect. He said that no matter what, a yogi should keep focus on naad and from there make the required adjustments.

He added this.

Om namo Shivaya is the classic mantra for yogis but somehow by the grace of God, we got something which is even better. That is naad sound. The intellect loses its hold on a yogi when he takes shelter under naad. It is wonderful.

I Saw a Little Man

This morning my practice was a bit lacking because of some things I did late last night. One thing about yoga practice in the morning is that it begins with the way one rested the night prior. If one did not get to rest at the proper time and if the mind was not set in a way for meditation at the time of resting then automatically the practice the next morning will not be up to par.

There is no point complaining about this. Due to pressing obligations, one will not practice in the most efficient way every day. That is tolerable. Realize that in this existence that is normal. Due to past life acts, and due to fresh demands of time and destiny, one must submit to some disruptions. One should do so with no complaint. However, one should certainly not use the disruptions as an excuse to permanently become derailed from steady practice.

I have a commitment with Rishi Singh Gherwal to rise for practice at 3 am. This morning at 3 am, I was not in the mood for rising because I spent part of the night tending to other matters. I did not rest early. In my mind, at 3 am, I saw a little man get up. He did yoga exercises. It was Rishi Singh Gherwal but then when I checked again, I noticed that it was an energy he left in my mind to act this out if I did not rise on time. I noted this and rechecked the mental and emotional energy, made some adjustments, instructed kundalini to abandon reluctance to rise early despite a lack of sufficient sleep. I got up at 3.15am. It took fifteen minutes to get the psyche in some order to rise.

During practice kundalini rose in an unusual way which is to rise through the organs in the gut of the body, in the central trunk. Usually kundalini will rise through the spine, or rise on the left or right of the spine. Getting it to rise through the center and run through the organs is great. Kundalini rose and went into the shoulder blades. A nice experience was when kundalini went into the front top part of the brain. When it got there, it expressed a cooling tingling sensation as if menthol or camphor was there.

At about that time, Rishi Singh appeared. He disappeared without speaking.

When I sat to meditate, I found naad quickly. It was at the top right back part of the head. It had a fine high treble frequency with some other tiny sounds around the main frequency which was high pitched. It came from a great distance and somehow struck and scattered on the top right back part of the head. I could not reach its source point. I went to where it struck the psyche and remained there. Naad is such that one can take advantage of its presence in more than one way. It works even if one cannot get to its source. It is something that one will never control, but one can always take shelter in it and use it as the reference.

Staying in naad was like being on the roof of the world, high-up, distant from everything and sealed from the thought rigors in the mind.

Sensual Energy Withdrawal

Sensual energy withdrawal is the fifth stage of yoga, *pratyahara*. In Sanskrit *prati* means against, while *ahara* means consumption or eating. *Pratyahara* means a sensual action which is the reversal of consumption. Instead of pursuing sense objects in the physical world, the yogi retracts the interest in those objects. He observes the placement of his attention energy into the core of his consciousness. This allows the realization of the coreSelf.

It leads to the need to pursue that core with the same intensity and interest which was used to pursue the sense objects.

Self as Light

Meditation this morning was a bit strange. I did an intense session of rapid breathing, Kundalini rose and spread in different directions repeatedly during the practice. At one time kundalini rose under the armpits. It shot through the arms. Once it shot downward into the pelvic area. It spread there like tiny laser beams which had a bliss feeling.

For about fifteen minutes at the end of the exercises, I worked on the head of the subtle body. There were foreign thoughts in the subtle head. Usually these thoughts are in the frontal lobe of the brain. Usually they attached themselves to the intellect which is in that location. These thoughts sensed that the intellect resisted them. They stayed high in the head of the subtle body. Even though they did not contact the intellect directly, they used mental space and mental energy to manifest themselves to me. During the earlier part of the exercises, even though I ignored those thoughts they persisted even though I focused down through the neck.

Just when I decided to deal with these ideas, I sensed the presence of two astral persons. These were the source of the thoughts. I sensed some energy from Rishi Singh Gherwal, which he left in my subtle body. That energy had an instruction in it, saying that thought which manifest without the assistance of the intellect, should be dealt with in the same way just as if they were manifest by the intellect. I moved close to one thought and infused the space it was in with rapid breathing. That one disappeared. I used the same technique on the other thought.

The two energies hung in the mind like jelly fish floating in the ocean with long tentacles dangling from their bottoms.

As soon as I sat to meditate, I noticed naad sound in the back top of the head. At first, I was distracted by a tiny thought energy which was about to be enlarged. I confronted it. It disappeared. I went to the top back of the head. When I got there, I became part of light which came from where the naad sound resonated and which was spread through the subtle head. I was part of this light subjectively.

Even though I was part of the light, I could not use it. It was as if I was a tiny part of a ray of it. There, I was not in a position to use the light or to objectively view it, because I was a composite part.

Since I was radiated forward from the source, being pushed from it without the ability to turn about and view it, I could not turn to see it. I could see the other rays of light near to the ray of which I was a part. I could see the ray energy of the ray I was in.

Time wise, I was in that light for five minutes. Suddenly, I was dropped out of it into a dark mental space.

Seeing Krishna

The exercise session this morning was great. I directed kundalini into a little blank space which is above the genital area and in the center of the body. Kundalini also rose into the chest and then into the head repeatedly. This happened thrice.

Near the end of the exercises, Rishi Singh Gherwal was present. He had little to say. During the exercises I had a problem with the intellect. Within it, there were three bruised areas. I infused breath to get rid of that. It took some time.

Rishi had an attitude of checking to see if I did the exercises attentively. After this session, I sat to meditate. Rishi disappeared at that point. It took about fifteen minutes to reach naad in the back-left side of the subtle head. This happened because I entered the intellect to do battle with some social energies which were in it. After fifteen minutes, those influences vanished.

I meditated for one hour. I had a feeling to recline the body and continue meditating in that way. Then my subtle body disengaged from the physical form. I found myself in a dimension where Yogeshwarananda floated. The subtle body he used looked like a physical body at about the age of thirty-five years. Above him was Lord Krishna, way in the distance. There was a thread of energy going from Krishna to the yogi. When I saw Krishna, he had an attitude which said that I should listen to the yogi and not try to communication with Krishna.

Yogeshwarananda spoke to me. He was annoyed. Even though I am not a person who goes to tears, somehow, I too cried. Yogesh complained about the lack of practice of yoga by human beings. He was critical because many persons do a little yoga, have no serious interest in it. They do not learn even elementary yoga, the first five stages as listed by Patanjali. Yogesh said that without mastering those five stages, people waste time and show insincerity. His remarks were distressing.

Little Self and Itself

During this morning session Rishi Singh Gherwal was present but as a presence only, not using a subtle body or a miniature subtle form as most yogis do when they enter the head of a student. As I practiced there was a lady from the Virgin Islands who want to discuss her cultural background.

During the night she showed me the area where her body grew up and also the cultural nuances of that place. After I decided to listen to what she said I made the decision to begin practice at 4 am instead of 3 am. That is another effect of association, where when a yogi associates with non-yogis either physically or astral, the practice is affected.

The lady was hurled on my path through this life by fate. I could not ignore her but all the same I was aware that the association sabotaged the practice.

In any case, Rishi noticed the lady. He realized what she said. He looked into the memory imprint which was in the intellect. He read its contents. Without the lady's knowledge he said that it was okay for her to be there during the exercises but he directed me to shift attention to another part of the intellect. When I did that, I became less conscious of her speech but she was not aware that my attention shifted. Soon after she disappeared.

A yogi who is serious about spiritual life or who thinks that he or she is serious, should understand clearly that social associations with people who have no strong interest in cultivating spirituality, is a great danger. If one is not careful with such associations, one's spiritual efforts will be nil.

Once the lady left, Rishi discussed the importance of having a yoga guru and of being obligated to that person to make spiritual progression, to get up early to practice, to be attentive during practice, to be consistent and loyal to practice. He said this.

The construction of the human psyche is such that one cannot make full progress unless one has an obligation to a greater person. No limited person can make full progression all by himself or herself without a connection to a greater yogi.

For the self, it cannot motivate itself enough. One needs a yoga guru to push one and to demand a certain amount of practice. In your case, you have me. You have Yogeshwarananda. You have Swami Atmananda, Swami Shivananda and others. You cannot afford to be lazy with practice.

If teachers are deducted from the equation, what will be left, except the little self? How much can that self demand of itself. How much can that self elevate itself.

Remember Arjuna. Krishna told him to lift himself, to elevate himself spiritually, to act in a manner for his long-ranged spiritual wellbeing. Even to use himself to help himself, Arjuna needed to be inspired and pushed by the Supreme Being.

Kundalini Down Rise

During the breath infusion session, kundalini arose in a rare way which is to rise into the *nadis* which are in the thighs, legs and feet. This feels as if there are cramps which have a bliss energy rather than an annoyance feeling.

In that experience kundalini rises but travels in a downward direction. Beginners doing bhastrika pranayama are usually familiar with kundalini rising up the spine. If one continues to practice, one becomes aware of kundalini rising up the front of the body or up the middle of trunk and in other parts, but rarely does the aroused kundalini rise and travel in a downward direction.

During the exercise session I did thigh stretches. Rishi showed how to blow breath energy into the thighs to remove the lusty energy which accumulates there.

When I sat to meditate, I was alert to naad. After two seconds I focused on it. I could not find its source point but it was positioned by the right ear. Rishi then said, "Be attentive to naad. Ignore everything else." After that he disappeared.

My Selfless Acts Squashed by Fate

This morning meditation was interrupted by two persons. One was a yogi who is in another country and who wanted advice on how to practice. The other was a deceased man whom I associated with as a neighbor some twenty-five years ago. This person contacted me during the night. From a relative he got an astral link to me.

At first, he wanted to speak about old times, about the things he did during the life of his last body and about some things he did in my association but then after some time it came to the punch line which was if any of my descendants could sponsor him a body. I told him that I had no objection to it and that if he needed my approval, he already had it.

He was happy to hear that. During the exercise session which lasted for fifty-five minutes, he was present. As he talked, I practiced. After a while he left. His astral body disappeared. Even though his astral body made its last exit from the physical one some twenty years ago, there was no change in this person's attitude or desire.

One thing of interest is that I knew this person in Poplar Bluff, Missouri, where he was a neighbor. In the astral world he lives in a similar building with similar construction and objects. It appears that wherever his astral body goes, his home environment goes with it. When he visited me, he showed how his stuff is arranged in the exactly the same way as before. His astral form did not move to go to Missouri to do this. It did this where he located my astral body.

Another feature of interest is that he has zero spiritual interest. He is happy like he always was on the physical plane with the routine mundane activities. Even though he is conscious that he is not in the physical world and that he would like to be part of the physical history of the world, he has no interest in the spiritual self or the astral body. His only interest is to be on the physical side. He has no curiosity about the subtle body. He does know however that he needs to get near somebody who would be his parents. That is the only part of reincarnation that holds his interest.

The most important observation about this person is that when he was a neighbor, he offered assistance now and again with one or the other things. I helped him in turn. During the conversation with him, his mind remembered the favors he did. He put those things forward as basis for which he should get a body through my descendants. The point is that even if someone does something selflessly, his intent has no meaning because he does not have control over destiny.

Fate may require that one uses such selfless acts as a bargain in the future when one is needy and must trade such selfless service for some opportunity.

Being selfless with full good intent is a great quality but providence may handle that energy differently. It may confiscate a selfless act or the resulting piety generated and use it as a bargaining chip in another circumstance.

This is like when a person saves up money in a bank account during his working years. Then in the elderly years, the person falls sick and enters an institution in a crippled state. The hospital administrators take action to use the savings to pay for the medical services rendered. Even though the account was deposited for other reasons, the patient can do nothing to stop the hospital from taking the money.

Making a selfless act does not in any way take away from fate its upper hand in squashing a person's plans. Fate could turn a selfless act into a selfish one by using the said energy in a selfish way for the person's interest at some future time.

Seeing Stars

In general, if one perceives starfield behind closed eyes, these are subtle energies which move constantly in the mental environment. Just as we have clouds moving in the atmosphere, and we have dust particles, solar radiation and many other types of energies in the local atmosphere and also in outer space, we also have many energies in the mental environment.

There are various dimensions. One's perception can jump into any of these levels where one may see this or that reality or energy. It does happen in some cases of a yogi where his perception becomes psychic or supernatural. He sees microwave energy, infrared or light frequencies which are not perceptible with physical vision. Some of what is seen through electron microscopes and other imaging devices may be seen by yogis. This is why there is a listing of transcendence states in the *Yoga Sutras* and also in the explanations given by Krishna in the *Uddhava Gita*.

The main objective is to find the components of the psyche. Many people set out in haste to find a unity with everything or a mergence with bliss energy or with cosmic energy. They deny themselves the right to objectively map the components of the psyche.

There are many persons who meditate and who speak about a mergence-into-everything experience but the same persons can locate the car key, credit card or passport. Yet, if asked about the components of the psyche they are at a loss for words.

Where is the self which perceives the starfield? Is that self in the starfield like a bird which flies in a star-lit night? Can the bird move in the starfield? Is it stationary like a tree?

Meditation Details

This morning exercises lasted for one hour. This was followed by a one-hour meditation. In a way, it may be stated that one hour of exercises supports one hour of meditation, meaning that the infused energy dissipates after the equivalent time of meditation. Then one finds the self on the normal social level once again facing the challenges of human life in a world filled with nature's intrigue for the evolutionary ravages forced on the creatures by the disciplinary dictatorial time factor.

A yogi friend from Guyana sent a text message by phone yesterday. He requested that I call. I did so last night before resting. This same person was there with me in the astral world before I arose for meditation. He was present during the exercise session and then left soon after. He was not present during the meditation session.

He is involved with various social issues. Even though sometimes I advise him on more efficient ways to discharge social responsibilities, I told him that my business with him concerns yoga practice and nothing else.

During the exercises, I aroused kundalini into the chest region. It rose into that region as sharp bliss energy needles. I did more infusion and rose kundalini into the central head twice. Once it ascended into the shoulder and arms. Due to that I held the arms in special postures to allow the kundalini to pass into the arm *nadi*s more efficiently.

Rishi Singh Gherwal expressed the opinion previously that the entire psyche must be dealt with, not just the head and spinal column. His view is that if any part of the psyche is not energized, it may cause a yogi to remain on a lower level, even if other parts of the psyche were elevated to higher planes. The entire psyche must be energized, not just a part of it.

Those yogis who deny that they have an individual psyche and that they are individual spiritual units are in for a rude awakening because if they fail to purify that psyche and if they think that they will become nothing at some stage and will be devoid of individuality, they will be disappointed after leaving the body.

During the last twenty minutes of the exercises, I focused on the head of the subtle body. During the last ten minutes I worked on infusing the intellect. It was not intrusive. It did not produce thoughts but it had a bruise-spot on its front right side. This was from contact with the thoughts of my friend in Guyana.

The other psychic component which was troublesome was a memory bubble which was above the intellect. It had within it an image of a news report I viewed yesterday. I directed some infused breath energy into the bubble. That demolished it.

At first when I sat to meditate, for about fifteen seconds, I was disoriented in the mental terrain. I was like a person who suddenly arrived in a forest and did not know north from south. After those fifteen seconds my instinct for finding naad sound resumed. I located nada behind to the right. Like a lost explorer who finds his compass (GPS) and gets his bearing, I went to it immediately.

After getting into naad, I checked the mind chamber which is the head of the subtle body. There were no disturbances. I settled deeper in naad. There was a soothing fog light which descended from above. I decided not to trace it since these lights have a way about them where they disappear as soon as one tracks them. This light stayed for a time. After that there was another light which spread in a rectangular way.

Meditation lasted for one hour. I noted when I began and then noted when it was finished. This is the preferred way to meditate, rather than to set a specific limit.

Time of Death Procedure

Exercises this morning lasted for over an hour. The left lung, being smaller, takes in less air than the right one. Whenever the right nostril is blocked it takes longer to infuse breath energy because with each draw of the breath one compresses less air.

The main reason for shut down of the right nostril is a lack of solar energy. The main reason for the opening of the left nostril is the preponderance of lunar energy. When the solar and lunar energies are in balance, both nostrils remain open to the fullest.

At different stages during the exercises, I saw different yogis but initially a yogi friend who lives in Guyana was present with his spouse. They spoke as I practiced. The lesson is that one should not allow astral associations to discourage practice. One should practice on schedule and complete it even if one is in association with astral people while the physical body sleeps. Those persons will remain on the astral side. One can still hear their conversations and perhaps even see their subtle bodies while doing the breath infusion. At least if one has no clairvoyant perception of their subtle forms, one can perceive their thinking energy and can think answers in response to their psychic speech.

Rishi Singh gave a rule that during the exercises, one should not think answers in response, but he never said that one should not hear what others say during the exercises. He thinks that if one thinks in response it may hamper one's focus for arousing kundalini.

During the exercises, I first saw Yogi Bhajan, then Yogiraj Yogeshwarananda, then Rishi Singh Gherwal, then Swami Atmananda. In all cases, I perceived them when kundalini rose and penetrated the trunk of the body and the head. This happens when kundalini moves the psyche to the level of existence where the particular yogi resides.

After I finished the exercises which took more than one hour, I sat to meditate. The yogi friend and his spouse were there at the beginning. They soon departed. I could not relate to them because I complied with Rishi's instructions about not responding during a session.

However, Swami Atmananda left an energy before my subtle body de-energized from the plane of existence he is currently on. That energy was for someone else to show me the passage the subtle body takes when the gross body dies.

Soon after, Rishi Singh and Yogi Bhajan explained the procedure for moving the subtle body away from the physical system and for directing the subtle body to reach where these yogis are.

The procedure is to leave behind some of the subtle energy which the subtle body has now and to collect the energy of it which is its higher level. Once that is done the yogi should express a repulsion force, which will cause the subtle body to drift through lower dimensions and reach these yogis in the places which are called siddhaloka. These are places where the only interest fostered is higher advancement through higher yoga practices.

Just as in this world we are preoccupied with social desires and fulfillments and that keeps us involved day and night, in the siddhaloka places the absorption and interest is to get the kundalini energy fully upgraded, and to remove all polluted energies from the subtle form and then discover and map the higher supernatural levels and make efforts to migrate to the divine world.

During the meditation, the intellect was all but non-existent in the sense that it did not foster thoughts and did not create images. It was silent. Naad blasted on the right side of the head. Lower memories were absent.

Rishi Singh Gherwal was the most present yogi during the meditation. His attitude was like this, "Your time is limited. Practice ardently. Reduce social interest."

The procedure left for me by Swami Atmananda is for having disinterest in social energies when the physical body dies and only taking that part of the subtle body which has the interest in yoga practice. Of course, that procedure is not an easy one, because kundalini's natural habit is to maintain strong interest in social affairs.

After death, a yogi can gravitate to the siddhaloka place. He can stay there only if he does not carry the aggregate social energies which the subtle body usually has. But if after getting there, one again gets ideas which related to one's previous social connections, those feelings will serve as a repulsion force, which forces the subtle body to leave siddhaloka and appear on a lower astral plane where one can interact with normal people. From that place one will assume an embryo.

The yogi is exempt if he can restrain from connecting with the aggregate social package of his energies which were left behind at the time of death. Unfortunately, those energy even though he separated from them, still exist on the lowered social planes. Those same potencies repossess him if he is unable to relieve himself of the social connections.

In this world a similar thing may happen to a person who leaves for a foreign country after living in his native place and developing various obligations there. So long as he remains in the foreign land, there is nothing to worry about in terms of the previous obligations but sometimes he may think of something in the native country and may for some reason or the other be drawn back. As soon as he returns people recognize him, especially those persons to whom he was obligated. They demand that he fulfills obligations.

Rishi Singh Gherwal alerted that if I do not erase the social connections and their related obligations, I will be unable to do it in the years to come. It takes a certain amount of time to put such energy into a neutral state from which one can repel it when death is near.

Lights in Meditation

During exercises this morning I dealth with a few thoughts. These came from persons who were nearby in the astral world. They spoke to me even though they were conscious that I did breath infusion practice.

Thoughts are all-pervasive on certain levels. Remaining on those levels and fooling oneself, thinking that one can banish them, is the same as if someone wanted to stop insects from buzzing. It is a lofty aspiration but it illusory. If a yogi wants to stop thoughts, he should get out of the dimensions in which thoughts prevail.

Some ancient yogis did exercises and also slept in the same spot in a cave, room or shack. These days, I do exercises in one place and meditate in another. When I finished the exercises and went to meditate, those persons followed me using their astral forms, but since I jumped dimensions, they could not relate to me as their thoughts occurred on a level from which I escaped.

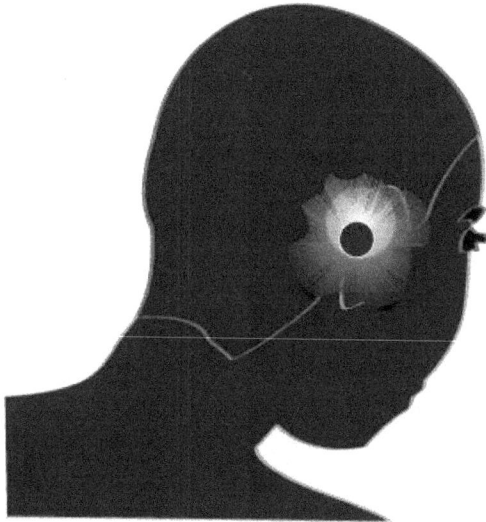

naad sound in default position
by right ear

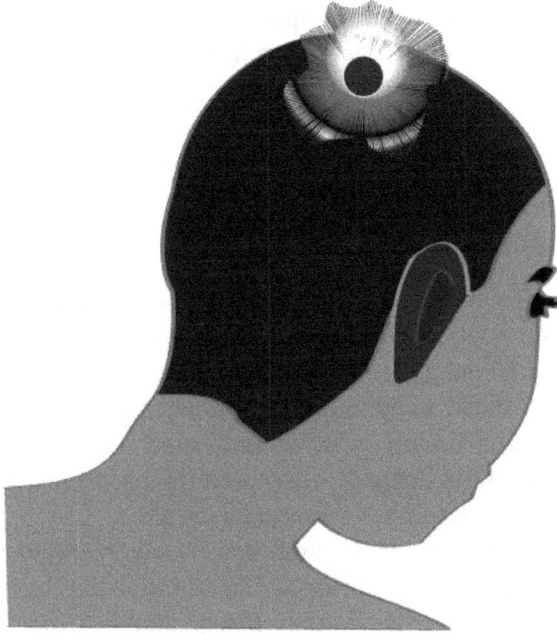

naad sound in shifted position
at right top back of head

During the meditation, naad sound was in the high back part of the head but its source point was out of reach. I remained near naad for a time. Then I found myself in the middle of the subtle head. There the intellect was quiet as if it did not exist. I stayed there for some time. Suddenly there was a bright astral light which shun in every direction in the subtle atmosphere. It looked like a frosted light bulb. Since these lights usually disappear if one turns to view them head on, I did not look to it. That light stayed for about three minutes for the most. Then it disappeared. Five seconds after that, there was a flash which spread as if it had a rectangular shape.

Even though such lights do appear in meditation momentarily, Yogeshwarananda reported seeing such lights for hours on end, while meditating and even after resuming physical presence.

One thing to know is that the disappearance of such lights is actually the disappearance of the yogi from the plane in which the light exists. In other words, the yogi reaches a higher astral dimension which is lit in one way or the other but he stays there for some seconds or minutes. Then his subtle body de-energizes and he is deprived of the experience. But his mind may interpret incorrectly that the light appeared and then disappeared because the mind uses itself as a reference, even though it is a relative psychic object.

During the exercise session early on, kundalini ascended the front and central part of the trunk. After this with more breath infusion, kundalini moved into the central head. The exercises lasted for about one hour. Then a meditation lasted for the same period.

Meditation Disturbance

This morning meditation was a disturbance in the sense that I had to deal with some social relationships having to do with some deceased persons whom I knew in Trinidad some years ago. It was however a good practice session, because these people, being now deceased, changed their view about the value of breath infusion and meditation. They realize that Christianity's idea about going to heaven on the basis of church attendance and being saved, turned out for them to be invalid.

They are now on the astral planes. When I was in Trinidad around 1973, I explained reincarnation and the value of meditation but these persons were on the course of improving the social status. They ignored such conversations.

The exercise session was good. It ran for forty-five minutes (2.45 am - 3.30 am). Immediately after I sat to meditate. During the infusion, I managed to raise kundalini through the chest, on the right side, on left side, through the center and then into the brain. This passage through the chest is called middle front kundalini as compared to through the spine which is spinal kundalini. It is the same kundalini from the base chakra but it goes through different *nadi* subtle passages, like a train leaving a Central Station and going in different directions at different times.

This happened while these persons, who are on the astral side only, spoke to me. I practiced even though they preferred that I relate to them. In yoga one has an obligation to a teacher(s). Even if others demand attention one cannot afford to cease the practice.

When I sat to meditate, those persons on the astral side backed away for about thirty minutes. Then they pestered me again. During the thirty minutes when they backed away, they observed my subtle body and noticed changes in it in terms of how kundalini energy was surcharged and distributed. One person compared the lights in my subtle body to theirs. He said that perhaps he could be a great yogin.

Even though they were present near me, I overheard their conversations from a distance, since my subtle body was so infused with energy that dimensionally it was distant from them.

During the first thirty minutes, I heard naad but it moved from its default position by the right ear to the top right side of the head. It sounded distant. When I tried to go into the source point, I could not reach that place. I then decided to stay where I was and listen to it.

The intellect was silent. The frontal part of the head was blank. I saw none of my yoga teachers. After those first thirty minutes, my subtle body lost the breath infusement charge which elevated it above where those astral beings from Trinidad were. It returned to the dimension they were in. They were happy about that. They began speaking of this and that, on and on. I pretended to be involved.

Except for one person in the group, the others had no spiritual aptitude. The idea that we are all the same and there is no difference and that we all have the same spiritual potential, is incorrect. Some spirits are so earthbound that not even God can transit them from these lower planes. Each is not the same. There are different grades of spirits just as we see physically, we have some persons who are brilliant scientists and other who are just plain dumb.

I do subscribe to the idea that people should be treated fairly and that everyone should be given due concern but that will never cause equalization in full terms because existence itself is against that. After this creation evolved for billions of years both in the physical and supernatural levels, no being will change this.

One can be as kind as Jesus Christ and as non-violent as Mahatma Gandhi, and still this existence will continue with manifest disparities. There is absolutely no evidence that everything will be equalized and that everyone will have the same value. Perhaps that is the very reason why we have to be so careful not to exploit if we gain the advantage.

Yogi Bhajan: Viewing Video Media (May 8, 2011)

Today when I sat to meditate, Yogi Bhajan was present. He commented on what happens when one views video media. He explained.

If the mind is strongly attracted to the media, it is tracked on the intellect. The track may be a deep or shallow recording. It depends on the strength of the attraction the person feels to the scenes viewed.

For yogis it is no different. A yogi should not feel that he can view media without a corresponding negative effect on meditation. If one views media one should expect a setback in meditation. If images are deeply etched into the intellect, do not think that there is a magic erasure for it. Do not view media unless you are prepared to scrub it from the intellect and memory at a later time when it obstructs the meditation session.

The methods of removing the sense media which is in the intellect or which penetrate it from memories during meditation, vary from person to person.

It is like the three guys who committed a robbery. They were arrested. One was the son of the governor. He called his father. He was released immediately. Another called his friend who was an attorney. He sprung from jail by paying a bond. The other one, who had no connections remained in jail until the trial. He had no money to pay a bond. He had no political connections.

This was further illustrated at the trial. The guy who was the governor's son got a suspended sentence but he paid a fine of ten thousand dollars. The one whose friend was an attorney was confined for a week. He paid a $5000 fine and did community service for one month. The other one got a three-month sentence with one week of hard labor.

Meditation is very similar in that one person has it easy and another has difficulty, depending on the focus of practice, the past life yoga efforts and the present circumstances.

Right now, I enjoy myself in meditation like the governor's son. If there is an image, I go into the intellect. I directly confront the information. Or I may not go into the orb but may go to a distance from it, like going into the naad sound. Then the orb becomes silenced since its power supply ceases if I am not connected to it. Another method which I use is to infuse breath energy into the place in the intellect which has the thought energy.

For beginners, it is best not to confront the thought or image which is the distraction. Initially because of not having power over the intellect and not knowing how to deal with it, one should get at a distance from it. This means psychological distance, distance in the mystic terrain of the mind.

Go at a distance and remain there until the intellect stops producing thoughts and images. Because the self is attracted to the intellect's fascinations, this is not as easy as it sounds. It is natural to be attracted and curious about images and ideas which arise in the mind, hence one must fight this attraction power in the psyche by learning how to turn away from what is desired and still be happy without that idea or commodity.

Just as we are attracted to sweet foods and we helplessly eat these even though we may be afflicted with suffering as a result, so we are attracted to mental ideas which we should abandon as soon as we realize we are under their sway. It is an uphill battle for each yogi.

Intellect Bruised

This morning in meditation, I jumped into the intellect at its default location which is in front of the coreSelf, towards the front of the head, toward the brow chakra.

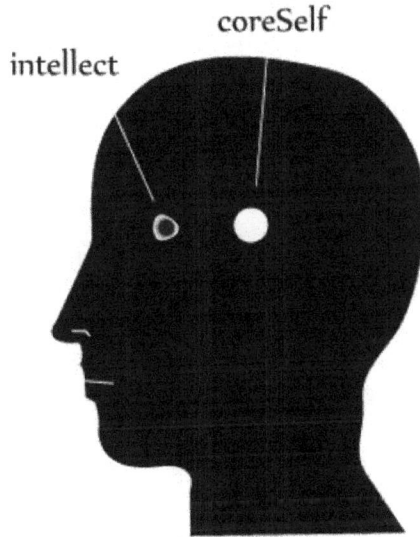

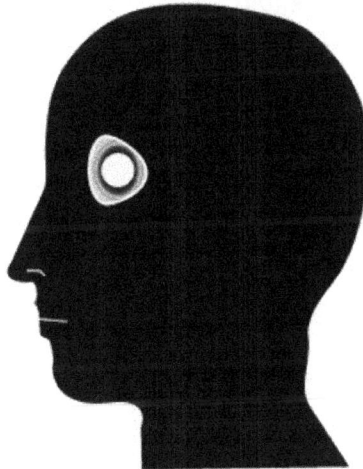

coreSelf interspaced
in intellect

When I entered it there was a bruise spot. This is like entering a semitransparent globe or oval shape object. The bruise was on the surface membrane. It did not penetrate the orb. I disregarded it. It was from a thought which reached me from some persons who wanted to contact me yesterday.

Because I avoided contact, those persons felt neglected. They sent a harmful energy which bruised the orb. Such is this social life that one must tolerate these incidences and not get upset because others make unreasonable demands.

The intellect was clear inside. It has no thoughts, images or other types of psychic expressions. This is the state which *Patañjali* feels the intellect should be in during every meditation session.

Intellect Jump

This morning after doing forty-five minutes of breath infusion in various postures, I sat to meditate. The last fifteen minutes of breath infusion was done to infuse various parts of the subtle head, such as the back top, the middle region and the intellect in the frontal region.

Before infusing the head, I raised kundalini through the spine. It released energy into the chest region with tingling sensations. It entered the head through the spinal column in the neck.

When I first sat to meditate, there was fresh energy rushing here and there in the subtle head. I checked for naad. After identifying that, I moved into the location of naad. I noticed that Yogi Bhajan was in the subtle head. He directed me to move back to the default coreSelf position which is in the center of the subtle head. As soon as I did so, the intellect jumped to a position above the core.

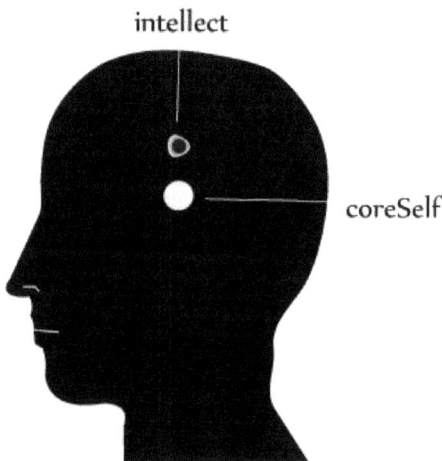

intellect

coreSelf

I cannot remember the intellect taking that position. I checked to see the cause of its relocation and saw that it did so because of the way the subtle energy struck and entered it.

During the breath infusion session, Yogi Bhajan instructed that I force fresh energy into a band which was around the intellect. This is what caused the orb to jump to a position above the coreSelf. The orb also had peaceful bliss energy in it.

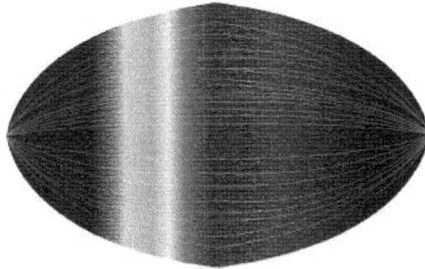

Resistance to Responsibility

Yogi Bhajan came during the breath infusion this morning. At first, he defended the Indian yoga chakra system saying that it was only the visualization and passive meditation people in India who were mistaken about the kundalini and the navel chakra. He asked me if I remember his stress about flushing that front expansion of the chakra during the late 1960s and the early 1970s. I did recall what he said about it and that he stressed it.

Yogi then went into the topic of why so many of his Western disciples did not remain consistent at the practice. Many returned to their former social ways. He said this.

The males who came to me, were mostly afraid of responsibility. Even though they practiced, when females would approach for relationship, they considered the approach to be sexual only. They were afraid of commitment for a family with children.

That was the impediment. I encouraged them to take a spouse, raise a family and be a responsible member of society. I even showed how to start businesses like health food stores, boutiques and contractor services, but they could not stick with anything because they did not perceive the value of responsibility. In India, responsibility for family is stress under the name of dharma. Without family one cannot get a body and without a body one cannot use a human form for self-realizations.

While in the West family life is seen as a necessarily social utility, in India, it is also considered the same way in addition to its value for spiritual realization. If someone does this breath infusion daily, and meditates, he will see his way through the morass of social life and will have spiritual elevation during this life.

Mental Chatter

Please read this verse from Patanjali's *Yoga Sutras*. This happened during meditation this morning:

प्रवृत्त्यालोकन्यासात्सूक्ष्मव्यवहितविप्रकृष्टज्ञानम् ॥२६॥

pravṛitti āloka nyāsāt sūkṣma

vyavahita viprakṛṣṭajñānam

pravṛttyālokanyāsāt = pravṛtti – destined activity, the force of cultural activity + āloka – supernatural insight + nyāsāt – from placing or applying; sūkṣma – subtle; vyavahita – concealed; viprakṛṣṭa – remote; jñānam – knowledge.

From the application of supernatural insight to the force producing cultural activities, a yogi gets information about what is subtle, concealed and remote from him. (Yoga Sutras 3.26)

Even though this happened it did not occur on the basis of how *Patañjali* presented the verse. His presentation concerns the direct application of supernatural insight to cultural activities. However, a yogi cannot directly apply insight unless his insight is well developed and steady. If the yogi is not isolated and is not fully developed in the supernatural body on the appropriate level, he cannot do what *Patañjali* described.

This does not mean however that a yogi who is not as developed will never have such experiences. He may but it will happen by the grace of providence, as if it occurred accidently, by chance or good luck. It is very important to report honestly about yoga and not to canvas people with a pretense of advancement that one does not have.

After doing some forty-five minutes of breath infusion, I sat to meditate. At first, I noticed two factors. One was naad sound which was higher in frequency than usually. If naad is higher in frequency or if it changes frequency there is a reason even though a yogi may not know why that occurred. In this case, naad assumed a higher frequency because the kundalini energy shot out the top back of the head. It grazed the naad sound on the right side of the back. This grazing caused naad to have an alteration.

To assess kundalini's vibration, I positioned the self in the kundalini energy. It was like if a person moved into a path of air flow which under pressure blew through a vent. The kundalini energy was clean and clear like sunlight. It moved with force through the back top of the head. It was in a rectangular channel

Most reports from yogis about kundalini is its movement through the spine in a cylindrical central channel called *sushumna nadi*, but this was rectangular shaped about two inches by four inches passing out the top back of the head. This is a case of having an experience which is different to the convention. This is why I asked students not to do meditate with preconceived notions and to be open-minded and report what happens rather than to visualize what was described in a book. Cease visualization. Be patient. Wait for these experiences to happen objectively.

After observing that I moved into naad. Being in naad as usual, something suddenly happened where I saw a flash of a scene in Australia of a lady in an orphanage with aborigine children. The lady used a white body and the children were dark skinned.

When this flash occurred, it was as if I was physically in Australia. The subtle body synchronized into the physical frequency there. This did not last for long. It was not more than about three seconds but it was definitive and distinct.

I was then transferred into naad sound. I realized that this was an example of what *Patañjali* wrote in the *Yoga Sutras*.

प्रवृत्त्यालोकन्यासात्सूक्ष्मव्यवहितविप्रकृष्टज्ञानम् ॥२६॥

pravṛitti āloka nyāsāt sūkṣma

vyavahita viprakṛṣṭajñānam

pravṛttyālokanyāsāt = pravṛtti – destined activity, the force of cultural activity + āloka – supernatural insight + nyāsāt – from placing or applying; sūkṣma – subtle; vyavahita – concealed; viprakṛṣṭa – remote; jñānam – knowledge.

From the application of supernatural insight to the force producing cultural activities, a yogi gets information about what is subtle, concealed and remote from him. (Yoga Sutras 3.26)

What is the psychic mechanism which operates this type of mystic transfer which could be done deliberately by an advanced yogi?

The answer is that this is operated by providence, where certain stored energies are released out of the deep memory when a yogi accidentally reaches a certain plane of consciousness through breath infusion or by some other means.

Why those specific stored energies or fated circumstances? Because those ideas are the ones which are to emerge next from the subconscious reserve.

In other words, if it could, providence would transport me to that orphanage to serve there as an assistant to that lady. Sometimes a yogi utilizes such information and goes to service a situation in his subtle form, thereby satisfying a providential account on the astral planes.

Initially a novice can expect that there will be mental chatter during practice. There may also be hesitation from not knowing which sequence to use. However, once a yogi gets a set sequence and consistently does it, he will find that this problem fades away. If he is not consistent this problem will never go away.

Mental chatter is nature's harassment. Even other species of life even the most primitive have that problem. All species think even though all species do not have the equipment to vocalize thoughts.

Thus, by nature's grace mental chatter will never cease. It will leave only by long endeavor along the lines given by Patanjali. One can just imagine how serious of a problem it is, that *Patañjali* declared both correct deductions and erroneous notions, as impediments in the clarification regarding what our psychic components are. It is a serious problem. The more one tries to meditate, the more it will be obstructive, even though in fact what happens is that the more one meditates, the more one observes how one is spellbound by thoughts.

Any beginner who gets the idea that overnight he/she will conquer this thought harassment system will be disappointed. It will happen after long consistent and sincere practice for many years. As soon as one does not apply the discipline, nature will resume the harassment.

Even though during the infusement when one is occupied infusing the breath energy, one does not notice thoughts or one hardly notices thoughts, there will come a time if one persists where one will infuse the system and will notice thoughts. Not noticing thoughts does not mean there are none. In fact, the stage of no thoughts is rare, just as when people say that they do not dream, the fact is that they recall no dreams.

When one does breath infusion, the attention is occupied doing that. Even though thoughts arise one may not perceive them.

When one reaches the stage where one becomes aware of thoughts during the infusion, one should send some infused breath into the location in the subtle head where the thoughts appear.

Glow of Light

Regarding a glow of light which disappears or recedes when one tries to observe it, the light itself informs the yogi that if he tries to see it head on, it will vanish. It informs him that it will not be controlled. The yogi should be satisfied that the light is present. He should be happy without trying to grasp or focus on the light.

When one sits to meditate if one becomes aware of the light, one should train the self to move into the naad sound, and then look forward gently without grasping the light, without trying to possess it or trying to cease its movement.

Naad Shift

Naad sound is usually heard from the inside of the head as if it is coming from the outside through a space near the right ear. In this morning meditation, naad was heard from a shifted position which was above and a little to the back of the right ear.

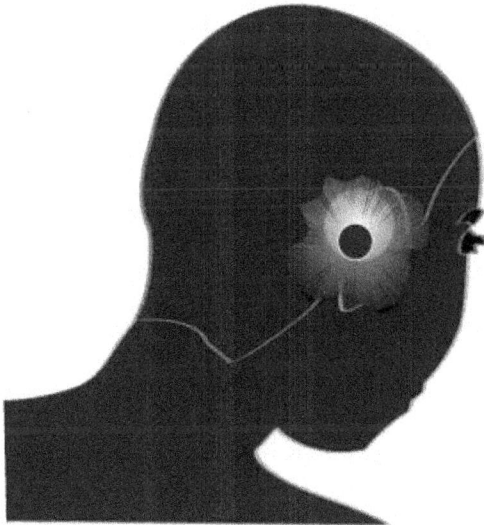

naad sound in default position
by right ear

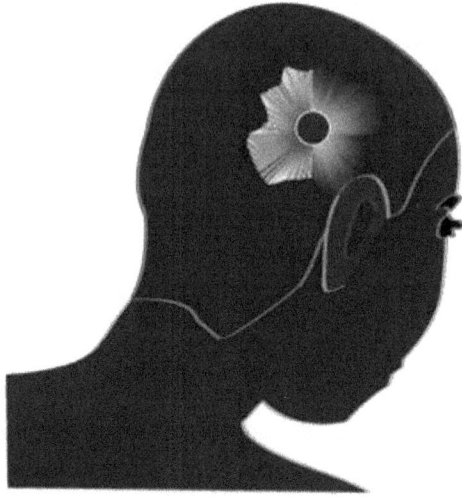

naad sound shifted above right ear

After doing breathing exercises and sitting to meditate, and after assuming a position in naad, shifting the coreSelf from its default position, I went forward again, after about ten minutes in naad, to see if the intellect was in a stilled condition. It was. Soon after there was a flash of light as if a piece of glass was illuminated. That occurred about two feet ahead of me. Then there was pitch darkness in the intellect. (That two feet distance is mystic distance, not physical measure.)

There were a series of lighted random lines and a lighted rectangular mirror-like object through the third eye. That lasted for six seconds. Then it disappeared.

I resumed focus in naad and moved to where naad was located. Periodically I found myself out of naad. Then I resumed naad focus. The intellect created no images.

I did however see Rishi Singh Gherwal in another part of my subtle head. He was not concerned to give directions.

Physical distance is perceived through the physical body, where one perceives an object and estimates its distance. Mental measure is a psychic estimation. Some people feel that everything one does is relative to one's perception and bias, but physical reality is not dependent on individual preference. This is why you can be given a measure of a certain number of feet or miles, and verify it with a standard measure.

Mystic distance is when you do not use the physical eyes. You make observations, form conclusions and make judgment or analyze on the basis of other perceptions such as intuition, subtle eye vision, third eye vision and intellect vision.

In the experience mentioned above, the psychic objects were at a two feet distance from the intellect but it was as if the third eye was like a glass pane sitting on top of the objects. If you perceive something through the intellect or through the intellect and then through the third eye, like seeing through two lenses of a telescope, the distance can be judged on the basis of measures used in this world but in actuality those measurements are not physical. They are psychic distances.

The application of this is as follows:

In the astral world you may cross the Atlantic Ocean to travel from Africa to North American in a matter of two seconds. Sometimes when the astral body does this, it happens so fast that one only knows that one was in Africa and then one was in America. One does not perceive the distance because the rapidity of travel of the astral form is such that it moves faster than one can measure.

There may be another experience where in the astral body, one tries to move it one inch and cannot move it or one takes ten minutes of physical time to move that one inch. In the physical world, we do not usually have such experiences. I stated two feet but it does not mean that it is two feet. I wanted to give some idea of where the perception occurred since location is important in advanced meditation practice.

Yoga Explained

Rishi Singh Gherwal gave this explanation about the layout of the eight stages of yoga.

The first two are yama and niyama, prohibited activities and recommended behaviors. These are the base for a human being. Initially, these concern social involvement. One uses the internal psyche to control physical behavior. At first, this is an external occupation.

These two elementary stages are internalized in the higher level of practice but initially these concern cultural activities and one's behavior in the physical environment. Practically all religions have moral taboos and approved behaviors because in a social setting there should be agreement for approved conduct just for the sake of living with others in peace.

The third level is the asana postures which concern the physical body. Yoga begins with monitoring the behavior of the physical form in a physical environment. Then we regard the body itself to monitor the behavior of the various limbs and organs in respect to each other.

At first yoga begins with an extrovert process. It graduates to an introvert observation beginning by paying attention to the relationship between the limbs and organs of the body irrespective to what one must do to manage behavior with others in the extrovert relationships.

If one drives a wagon or an automobile and if one did not create the machine, one may never have a mind to study the design nor the relationship between the parts.

That would be like if a person began to practice restrictive moral behaviors and approved relationships and went no further. In fact most religions do just that. They require no more from the believer.

In yoga that is the beginning. In addition, you are required to study the relationship of the limbs and organs of the body in terms of the body itself and how its parts are operated collectively.

The mastery of the asana comes when the student intimately understands how the various parts of the body are interrelated and what to do to cause these to function more efficiently.

The fourth step in yoga is breath infusion pranayama which concerns studying the effects of the basic energy of the body. This basic energy is air. The body cannot exist on air alone but air is the most essential ingredient. Air allows the body to distribute its energy reserves. If there is energy in one part of the body and it is needed in another part of the system, air is the substance that facilitates the transfer.

By studying the conveyance of air to various parts of the form, a student gets some idea of how he/she can better distribute energy through the body and through the psyche or the psychological components which comprise the body. The advantage of this is that a person can select which type of area of the body, he/she wishes to energize.

Nature teaches a technique through sexual indulgence. In sex activity, nature directs the air energy into the genitals. The person directly experiences the intense feelings which are created as a result.

In yoga however we are not interested in further use of sex but rather, we want to take the air to other parts of the body particularly up the spine and into the brain. We desire to experience blissful states of consciousness in that way as contrasted to overwhelming feelings from the genitals.

Yoga begins with restrictive moral behaviors and approved conducts. Then there is observation of the limbs and organs of the body. Then there is breath infusion.

This is progress from extroversion to introversion.

The fifth state is pratyahara which is sensual energy withdrawal. This is an emotional arrest, where the person retracks his or her sensual interest from the outside world. Initially this is a struggle because it goes against the natural way which is to procure information from the external environment.

As soon as a creature is born, it researches the external environment. It has to put itself into a safer position. If it fails to do so, it may be devoured by other creatures. Thus, when the yogi first attempts to curtail the interest in the external world, he/she feels strained psychologically because it is unnatural to turn the senses inwards.

Kundalini lifeForce is concerned to protect the body from external assaults. When a yogi begins pratyahara sensual energy withdrawal practice, he/she struggles with kundalini since it instructs the senses to disobey the introvert interest of the yogi.

As the main protector of the body from its inception, kundalini does not respect the coreSelf's decision to reduce external interest. When a yogi gets serious about sensual withdrawal practice, there is a power struggle on the psychological plane.

Nature designed the senses to help to protect the body from external assaults. If one wants to use the senses for other purposes, one will have to fight against the natural tendencies. Even the use of the senses for sexual enjoyment is a function of that protection system because the intentions of nature for sex enjoyment is reproduction. As soon as there is success in that, the protection systems become relevant all over again.

Initially in sensual energy withdrawal which is the fifth stage of yoga, a person becomes obsessed with escaping from the external environment but when he is successful at doing this, he is forced to face another problem which is that within the mind and feelings there are sensual deviations which seem to be beyond his or her control. At this stage a yogi realizes that he must get assistance from advanced yogis.

He then gets an instruction about the sixth stage of yoga which is dharana, or focus on something higher. What something? That varies from student to student and from teacher to teacher. There is a need for focus because that happens to be part of the essential being. Thus, merely to suspend the senses is not the complete process.

A ship needs an anchor. A living being needs something to rely on. There arises the need for focus. The process of finding something or someone on the psychological plane to focus upon is known as dharana. Various leading yogis give different objects of focus. There is disagreement as to the object of such focus.

Let us assume that a beginner retracts his or her sensual energies, then what?

He/she will find that the energies may sometimes relax and be satisfied to remain in a dormant or quiescent stage but sometimes they rush outwards forcibly again. This is daunting. Many beginners turn away from yoga when they face opposition from the senses.

Dharana is deliberate focus on something out of this world, something transcendental. This may be a person or thing. In this, the sixth stage of yoga, the yogi directs his retained focus to something or someone other than the objects in the physical environment. He/she shifts focus into other levels of consciousness or other higher dimensional environments.

The seventh stage is dhyana which is the proficient level of the previous stage of other-world focus. In dhyana, that other focus happens but without effort. This is like getting money in an honest way without working for it. An example is like when a person wins a lottery, or gets a large inheritance.

Most people work for a living but some get lucky. Some yogis struggle to maintain otherworld focus while for others it comes easy without mental exertion.

The eight stage is samadhi which means that the yogi experiences an otherworldly focus for a long time and without any effort on his part. Somehow the yogi finds that his psyche retains spontaneous interest in transcendental focus.

What is the purpose of inSelf Yoga™?

It has to do with destination and transmigration. A living being in this world is a nomad, a self which wanders through the corridors of existence. Most selves do so without a clue as to selection or preference.

Yoga can show a person the selections which are available after death of the body. Thus, the yogi can focus on the preferred hereafter environment.

Morality becomes an internal behavior when the coreSelf supervises the interactions of the adjuncts in their relationship with the core. The different is clear because initially the restrictive moral behaviors and approved conducts concern one's physical behavior and that of others in the social environment, while now it concerns no one but the student himself or herself, between the coreSelf and the adjuncts.

When Narad spoke to King Prachinabarhi about Puranjan, Narad said that Puranjan had married a woman who was a queen. Puranjan had numerous children by this queen. Later when Prachinabarhi asked Narad about the pedigree of Puranjan, Narada explained that Puranjan was the coreSelf and the Queen to whom the king was married was the intellect.

Our tendency is external social regulation but that is misleading. The priority is regulation of the psychic adjuncts by the coreSelf.

Part 3

Third Eye Beam-Light

In meditation this morning the following occurred. (This was meditation after breath infusion which raised kundalini into the head and then breath infusion which caused the intellect to be directly struck by the breath energy.)

At first, I instinctively identified and moved into the naad sound. I noticed small thoughts hitting the intellect which did not respond to the thoughts because it was struck by the infused breath energy which I did just prior to sitting for meditation. The orb was still under the spell of that energy. It did not resume its usual acceptance of thoughts which struck its membrane.

I remained in naad. Suddenly ahead of me, there was a light which shone in a vast darkness. This changed into a third eye light which shined like a search beam in a dark sea which had fishes. They were startled by the light. A few swam to the light but the light moved away from them and kept moving at a speed of about five miles per hour. I could not tell the depth of the water. As this happened my central consciousness was still in the physical body but its full focus was on the light and what the light revealed.

This lasted five minutes. Immediately after, the subtle body, suddenly and without notice, separated from the physical one. Both bodies were in lotus posture. The subtle body maintained that pose.

Suddenly I was in the air near a place where people walked by a beach. There was a dike made out of rock and concrete, the subtle body moved at about 20 miles per hour. It rushed towards the rock. I knew that it would not crash into the rock but still when it got near the rock, the rock emitted a fear energy as if it did not want the body to crash into it.

The body then rose just before it hit the sea-wall. After this it coursed through the sky and went to a place where people strolled near some tall buildings.

While this took place, the subtle body used third eye vision and not dual subtle eye vision. This was unusual. Normally, when one is in the subtle body during astral projections it uses dual subtle-eye vision.

I modified but could not fully control the speed of the astral body. It went on its own. It acted as if it was programmed for these movements. After about ten minutes, it fused into the physical form.

Special Note

This experience shows that the subtle body may sometimes act on its own. Rishi Singh Gherwal's idea is that if one energizes that body by raising kundalini and also energize the intellect which is in the head of the body, one will get such experiences. He said that it is the influence of laziness and inertia which discourages yogis, preventing and effectively discouraging them from practice.

Instead of thinking that one can order the subtle body to have these experiences, one would get success in a rapid way if one infused sufficient energy into the subtle system. One must challenge the laziness energy in the psyche. It influences the individual. This is why one person practices and another does not.

Sometimes people think that I am lucky and perhaps that is true. Still, I must deal with laziness. I too must confront it and put up a daily fight. The laziness energy does not go away. It is an intrinsic part of nature. One has to understand that a daily fight will occur if one is to effectively counteract it.

Read this conversation between Krishna and Arjuna.

अर्जुन उवाच

अयतिः श्रद्धयोपेतो

योगाच्चलितमानसः ।

अप्राप्य योगसंसिद्धिं

कां गतिं कृष्ण गच्छति ॥६.३७॥

arjuna uvāca

ayatiḥ śraddhayopeto

yogāccalitamānasaḥ

aprāpya yogasaṁsiddhiṁ

kāṁ gatiṁ kṛṣṇa gacchati (6.37)

arjuna — Arjuna; uvāca — said; ayatiḥ — indisciplined person; śraddhayopeto = śraddhayopetaḥ = śraddhayā — by faith + upetaḥ — has got; yogāccalitamānasaḥ = yogāc (yogāt) — from yoga practice + calita — deviated + mānasaḥ — mind; aprāpya — not attain; yogasaṁsiddhiṁ — yoga proficiency; kāṁ — what; gatiṁ — course; kṛṣṇa — Krishna; gacchati — he goes

Arjuna said: What about the undisciplined person who has faith? Having deviated from yoga practice, having not attained yoga proficiency, what course does he take, O Krishna? (Bhagavad Gita 6.37)

कच्चिन्नोभयविभ्रष्टश्

छिन्नाभ्रमिव नश्यति ।

अप्रतिष्ठो महाबाहो

विमूढो ब्रह्मणः पथि ॥६.३८॥

kaccinnobhayavibhraṣṭaś

chinnābhramiva naśyati

apratiṣṭho mahābāho

vimūḍho brahmaṇaḥ pathi (6.38)

kaccin = kaccid — is he; nobhayavibhraṣṭaś = na — not + ubhaya — both + vibhraṣṭaḥ — lost out; chinnābhram = chinna — faded + abhram — cloud; iva — like; naśyati — lost; apratiṣṭho = apratiṣṭhaḥ — without foundation; mahābāho — O Almighty Kṛṣṇa; vimūḍho = vimūḍhaḥ — baffled; brahmaṇaḥ — of the spirituality; pathi — on the path

Is he not like a faded cloud, lost from both situations, like being without a foundation? O Almighty Krishna: He is baffled on the path of spirituality. (Bhagavad Gita 6.38)

एतन्मे संशयं कृष्ण

छेत्तुमर्हस्यशेषतः।

त्वदन्यः संशयस्यास्य

छेत्ता न ह्युपपद्यते ॥६.३९॥

etanme saṁśayaṁ kṛṣṇa

chettumarhasyaśeṣataḥ

tvadanyaḥ saṁśayasyāsya

chettā na hyupapadyate (6.39)

etan = etad — this; me — of mine; saṁśayam — doubt; kṛṣṇa — Krishna; chettum — remove; arhasy = arhasi — you can; aśeṣataḥ — without reminder, fully; tvadanyaḥ = besides you; saṁśayasyāsya = saṁśayasya — of doubt + asya — of this; chettā — remover of doubt; na — not; hy (hi) — indeed; upapadyate — he exists

You can, O Krishna, remove this doubt of mine fully. Besides You, no other remover of doubt, exists here. (Bhagavad Gita 6.39)

श्रीभगवानुवाच

पार्थ नैवेह नामुत्र

विनाशस्तस्य विद्यते ।

न हि कल्याणकृत्कश्चिद्

दुर्गतिं तात गच्छति ॥६.४०॥

śrībhagavānuvāca

pārtha naiveha nāmutra

vināśastasya vidyate

na hi kalyāṇakṛtkaścid

durgatiṁ tāta gacchati (6.40)

śrībhagavān — the Blessed Lord; uvāca — said; pārtha — O son of Pṛthā; naiveha = na — either + eva — indeed + iha — here on earth; namutra = na — nor + amutra — above in the celestial regions; vināśaḥ — loss; tasya — his; vidyate — it is realized; na — not; hy (hi) — indeed; kalyāṇakṛt — performer of pious acts; kaścid — anyone; durgatiṁ — into misfortune; tāta — O ideal one; gacchati — goes down permanently

The Blessed Lord said: O son of Pṛthā, it is realized that neither here on earth nor above in the celestial regions, does the unaccomplished yogi lose his skill. Indeed, O dear Arjuna, no performer of virtuous acts, goes down permanently into misfortune. (Bhagavad Gita 6.40)

प्राप्य पुण्यकृताँल्लोकान्

उषित्वा शाश्वतीः समाः ।

शुचीनां श्रीमतां गेहे

योगभ्रष्टोऽभिजायते ॥६.४१॥

prāpya puṇyakṛtāṁllokān

uṣitvā śāśvatīḥ samāḥ

śucīnāṁ śrīmatāṁ gehe

yogabhraṣṭo'bhijāyate (6.41)

prāpya — obtaining; puṇyakṛtām — of the performer of virtuous acts; lokān — celestial places; uṣitvā — having lived; śāśvatīḥ — many, many; samāḥ — years; śucīnām — of the purified person; śrīmatām — of the prosperous person; gehe — in the social circumstance; yogabhraṣṭo = yogabhraṣṭaḥ — fallen from yoga; 'bhijāyate = abhijāyate — is born

After obtaining the celestial places where the virtuous souls go, having lived there for many, many years, the fallen yogi is born into the social circumstances of the purified and prosperous people. (Bhagavad Gita 6.41)

अथ वा योगिनामेव

कुले भवति धीमताम् ।

एतद्धि दुर्लभतरं

लोके जन्म यदीदृशम् ॥६.४२॥

atha vā yogināmeva

kule bhavati dhīmatām

etaddhi durlabhataraṁ

loke janma yadīdṛśam (6.42)

atha vā — alternately; yoginām — of the yogi; eva — indeed; kule — in the family situation; bhavati — is born; dhīmatām — of the enlightened people; etad — this; dhi = hi — indeed; durlabhataram — difficult to attain; loke — in this world; janma — birth; yad — which; īdṛśam — such

Alternately, he is born into a family of enlightened people. But such a birth is very difficult to attain in this world. (Bhagavad Gita 6.42)

तत्र तं बुद्धिसंयोगं

लभते पौर्वदेहिकम् ।

यतते च ततो भूयः

संसिद्धौ कुरुनन्दन ॥६.४३॥

tatra taṁ buddhisaṁyogaṁ

labhate paurvadehikam

yatate ca tato bhūyaḥ

saṁsiddhau kurunandana (6.43)

tatra — there; tam — it; buddhisaṁyogam — cumulative intellectual interest; labhate — inspired with; paurvadehikam — from a previous birth; yatate — he strives; ca — and; tato = tataḥ — from that time; bhūyaḥ — again; saṁsiddhau — to perfection; kuru-nandana — O dear son of the Kurus

In that environment, he is inspired with the cumulative intellectual interest from a previous birth. And from that time, he strives again for yoga perfection, O dear son of the Kurus. (Bhagavad Gita 6.43)

पूर्वाभ्यासेन तेनैव

ह्रियते ह्यवशोऽपि सः ।

जिज्ञासुरपि योगस्य

शब्दब्रह्मातिवर्तते ॥६.४४॥

pūrvābhyāsena tenaiva

hriyate hyavaśo'pi saḥ

jijñāsurapi yogasya

śabdabrahmātivartate (6.44)

pūrvābhyāsena = pūrva — previous + abhyāsena — by practice; tenaiva = tena — by it + eva — indeed; hriyate — he is motivated; hy (hi) — indeed; avaśo = avaśaḥ — without conscious desire; 'pi = api — even; saḥ — he; jijñāsuḥ — persistently inquiring; api — even; yogasya — of yoga; śabdabrahmātivartate = śabda — spoken description + brahma — spiritual reality + ativartate — instinctively sees beyond (śabdabrahma — Vedas)

Indeed, by previous practice, he is motivated, even without conscious desire. He who persistently inquires of yoga, instinctively sees beyond the Veda, the spoken description of the spiritual reality. (Bhagavad Gita 6.44)

This means that a person who did not perfect yoga practice in a past life, must take another human body sooner or later, and will more than likely begin the practice again even if that person has no training in the new life and even if that person is born in a family or society where yoga is unknown.

Krishna said that the yogi is inspired with the cumulative intellectual interest from a previous birth. He strives for yoga perfection. By the grace of previous practice, that person gets experiences and feels inclinations to yoga. He must however consolidate the practice. A question arises as to why the psychic capabilities do not manifest in the infant and childhood stages and may only become known in the young adult stage.

These matters need be investigated. When one gets a new body, it is so arranged by nature that one loses awareness of past lives. That risk is there every time one assumes a new body. One will be out of touch with the information and learned behaviors from the previous life.

Social contact, family life and the like does have value. It is just that it has mostly nil spiritual worth. If one must take another body, one must take recourse to one's social contributions. One will get the next body on that basis. The social life has value in terms of the allowing choice opportunities for rebirth in selected families and under select conditions.

As yogis we do not have to care about that value, because when all is said and done one cannot get out of material existence by patronizing family and society. It only increases one's involvements and causes one to be more intertwined in the various providential complications.

All the same one should hurt no one because that will create unwanted backlashes from nature in this or future births. Nature may appear to be haphazard and random but you can take my word, that it is methodical and mathematical. It is exacting in dishing out reactions for our beneficial or criminal acts. One does not know who will be the mother or father. It is worth it to be responsible to any and everyone on the social plane.

Naad Location

Naad sound may be heard on the right side by the right ear. It is heard on the left side. Sometime it switches back and forth between right and left.

It is a high-pitched frequency which resonates continuously. Yet someone may not hear it because of distractions. The high-pitched frequency changes if one meditates on it. To some persons it is a boring sound. To others it is a nuisance. It is a source of shelter to yogis. It allows a yogi to escape from mental harassments in the frontal part of the head. Naad is the ultimate free mantra which one can hear. It assists in tuning the coreSelf.

The key issue is location. Where was the sound sourced, from which direction? Could one enter it? Was one repelled from it?

Non-Essential Yogi

During meditation this morning Rishi Singh Gherwal requested that I mention that a yogi should realize that his/her existence in this physical world and also in the lower adjacent astral world, is unnecessary.

He said this.

So long as one thinks that one can be useful in these creations one will not make a full effort for yogic success. One will not feel the necessity to take the disciplines of the eight-part yoga process. One will play with yoga practice, doing it now, doing it then and going along like that until one finds that one is no longer allowed to be the physical body.

As great as one may be, the plain truth is that this creation does not need one. One is not essential to this. This will continue in one's absence. One will never affect this permanently in a significant way.

What do you think?

Do you feel that you are necessary? If you know that you are not, why invest in this even though whatever you do will lack significance?

Did you not notice that Rama, the son of Dashrath and Kausalya, was here? Krishna, the son of Devaki and Vasudeva, was here. Jesus, the son of Mary and Joseph, was here. This system continues in a stubborn way without lasting impact being made by those super-persons. How will you permanently affect this?

Wise up! Understand that it will continue in its own way. Turn away from this.

Sense of Identity Control

The connection between the sense of identity and the intellect is made by a dart of energy which pours out of the sense of identity in the form of a ray of light.

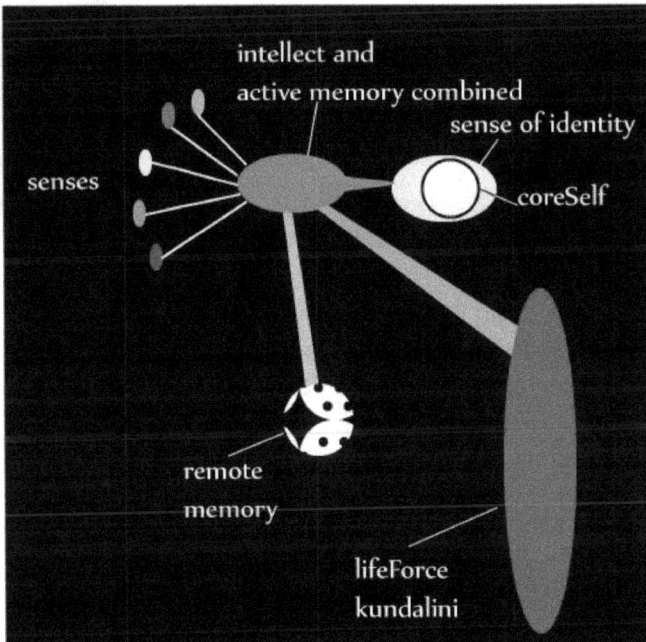

Even though the sense of identity surrounds the core in all directions, still for there to be communication between the identity and the intellect, the identity fires out a dart of energy. This dart makes contact with the intellect and from that the vrittis or mental and emotional modifications comes about.

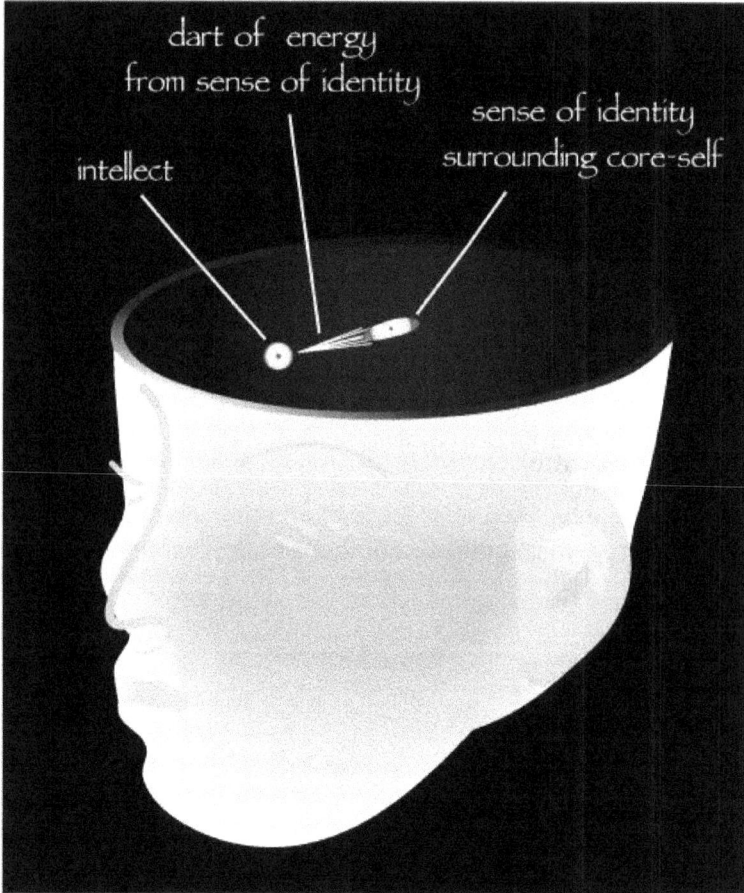

If the coreSelf could control the ray which the sense of identity emits, the core could isolate itself from the ravages of the intellect which really means being protected from being influenced by the senses, kundalini and memory.

Many meditators think that if they get rid of the ego, all problems will be solved but that is a losing battle because no individual will get rid of the sense of identity. One may disable it for a small period of time but that is all. Actually, there is nothing wrong with the identity. By itself it is a neutral psychic aspect. The problems begin when it connects haphazardly to the intellect.

Since we are endowed by nature with a lack of control of the very psyche which we are, there has to be an effort to change that natural arrangement. A yogi must aspire to control the energy which leaves the sense of identity and contacts the intellect.

In meditation when there is a thought, what is the process of the generation of the thought, the perception of it in the mind, and the rejection of or submission to it by the coreSelf?

For this discussion the part which concerns us is the part where the sense of identify contacts the intellect. How does the ego get information from the intellect? Can the ego be segregated? Can the self restrict the ego so that it has no freedom to contact the intellect without first getting permission from the core?

Blank Mental States

It is possible for the grasping tendency to collapse and go into dormancy for a second, minute, hour or for longer duration. But it will reassert itself. The assumption that it will not, is illogical. There is no sense in saying that if one realizes the extent of the cosmic potencies and their penetrating influences, one will be permanently enlightened. When the dormancy runs its course, we will find ourselves with the penetrating influential grasping tendencies again.

Yogeshwarananda dismissed the idea of permanent liberation by asking one simple question.

Were you conditioned before?

This is followed by these questions.

Who or what conditioned you?

Is that authority or potency still existing?

Are you confident that it will never again get the better of you?

Then he would say like this,

"If it happened before it can happen again if the cosmic circumstances produce it. What will you do when it occurs again? Will you be in a position to stop it? Are you not a subordinate part of the cosmic production? Or are you the cosmic producer?"

Being in blank stillness is compared to being in deep sleep or in a fainted state. It is an ignorant condition.

On the other hand, stillness with clarity contains personal experience and certainty of knowing.

The clear type of stillness is the superior type.

A person can center a state in which all grasping ceases for that person, where that psyche ceases craving and does not manifest the symptoms of grasping. But that person may have no insight and may be in a blankness which is actually stupor. Not everyone who attains blankness in meditation is in an insightful state.

The mind exists on several levels. It adapts to the psychological environment of the particular level to which it is synchronized. The natural state of the mind is chaos when it is on a chaotic level. It is clarity when it is on a revealing level. It is stupor or ignorance when it is on a retardative level.

Clarity and emptiness, when emptiness means no ideation, no image forming, no thought creation, applies not to the mind's natural state but to the mind when it is on a certain level.

Its natural state is to become saturated with the level it is synchronized into or is influenced by. For instance, on the physical plane the mind flickers from one object to another. It is untrue that in every case the disappearance of thoughts causes clarity. Some people enter a no-thought state in meditation and derive no spiritual insight from it.

I do agree however that during meditation thoughts should not be pursued. The *Patañjali* method is to cease thoughts and quiet the thought producing psychic apparatus which is the intellect *(buddhi)*. The lower states are an integral part of reality.

In the *Bhagavad Gita,* Krishna said that the material energy, *prakriti*, is *brahman*. It is a type or class of reality. We get confused about it and think that it is trash because it is always altering or as Krishna said it is endlessly mutable. But even so it is here to stay.

Location in Meditation

Location is important. inSelf Yoga™ is concerned with clarity. In stupor states one can become disoriented. One may experience vague and indistinct states of consciousness.

If for instance I am located in London and I tell you that I am in Brazil or that I am the center of the universe, you can understand that something is amiss with my sensual perception.

If I believe that I am God, that I am everywhere and am everything, it will be difficult for me to get clarity and distinction. I will be happy with the absolute-me idea and my sense of omnipresence but it will be an abrupt departure from reality. Thus, location is important.

Naad sound comes from a certain place where the subtle material nature borders the spiritual nature. That place has a supernatural content. Its resonance is naad. According to how near you are to it or how far, that is how you hear it. Still, it will come from a certain direction because the material nature is manifested from a certain place on the edge of the spiritual nature.

The biggest problem for people who want to meditate is to realize the coreSelf and intellect. People usually think that the intellect is their understanding, their calculative intelligence, their sense of reason. They do not see it as a psychic object. One should strive to get clarification about it.

One does have a psyche but it has components. What are these factors? How do they interact? What are the functions? What is the relationship to each? What is a self with or without the components? Does the self lose power to act if it is separated from another component?

The Individual Psyche

During meditation this morning, Yogeshwarananda entered my subtle head. He made the following remarks.

Success in yoga comes about through a thorough effort to study the individual psyche. General statements and ideas do not help. The whole scheme, the process, was given by Patanjali. Krishna discussed the details.

The procedures given by these masters of yoga, serve as a map so that a beginner can realize what he attained and what he should strive to accomplish.

Only in the human species can one get the upper hand to challenge the layout one is given by nature but the human species is also the location for the greatest demands to be placed on anyone for social participation.

Therefore, unless one finds a way to efficiently take care of social obligations or to side step them without negative reactions, one will not be a successful yogi. A human body, once it is assumed, is only a means for social participation. One participates either as a rich or poor man, famous or unknown person. That is normal. But to side step that and study the psyche, that is an attainment which one must struggle for because Nature will not give one that easily.

In general terms the struggle for that may be termed as yoga, even though Patanjali ironed out a specific definition and process.

Some say that yoga is unity, but the flaw in that is this: Who or What controls that unity? If the individual is not ultimately the controller over his unification into or distinction from the Whole, then a discussion about unity is mere talk and nothing else.

You emerged and found yourself as a unit of energies. Did you cause your appearance? If you did not, the discussion over your permanent unification with the whole is baseless. Until we can communicate with the original cause of this diversity, the idea of advaita or ultimate unity is meaningless. The diversity is here to stay. No one can remove it. Even great yogis who merge into cosmic consciousness as they define and experience that, find themselves again as individual units after such experiences.

There is a place where one can go into cosmic energy and remain there but for how long? Since one is not the ultimate controller, one cannot be absolutely sure, that one will not again come out as an individual composite in one of these creations. One does not have that power. Why not admit it and work in a practical way to improve the individual psyche which you are.

This is why I stress that one may as well accept oneself as a composite unit and work from there to understand the ins and outs of the individual psyche. Why keep on hawking over something you did not control, cannot fully control now, and will not control in the distant future.

You have an individual psyche. That is what you are. Work with that. Bring that to order. Know that in detail. Get the best service from that. Reform that. Refine that. Keep that in the best condition.

Intellect Bruised

Here are some ideas given by Rishi Singh Gherwal.

His principle is that using breath infusion practice a yogi should first raise kundalini. Once kundalini is aroused and moves from the base of the spine into the head and into other parts of the body, the yogi should attack the intellect which is usually experienced as thinking constructions.

After kundalini is raised, the yogi should direct the infused breath to the intellect. Question is this: If one cannot see the intellect, if one never saw it, how should one direct the infused breath to it?

This is done by directing the infused breath to the thinking, imaging area in the head. As soon as an image appears, note where it is. Direct the infused breath energy there. As soon as a memory appears, note where it is and do the same thing. Eventually a yogi will know the general whereabouts of the intellect.

The intellect is egg-shaped. It is mostly crosswise in the head in the front part of the brain.

intellect in silent unseen condition

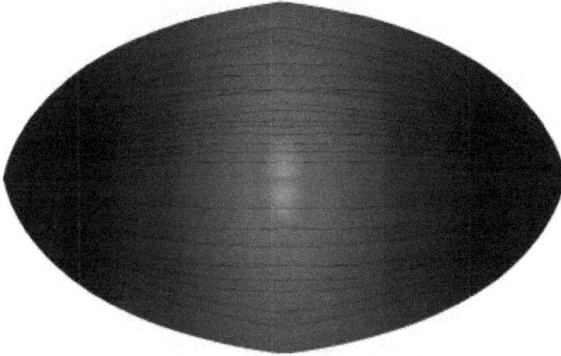

outer membrane of intellect
hit by thoughts from someone else

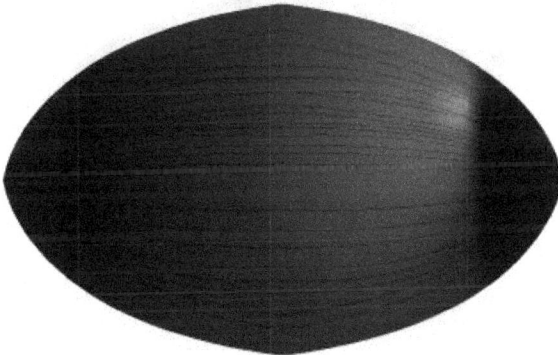

outer membrane bruised by external thought

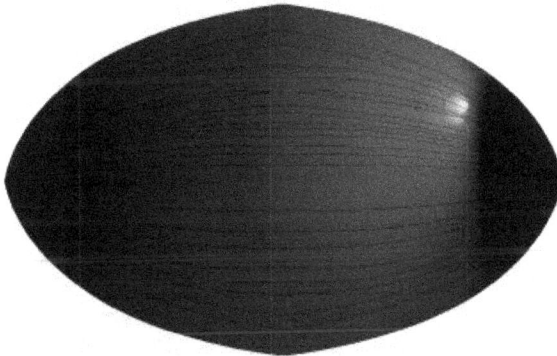

If the idea or thought came from someone else it will hit the membrane layer of the intellect. It will either bounce off or create a bruise mark like when a person is hit with a hard object, and a bruise appears on the skin of the body.

This bruise on the orb will produce an inner spike energy which will spread through the orb and become a thought, image or idea.

If the idea was from the meditator, it will appear inside the orb with no bruise on the membrane of the orb.

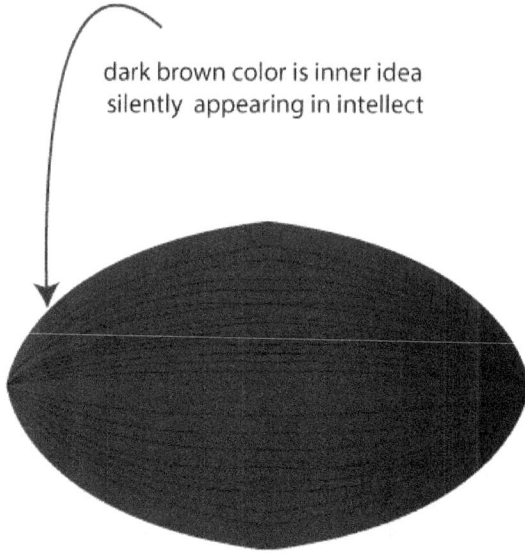

dark brown color is inner idea
silently appearing in intellect

inner idea developing spontaneously
it attracts the coreSelf to view it
core-self experiences the attraction
as a lack of total darkness in the mind,
and as a picture, idea or image emerging

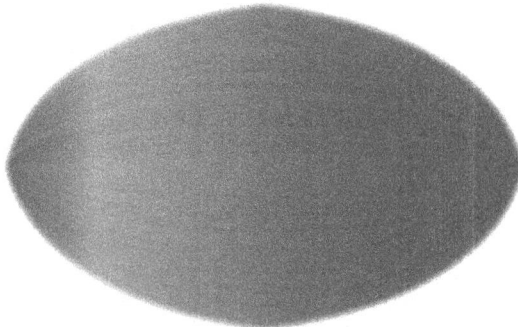

due to receiving energy input
from the attention of the coreSelf,
inner idea comes alive in the mind
the core for its part is fascinated with the image
which it sees as if it was positioned in the intellect

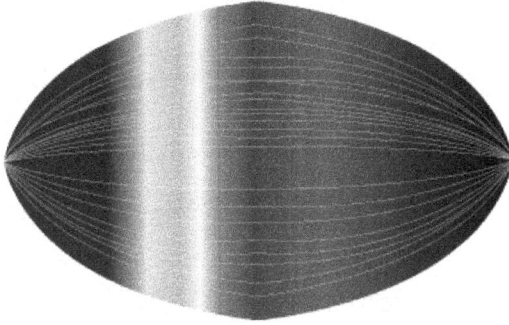

There are two sets of thought images which come from the outside of the orb namely, those which are totally foreign to the psyche of the meditator and those which are not foreign but which are elsewhere in the psyche and which for one reason or the other penetrate the orb.

People speak of finding God inside the self. How should that be done? Should one go into the self or into the subtle psyche in which there is more than one component, the self being only one of the components and one which is sometimes acting under directions from the other components?

I suggest that there is an outside which is inside. We know very well what is outside the physical body. That is an environment in which there are other similar bodies and other animate and inanimate objects. But there is a similar situation on the inside of the psyche where the self will find itself in a mental/emotional environment which is outside the coreSelf.

Just as in this world your body is outside my body, so in the subtle environment within my mind and emotions, my kundalini energy is outside of my coreSelf and so are my memory and other psychic objects.

Because most meditators have not developed psychic senses, they are oblivious to such psychic objects. For them it is all one without differentiation and so they speak of God within.

Actually, there is God within but it is not the individual limited coreSelf, you or me. The real God within is another person completely. When one has experiences of the divine world which is a divine environment with divine people and divine vegetation too, then one will really understand what God really means.

Thoughts and images which come from other psyches and which penetrate one's aura, immediately latch on to the intellect, just like when viruses enter the body, they latch on to cells and begin to make changes for their convenience. Thoughts which are foreign to your psyche slam into the subtle membrane of the intellect and bruise it. In that bruise, the said thoughts spread energy and take control of the intellect. It forces one to view certain ideas.

The thoughts which bruise the orb are those which come from an external psyche. But there are thoughts which come from outside the intellect but inside the psyche which also penetrate the orb without bruising the intellect.

Because these thoughts are native to the psyche they do not rupture, they enter silently. These other thoughts come from the kundalini, and from the memory compartments and also from seed energies in the causal body.

Think of a situation where I have two sons. My wallet is in my bedroom. One son enters the room and removes $100. Later the same night a burglar smashes a window, enters my room and removes $55. The burglar is like the thoughts from outside the psyche. The son is similar to thoughts from kundalini or from memory. In all respects everything outside the house is outside my room and everything that is in the house and which is not in my room is also outside the room.

My son did no damage to the structure of the room but the burglar did, and yet in another consideration my son stole more money than the burglar. By convention of nature, the self is compelled to view thoughts. The force of compulsion comes from the thoughts themselves. Mostly the self is helpless in this matter.

The thoughts and images do burst but not necessarily in the center. According to the nature of the thought it will burst here or there, appearing to be random even though in fact it is not random. Because we lack psychic senses, we fail to differentiate the location of particular thoughts.

The thoughts and images burst in the intellect. The self is compelled to look at the illustrations. It is forced to focus in the orb in a particular place in order to view images, just like when, you go to a multi-screen theatre, you are directed to enter a particular movie room.

If two thoughts hit the intellect simultaneously or if an external thought hits it at the same time when it will show an internal thought, there is a struggle between the two energies. One predominates, such that the coreSelf is forced to accept the priority of the stronger thought. Sometimes after giving that thought its demanded attention, one tries to locate the other thought but sometimes that other energy is destroyed in the clash with the other stronger thought which took precedence over the mind space.

Sometimes when this happens the coreSelf regrets that it lost contact with that other thought. It tries to retrieve it but if it was destroyed it regrets the loss, just like when a bird has two chicks and when she is away, one kills the other. She regrets the dead one but all the same she is compelled by motherly instinct to care for the surviving vicious chick.

Intellect Entry

This is an advanced practice which one may do if one gets the intellect into an attitude of submission. Rishi Sing Gherwal gave this procedure. A similar but more advanced technique was given by Yogeshwarananda in which the intellect moves under the crown chakra, is fused into that chakra and takes a bell-housing shape under it.

Yogesh's procedure is too advanced. One would have to be in isolation for some years to practice that method.

Rishi's method is as follows:

Always get kundalini raised into the head. Then use kundalini to attack the intellect. This means that kundalini is focused into the place where the intellect usually creates thoughts, ideas and images.

When during breath infusion one finds that there are thoughts created by the intellect or that it sensed a thought which was created by someone else and which hits it, one should direct the breath energy to the location where the thought contact occurred. One should aggressively do battle with the intellect to subdue it.

As soon as one ceases the infusion and sits to meditate, one should focus on the naad and move the coreSelf to be surrounded by naad. When this is completed and when one finds that the core remains in the naad and that the intellect is not troublesome and demanding but remains quiet like a mouse which is afraid of a cat, then one should as the coreSelf step into the intellect. This would mean stepping into the mental space where the thoughts and images would normally appear in the mind.

If one does this and one finds oneself in the center of the space of the intellect, it will feel as if one stepped into a transparent bubble. One will know if one achieved this because one could shift into the naad sound and then step into the bubble again.

One will not be able to do this if the orb is resistant to the core, in which case, one should remain with naad and continue the practice of being in naad in isolation from the intellect.

This practice is definite. Because of the location difference between the naad and the intellect, it is not imaginative. These aspects have their particular location just as an eye is located in one place on the face and the nostrils are located in another. In this experience one aspect is distinct from the other.

If one is unable to move into the intellect as described, one should not worry or feel undone. Simply keep practicing to move the coreSelf into the sound of naad. Keep confronting the intellect until you are no longer afraid of it, and until the core develops authority over it.

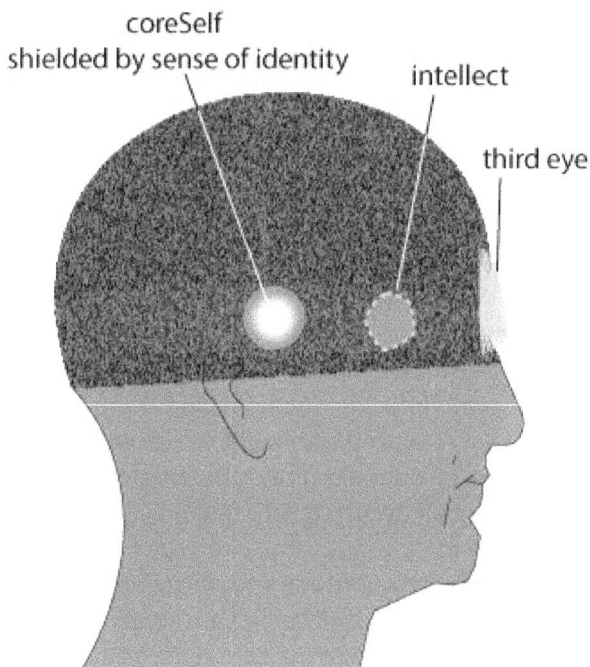

coreSelf
shielded by sense of identity

intellect

third eye

In that diagram, the standard locations of the intellect and the coreSelf are given. These are their default positions. Even if a yogi relocates these, they will resume these locations as soon as he/she relaxes the control.

Examine this diagram:

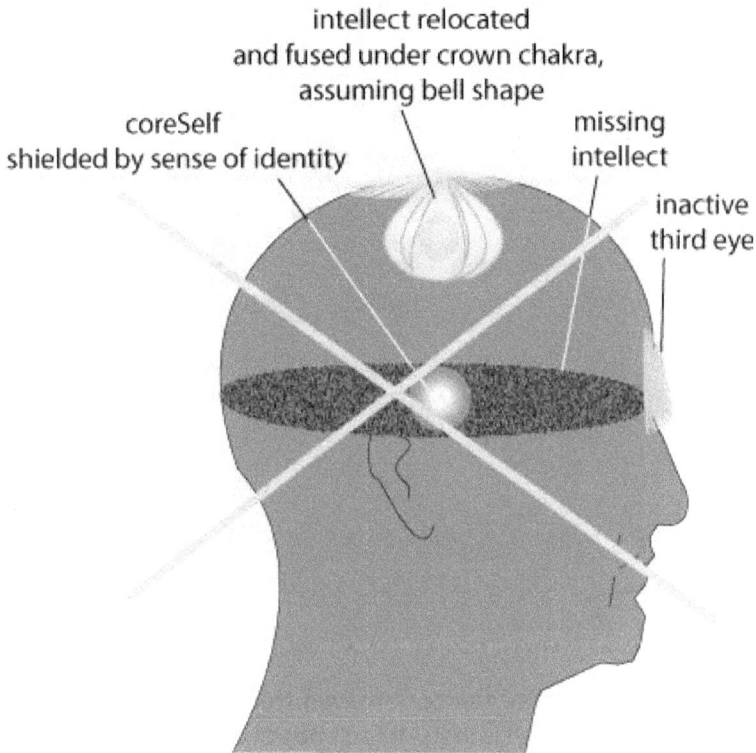

intellect relocated
and fused under crown chakra,
assuming bell shape

coreSelf
shielded by sense of identity

missing
intellect

inactive
third eye

In the above diagram, I gave a method shown by Yogeshwarananda some years ago. Unfortunately, this diagram is useless if for some years one was not isolation with the right techniques. In the diagram the crown chakra *(brahmrandra)* is activated and the intellect assumed a location under the chakra. In doing so the intellect took a bell shape.

Yogeshwarananda discussed this in his *Science of the Soul* book.

Please look at this diagram:

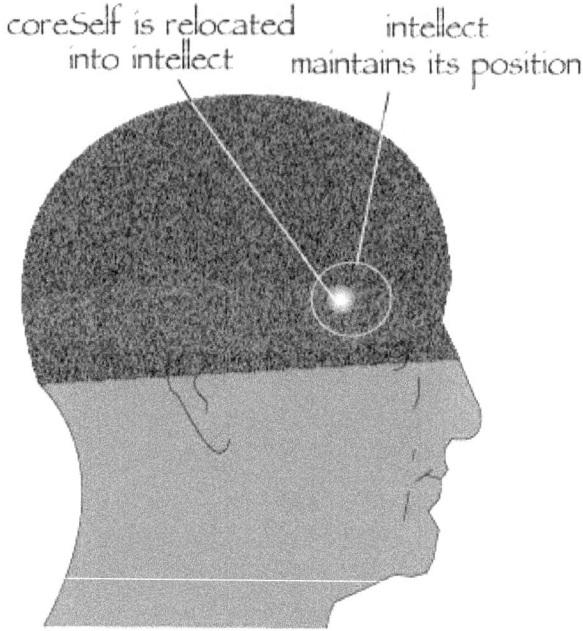

coreSelf is relocated   intellect
    into intellect   maintains its position

In the above diagram, the core moved from its standard location and entered the intellect which is in its default position. To achieve this, the core should first locate, listen to and then move into the naad sound. When the self detects that the intellect is submissive, it should make the attempt to move into the intellect as described.

Squaring up with Fate

Everyone has both bad and good consequences which are due to be applied by fate at fate's convenience. It is impossible in a world like this to have only good consequences. It is also impossible to have only bad results.

Some persons may have more bad effects on the average, just as some may have mostly good luck but all persons existing here are involved in mixed consequences.

Just to take a body, one must absorb some consequences from the parents and ancestors. There is no way around that. Even if one is a pure saint from past lives, or even if it is true that one came from a pure divine world, still one will be marked with negative circumstances from the ancestral line through which one took the body.

In this world even if one came from a divine origin as some persons claim to be, still then one has a perverse destiny unless one can prove that one got the body from a divine non-physical source.

In yoga one should begin with the assumption that one has bad consequences from previous lives and that fate will demand services to compensate for past criminal and careless acts. One must also assume that one has good consequences and that fate is so disordered that it will be sure to repay one in some way or the other but not necessarily at the ideal time.

Let me give an example. When I was sixteen years of age, I lived in Trinidad. It was a sudden change of fortune because I grew up under poverty-stricken conditions. Suddenly I was put on a boat with some sailors at fifteen years of age and was taken to Trinidad.

There I was greeted by the father of my body, a man who did not raise the body and whom I do not recall ever sleeping in the house I slept in from when I was a toddler on up.

This man was an alcoholic. He was brilliant as a seaman. He was hired as the first black man to pilot oil tankers in and out of Trinidad harbors. He had amply salary. He lived in a small palatial house. It had marble pillars and floors.

After I was at his house for about two months, a boy from a neighbor's house came to me. He queried "Is the captain here?"

I replied, "No, he is out at the moment."

The boy then said,

"You are doing a good job as his gardener. We like the way you tend the plants."

The boy felt that I was a yard boy.

By fate, palatial life was imposed on me for a few years. Soon after my father lost his job due to alcoholism. I was deprived of the comfort of that palatial place.

The point is that in my adult life when I could really appreciate and enjoy it, providence did not again give the opportunity. In fact, providence was sure to make low income and poverty my circumstance throughout most of my adult years.

One of the first things we come to realize on this path is that fate is cruel. It imposes both good and bad results on the basis of our good and bad acts from the past, but at its convenience without respect to one's desires, such that at some times it seems that time coincides with what is desired and at other times it seems to oppose outright.

Fate may be compared to the good shepherd idea. This good shepherd idea springs from nomadic tribal life, where a clan had sheep. They wandered with the herd to find new pasture for the sheep.

For their part, the sheep are completely ignorant of the intention of the shepherd which is to keep the sheep as a moving food source. The sheep think that under the protection of the herders they do not have to worry about vicious wolves. It is a fair trade-off. They stay close to the herders and go wherever they direct them. The herders gets the satisfaction of being a good protector.

This is all well and good for the sheep with their limited intellectual capacity but on close analysis it is faulty. Fate is cruel. It will enrich you, the way the herders fatten the sheep but fate's intention is to bring one to ruin just the way the herder will certainly put knives to the throat of the sheep.

Generally, we try to enjoy the events of life. We have ploys for escaping from negative events. But one must realize that both happiness and distress are impositions of destiny.

What bad consequences are due from past lives?

That question cannot be answered in full because fate is not interested in giving any limited person full knowledge of the past. I may assume that bad luck will find me. I also have good luck.

My only leverage is my response to life in terms of how I react to circumstances.

I should behave in the least inconsiderate way. If an opportunity presents itself for me to harm someone, I should if possible, use that opportunity to help the person instead.

Here is a case in point. A friend who lived on the Mexican-American border in Texas called to ask my view on his visit to a prostitute. I explained that visiting prostitutes is counterproductive in yoga practice.

I suggested that if he was compelled to visit the prostitute, he should instead go there, give the money intended and leave after explaining that he would take no sexual service but would donate the funds intended.

That is a case of an opportunity to degrade someone, being used to help that person instead.

A few months back I was in Florida. I arrived there on a bus but the person who was to greet me was late. There was also an elderly lady who waited on someone to transport her. She had a heavy suitcase. She was frail due to the elderly condition. She used a white body. I used a black one.

I could tell she was scared of me but I saw that providence gave an opportunity. I went to her and said, "I have a cell phone. You can use it to call your contact."

She then said, "There is no need to call. They will arrive soon. The only thing is that they will be on the other side of the parking lot."

I lifted her bag and took it to the other side.

That is how a yogi absolves previous obligations. Providence will show obligations from the past. If one is sensitive one can take these as opportunities to absolve bad actions of the past.

Unfavorable consequences mean that bad behavior in a past life resurfaced in this life as unfavorable circumstances, but it can be the antisocial acts of an ancestor. One can inherit bad or good consequences from the ancestors. Providence may pool things together, bundle them and then act in summary.

We experience this in a world war or natural disaster. At that time, providence bundles the reactions due. It inflicts wholesale inconvenience. That is like when a man fishes with a rod and when he does so with a net. With a rod the target is one fish. With a net several are captured.

Providence operates in a similar way. Just as the fish are helpless against the fisherman, we are helpless with providence having the upper-hand.

In regards to absolving faulty actions, that is not something one may do on one's terms. Fate is such that it will not sit with you and make a draft of the bad behaviors from many past lives and allow you chart how to absolve the complaints.

But what you can do is to try to be on your best behavior in whatever circumstance providence places you. *Patañjali* in the *Yoga Sutras* listed the first two stages of yoga, yama and niyama, as prohibited behavior and approved conduct. If one takes that to heart and trains the self to abide by that, one can settle past consequences on providence's terms at fate's convenience

Sometimes however by advancement in meditation, a yogi gets direct insight into some criminal and malicious acts from the past. Sometimes he sees his magnanimous acts and very kind notions from the past. Sometimes when great misfortune comes, a yogi has a flash in his mind where he sees the past act which caused a misfortune. That does happen but it does not mean that he controls fate.

No limited being regulates fate. The most we can do is to cooperate with fate as it manufactures the sequences of event on the stage of time. When something unfavorable comes, the yogi should willingly endure it. He should assume that it is due to him, due to an individual or collective past involvement. If good fortune comes, he assumes the same without being elated. He protects himself from over-indulgence by looking for an opportunity to again invest more good behavior instead of only enjoying the positive circumstances of fate.

In the final analysis a yogi realizes that no fortune is his individual destiny. Like a twig in a strong current, he just happens to be in the river of time. He does not control it. If he is removed from the river, like if he floats up on the shore and is deposited on dry land, the river will continue its course. He is not essential to this creation. He is dispensable in the social sense. He is not vital to this. This will continue with or without him.

When a great yogi leaves the physical universe, it is not after he reimbursed all bad acts and is rewarded all fortunes of previous good acts. In fact, he leaves much of the consequence energy in this dimension. Others take possession of it. They use it, just as when a wealthy man dies, his relatives divide and share the property.

In the final analysis consequential energy is circumstantial for the individual limited spiritual being. But that does not mean that one should be bad-behaved. So long as one is not liberated one should render the best behavior.

Kundalini Spike through Naad

After kundalini was induced to leave the base chakra, it coursed through various parts of the body. Gradually it passed through the neck into the head. Once it coursed into the neck, a yogi should restrict it. It should be directed to the brow or crown chakra.

In Sanskrit these chakras are called *ajna* and *brahmrandra* respectively. *Ajna* is Sanskrit for perceiving or realizing. With the brow chakra one can pry into reality and get objective perception of other dimensions and situations. *Brahmrandra* may be translated as hole of *brahma* or aperture through which one would gain a glimpse of spiritual existence.

Rishi instructed that at some point in development, a yogi should heed *Patañjali* and make the effort to eliminate the independence of the intellect. Sanskrit for this psychic organ is *buddhi*. In chapter two of the *Bhagavad Gita*, Krishna gave the discipline for curbing this orb.

It is known as *jnana-chakshus* and *jnana-dipa*. *Jnana-chakshus* is the organ which gives direct visual *(chakshus)* perception in an objective way *(jnana)*. *Jnana-dipah* is the organ, which by its own light *(dipah)*, gives perception in an objective way *(jnana)*.

The big mistake made by anyone who has no psychic perception is that he regards this orb as the analysis ability, as a part of the brain. Others who are yogis but who have not developed psychic perception consider the organ to be non-existence even though when questioned they assert that even though it is invisible it is an integral part of the mind.

Rishi instructed that the orb should be the main focus of attention. The yogi should take the independent operations of the orb, the relation the kundalini lifeForce has with it, and the self's lack of control, into account.

When kundalini rises into the head, if the yogi finds that he can direct this energy, he should for this practice, directing it to the orb. If kundalini is in the head and the yogi finds that he/she cannot direct it, the yogi should connect to the naad sound. From that perspective, he should determine what to do next.

There will be some times during meditation, when the yogi finds that kundalini entered the naad sound zone and caused a spiked energy to rise out of the naad zone. See this diagram:

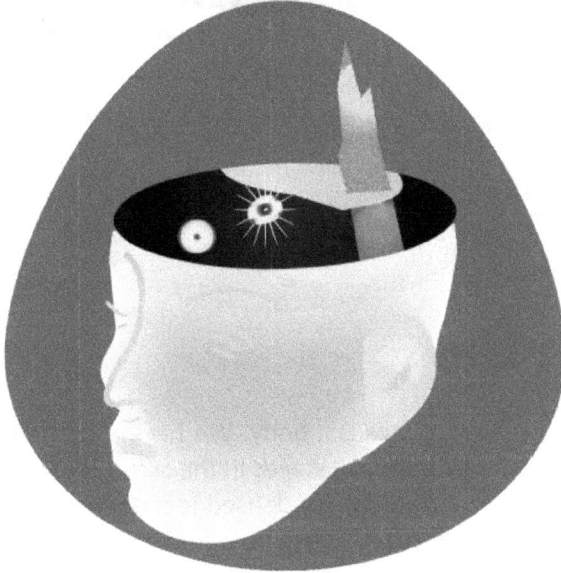

The yogi, after observing that the kundalini entered the naad zone and that kundalini's energy has spike upwards in the back of head, should enter the spike at the point where it shoots upward above the naad zone. The yogi should remain there and observe the texture of consciousness which results.

Desire: Its Origin

Desires come from the causal body. We have a subtle body which we experience in different vibrational stages in the astral existences, but there is another body which is a zone of condensed ideation energy. That is where the desires originated. Just as dry seeds in a sealed jar cannot sprout, on that level the desires cannot be fulfilled.

If the seeds are put into a moist environment they will germinate. If after they are placed in soil, they will grow as plants. When released from the causal body, desires first become known to us in the subtle body. Later, they motivate us to produce their manifest formats using the physical system.

Personal history is involved. Who can deny that? But in a way personal history is insignificant because the desires are like viruses in that they can penetrate the mind, causing the person to strive for their production as a personal achievement. From that angle we are hosts of the parasitic desire energy.

As humans we have a wide variety of emotions such as love, lust, shame, guilt, hope, attraction, anger and sorrow. Desire is one of many emotions.

Desire and other emotions, stem from early childhood and even before birth as part of our genetics. What we get from the ancestors in the way of genes plays a major role in how and what we think. Once we are born into this world another very powerful force influences our emotions. That is the environment. Internally our senses develop desires for certain smells, tastes, sights, textures, and sounds. Externally the parents, friends, enemies and teachers develop varied desires, wants and beliefs.

By looking deep into desires, we may gain insight about their origin. We can see that they come from either genetics or that they are learned. How do we look deep into our desires? By going into deep mindful meditation, we can eventually arrive at the origin of a desire.

By sitting quietly and focusing on a desire one allows the mind to regress into the past, experiencing the desire at its first recognition. However, the first recognition of a desire may not be its origin. One may need to regress even further to locate the root. For sex experience one may regress into memory to know the first time one indulged. One may review the first feelings. After the first encounter one may research the development for more sexual participation. If one regresses even further one may discover that one had sex dreams as an adolescent, long before the first physical experience. By meditating on the question, "Where was that experience before adolescence?", one may discover that it was present before one was born. If one goes deep enough one may experience being an ancestor and even being an ancestor of an ancestor. If that is the case, the desire for sex is primeval.

The zone of unfulfilled but known desires is different to the zone of unfulfilled unknown desires. Those which are known are like desires for more sex after one reaches puberty and had the experience. As soon as one has the first experience, other desires for it surfaces in the mind. One pursues sexual opportunities in order to fulfill the emerging pressures.

What of desires for sex in a three-year-old for example? At that stage there are dormant unknown desires which remain unmanifest to the infant. Another example of this is the eggs in the ovary of hen. Some hens lay eggs every thirty-six hours. But she is not aware of the eggs until they reach a certain stage of development. Once she becomes aware of them the sitting and clucking begins. She is not at ease with a particular egg, until it passes from her body. Those are like the unfulfilled desires.

However other eggs are in her body. Some are the size of a pin-prick, some are so small we need an electron microscope to see them. Those are like the unknown unfulfilled desires.

Origin?

That is a big question. One thing I can say is that the origin of the condensed unknown desires is in the pre-existence and as such it is causal, meaning that it exists in the energy which caused this existence. Hence transcending that, to find out about that, is near impossible.

Spiritual forces placed these factors of our pre-existence here. We are dependent on the sun, regardless of who or what placed it there. We can do nothing to either show that it makes sense or that it makes no sense. We are helpless in that regard. Cause and effect do not always make sense. The need for order and logic cannot bully everything into a logical sequence.

Part 4

Intellect Discovery - Three Phase Procedure

This is shared by Rishi Singh Gherwal.

Phase 1

In this phase, the yogi sits to meditate after doing breath infusion or even sitting without that practice. He/she finds that there is a high-pitched frequency (naad sound) on the right back side of the head. Sometimes this sound is heard on the left side or in some other area or zone.

The yogi becomes aware of his or her central presence in the head of the subtle body. This is the coreSelf. It is surrounded by an invisible energy which is the sense of identity.

Along with this there is the intellect which is the place where the thoughts, images and ideas arise and are shown graphically or otherwise in the mind. The objective of the yogi is to curb this psychic organ but initially the yogi must put aside that idea and listen to naad sound.

How long should a yogi remain in this phase 1? It varies from yogi to yogi. One should remain listening to naad and aware of the limits of the coreSelf's intense radiation and its contact with the intellect orb, for as long as it is necessary to feel that it is natural to be in contact with the naad listening zone.

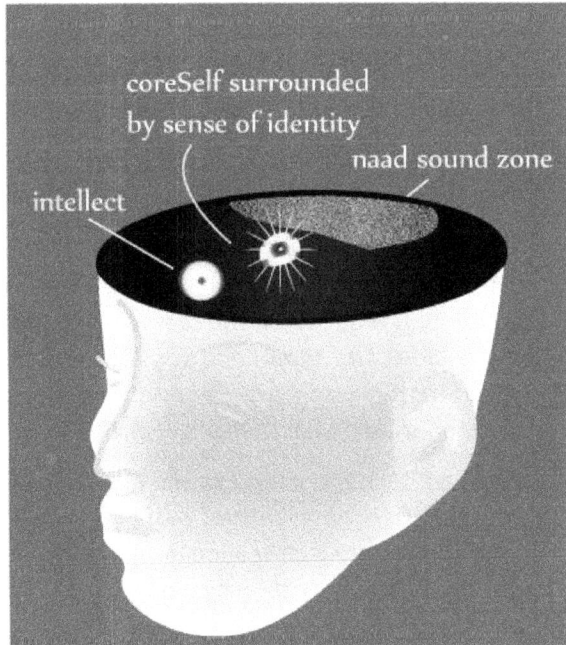

coreSelf surrounded by sense of identity

naad sound zone

intellect

default locations of intellect, sense of identity, coreSelf and naad

Phase 2

In phase 2, the coreSelf moved into the naad sound zone. It did this for its own protection so that it does not fall under the influence of the intellect. Since it is natural for the core to be under that unwanted influence, it must take help from naad to transcend the hypnotic effects of the intellect. Gradually as it listens to naad, it is nudged more and more into the naad zone. The intellect becomes almost non-existence. The coreSelf is free from its influence for the time being.

Rishi said that *Patañjali* instructed the yogi to attack the intellect outright, but Rishi said that initially this cannot be done. The coreSelf must develop the power to do this.

Rishi said,

In the Bhagavad Gita *there is a statement suggesting that the coreSelf is higher than the other mental components. It should dictate to those components. In reality, this is not the case. The reality is that one has a psyche which is out of control.*

To bring it in line with Krishna's ideas will require some adaptations and changes in the basic structure of human psychology.

The coreSelf has the power which Krishna suggests but initially it cannot realize itself as such. For instance, we know that an alligator is superior to a dog in strength but this statement is flawed.

A small alligator which is about one week of age cannot successfully bring down an adult dog but an adult alligator can.

Similarly, so long as a human being has not evolved sufficiently, he/she cannot control the components of the psyche. A certain degree of maturity is required. In the case of the infant alligator, it stays under the protection of its parent and dogs cannot assault it. In a similar way, until it can realize itself sufficiently to execute Patanjali's instructions, the coreSelf should take shelter under the naad sound.

The yogi should remain in naad and should do whatever is necessary to keep focus there. If it leaves that influence and then finds itself under the spell of the intellect, it should immediately shift to naad influence, just like the infant alligator which runs to its parents when it strays away and finds itself confronted by a vicious dog.

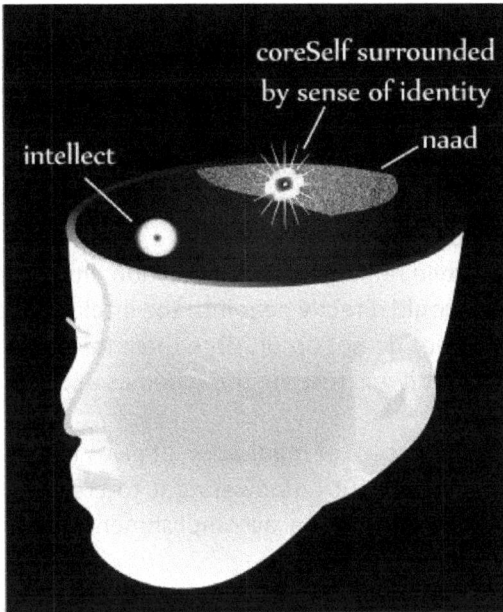

coreSelf retreats into naad

Phase 3

In phase 3, the intellect moved from its usual position in the frontal part of the head of the subtle body.

This action occurred because of the intellect becoming lonely for the association of the core. There is attraction between the sense of identity and the intellect. When the core which is surrounded by the sense of identity, moves into the naad sound and becomes absorbed there, losing interest in the intellect, the orb

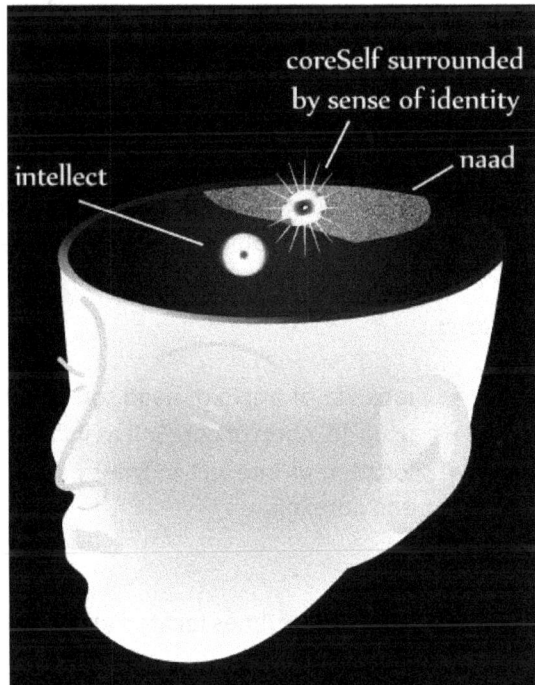

as attracted by sense of identity
intellect moved from default position

finds itself being pulled to the core.

Since these are not the natural locations of the intellect or core, both factors will return to their respective positions as soon as the yogi ceases to endeavor to keep the core in the naad zone.

So long as the intellect is nudged backwards away from its natural location, it will remain submissive to the coreSelf. It will make no effort to create compelling ideas, images or sounds.

Rishi said that while remaining in this position, in location with the naad sound, the coreSelf should directly peer into the intellect and should observe that its creative activities do not occur. Here the intellect is harmless without its diabolical habits, but it will resume the schemes as soon as the yogi shifts from naad.

This is an important stage of meditation. It gives the yogi an idea of how to handle the intellect without empowering it to create images, ideas and sounds which distract from spiritual accomplishments.

Intellect Submission

This is a meditation procedure shown by Rishi Singh Gherwal. This has to do with using naad sound to control and condition the intellect. Rishi said that this is done best immediately after doing breath infusion but it can be done without that, even though it will not be as thorough.

There are three psychic components and three locations to use in this meditation.

components:

- naad sound at the back of the subtle head
- coreSelf surrounded by sense of identity
- intellect

locations:

- location of origin of naad sound in back of subtle head
- usual location of coreSelf as it is surrounded by sense of identity,
- location of intellect in front part of head between brow chakra and coreSelf

Special notes:

Naad sound is sometimes located at the back center or back right or left of the head. Sometimes it is all-surrounding. It does not matter where it is located. One should reach its location wherever it is heard.

CoreSelf is surrounded by a sense of identity. Even though these are two distinct supernatural objects, they are regarded as one object in this meditation. This is similar to a filament and its surrounding glass bulb being regarded as one object, as a bulb.

In this meditation, no effort should be made to separate the coreSelf from the sense of identity. The sense of identity is not the nuisance. For this meditation the target is the intellect. It is invisible but it becomes manifest indirectly by its thought, idea and image constructions. The yogi should focus on the location from which these mental impressions and feelings arise. He should accept that the invisible intellect is located there even though it is imperceptible visually.

Just as when there are thoughts, ideas and images, the yogi knows for sure that the intellect functions, he can know that it is silenced when it does not generate impressions. But this organ has a higher useful function which will be manifested to the yogi if he/she adheres to Patanjali's instructions for practice. Then it is used as a visual orifice to see into higher dimensions. A yogi should be patient. Instant results may not be applicable.

With or without doing breath infusion before hand, the yogi should sit to meditate and should endeavor to connect with naad sound. If he finds that naad sound is the focus during the meditation and he is diverted to something else, he should note that after realizing that the meditation was dominated by distractions.

In some sessions, a yogi even though he/she began with an intention to meditate in a certain way found that some time passed with no idea of naad sound and with absorption in ideas which were impulsively produced by the intellect. When this happens, the yogi should make a mental note. He should use the experience to realize the power of the intellect over the self.

The natural arrangement of the psyche is that the intellect should dominate the self. The yogi should realize this and should endeavor to redesign this. Constant efforts at this in meditation will result in success over the long term but there will be disappointment and frustration time and again. Still a yogi should persist.

Here is the standard procedure.

- Sit to meditate
- Reach naad sound
- Double check to be sure that the coreSelf adheres to naad sound and is not being pulled to the frontal part of the subtle head to be under the dominance of the intellect's mental and emotional creations.
- Remaining in the naad sound, the coreSelf should reach forward and touch the invisible intellect. The core should make an

attempt to pull the intellect back. If it does not respond the core should re-establish itself in naad.

One of two things will occur.

- CoreSelf will retrieve its touching energy. The intellect will move to the middle of the head abandoning its intentions in the front area.
- The intellect will retain the self's touching energy. The self will feel itself being pulled to the intellect forcibly.

If the intellect is resistant, when self moves back into the naad sound, the self should insist of itself that it remain in naad. For that meditation session the core should abandon all attempts to influence the intellect. The intellect will go silent. It will be as if it does not exist. No thoughts, ideas or images will appear.

If on the other hand, the self finds that when it retracks its touch energy, the intellect willingly moves back, the self should remain focused in naad. It should retain only a slight observation of the intellect which accepted the naad influence.

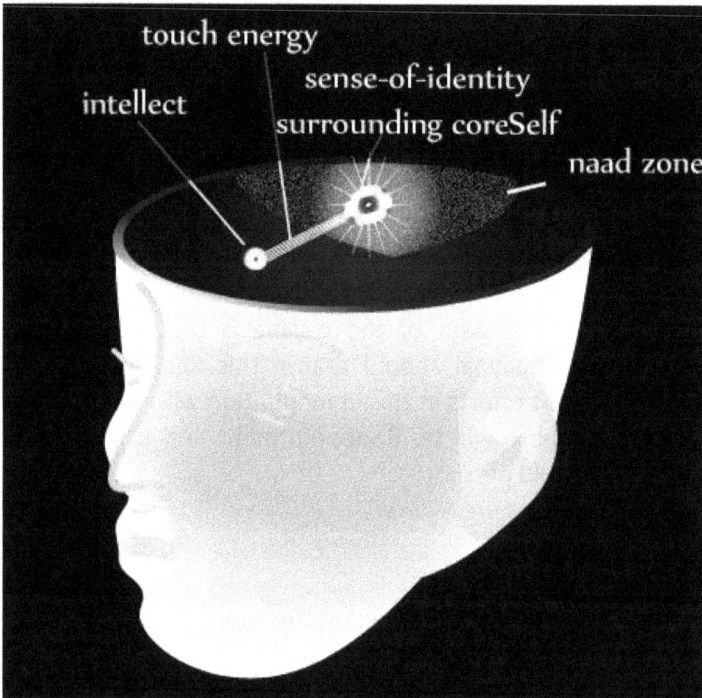

coreSelf in naad zone,
emitting touch-energy to intellect

Psychic Technology: Third eye / Intellect Differentiation

The third eye and the intellect are both uniVision apparatus. The third eye is a psychic apparatus but it is inferior to the intellect. For that matter, the third eye can only operate when it is assisted by the intellect but the intellect can operate with no connection to the third eye.

Both give uniVision, which is vision through one orifice as contrasted to bifocal vision which is what we use in the eyes of the physical and subtle bodies.

How to distinguish between the uniVision of the third eye and that of the intellect?

The distinction is this:

One must peer through the third eye to use it while one peers into the intellect to use that psychic organ.

Third eye is like a window through which one sees into other dimensions or into other places in the same dimension. The intellect is more like a crystal ball or like a wireless television device that one looks into to see into other dimensions.

To use the third eye, one must peer outside the psyche, just as to use physical eyes, the eye apparatus has to acquire information from outside the physical body.

To use the intellect, one focuses on it within the psyche to see what it perceives which is inside or outside the psyche. With the intellect, even though one uses it inside the psyche, one can perceive objects from other dimensions which are external to the psyche.

In this respect, looking within means more than seeing what is within. It also means seeing what is outside of the psyche. A similar experience is allowed when using televisions where a person in a room can see what occurs outside of the room. One can see outside the psyche while looking into the orb which is located in the psyche.

A question arises about the use and control of these mystic vision implements.

Consider if one can control the physical eyes. Consider how much one can control either eye?

Consider that the third eye and the intellect are pre-designed. These have certain capabilities. One's ability to control or even adjust these psychic organs will be limited just as one's ability to adjust physical vision.

Usually beings in other dimensions are occupied with their activities and are not aware of those yogis who view them from other places. The opening to another dimension from this place may be imperceptible to those being viewed.

Limited beings have limited consciousness, not only in this place but in other dimensions. You may have heard about cosmic consciousness on this planet but that does not mean breaking all boundaries and perceiving everything everywhere. If a yogi in another dimension perceives your existence, you may never know of it.

Use of the third eye does not mean that the yogi can interfere with what happens in other worlds. In this world for instance where one may have a closed-circuit video system around a house or business, seeing an intruder does not always mean that one can intercept the person. One may see the person and be unable to interfere in what he or she does.

A yogi may see into another world but he is not permitted to interact there unless his consciousness is transferred into a form which acts on that level. There are many divine beings who sometimes hover over this planet and who may see what we do but even if they know that we are being suicidal they can do nothing about it unless they take physical bodies or influence one of us who use a physical form.

Generally speaking, psychic perception, supernatural perception and spiritual perception means observing without the power to interfere. The history of those other places keeps on its progressive or destructive course despite someone's perception of it from another world.

To influence the events in another system, for better or worse, one must take a body in that place, either a physical one as on this planet, or a subtle one as in the heavenly worlds, and then by virtue of assuming that social identity one acquires some power to act. Subtle perception does not automatically mean the right to positive or negative interference.

Many people dream about an Age of Enlightenment but for such a thing to happen a divine being or a set of divine beings must assume physical bodies and then bring about those changes. They must adjust human nature before that can happen. This is why year after year, things keep progressing in a way that seems quite natural for animal beings, though unnatural for divine people.

This does not mean that a person in a higher dimension cannot influence someone directly without taking a physical body. In my own life for instance I am constantly being adjusted and advised by persons in other dimensions but their access with me hinges on my psychic perception of their domain and my submission to their advisories.

There were times when I saw a yogi meditating in a cave in some other place but I had no authority to converse with him. It is like seeing someone through a one-way panel where you can see the person and that is it. One cannot communicate.

Yogeshwarananda, of all my teachers, is perhaps the one who visited me most frequently but it is not that I can reach him. I cannot. My relationship with him is one of my trusting that if I need something that pertains to practice, he will render the assistance. I am unable to reach into the dimension where he resides.

He gave me a place where I can go and call for him from time to time, even though usually I do not use the method because of fear of interfering, being that with him he will come when he is of a mind to assist.

Sometimes while infusing the subtle body, it reaches his level of existence but still I do not call him. I continue the practice, because merely being outside a person's house does not give one the right to intrude.

Fourth Dimension Vision

The third eye is not always active when the physical eyes are being used. In most people the third eye is inactive but there is energy which moves through the brow chakra, even when the chakra does not function.

In most people the third eye is non-operational. There is however confusion among yogis where some think that the intellect or buddhi (Sanskrit) is the third eye. It is not.

Let us consider the location of these psychic organs. Third eye is between the eyebrows but the intellect is back in the brain about one inch at least back from the center of the eyebrows.

To locate the intellect, sit quietly and try to visualize something. Wherever in the mind space that visualization occurs is the intellect.

That location is not in the center of the eyebrows on the surface of the face. It is in the brain space about an inch or more back from the surface of the face.

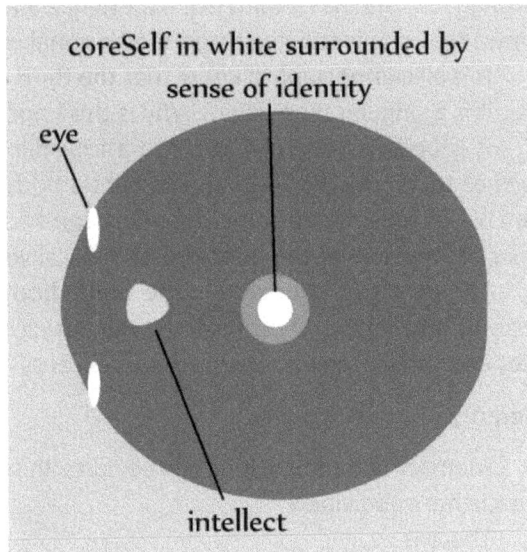

coreSelf in white surrounded by sense of identity

eye

intellect

In regards to seeing in the fourth dimension; if you develop that type of vision it will not interfere with physical perception. Right now, fourth dimension perception is off-limits. It will remain so unless one does austerities in higher yoga. It is not achieved easily. What is natural now is physical vision which was developed when one took the embryo body. Most of one's attention is geared to operate through physical access.

Because the physical vision is involuntary, moving into the fourth dimension will not shut down the physical three-dimension vision. A person who has fourth dimension consciousness must exert to maintain it because the psyche is honed into matter and prefers physical perceptions. Since that is the natural way there is no fear of losing it.

Third eye experiences may occur in a three-dimensional world like this or in a four-dimensional world. One can tell the different by the ability to see through objects.

When one is allowed a three-dimensional use of the third eye, one perceives things near or far but without being able to see through the objects. For instance, one may suddenly see a yogi in a cave in India or one may see someone in another physical dimension or in a low vibration astral world. But one cannot see through those forms, just as we cannot see through most solid forms here.

We can see through glass or clear water but we cannot see through most of the solid forms. If the glass is frosted or if it is too thick, we cannot see through it. If the water is agitated sufficiently or if it is deep, we cannot see through it. If one has a third eye experience and one cannot see through, one knows that one is still in a three-dimensional world.

It is also important to know that the third eye is uniVision which is to say that it is a singular lens vision. Why is this important?

It is because one can see into a four-dimensional world using the two eyes of the subtle body. Both the subtle body's eyes and the third eye are capable of four-dimension vision. One can know one from the other on the basis of uniVision of the third eye or bi-focal vision of the subtle body.

The third eye is located in the subtle body. It is not part of the physical system. However, one can used it while using the physical form because the subtle body is interspaced into the physical system.

Memory

Memory is complex. It has three parts. In some persons these three parts are further subdivided.

There is

- flash memory from this life
- stored memory from this life
- sublimally stored memory from past lives

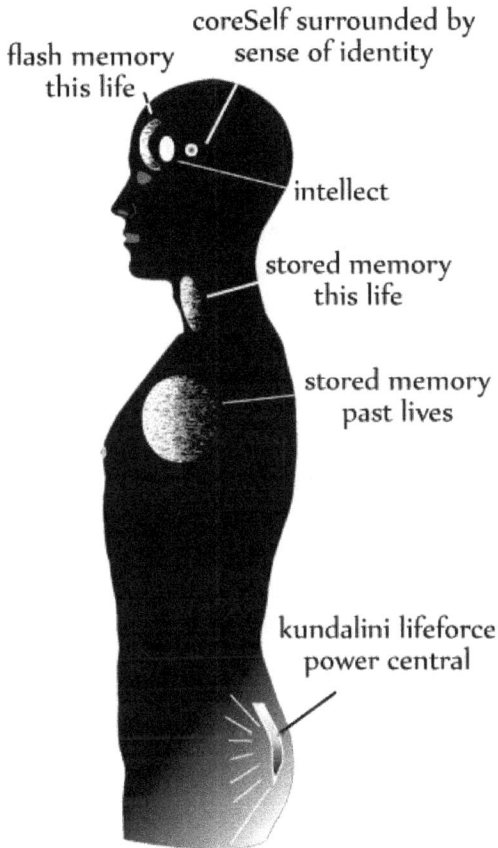

coreSelf surrounded by
sense of identity

flash memory
this life

intellect

stored memory
this life

stored memory
past lives

kundalini lifeforce
power central

The question is this:
How are memories accessed by the intellect?

- What format does it use to access memories?
- Are the memory compartments sensitive?
- What governs the interaction of a memory with any other factor?
- As a yogi the main concern is to destroy the social memories. *Patañjali* instructed that we wipe out the chittavritti, one of which is memory. Its spontaneous use is outlawed by him.

It is important to know that beyond the three types of memories there is another memory which is dangerous and which can override all other signals in the psyche. That is the *instinct*. Kundalini has a memory which we interpret as instinct. From our position in the psyche we do not regard instinct as memory because instinct does not arise as a visual or ideation presentation in the intellect, and yet, it is a potent form of memory.

Due to having this instinct, kundalini independently maintains and operates these bodies. It influences us into continuing in the mundane evolutionary cycle. Kundalini's effective weapon against the coreSelf is instinct, which is a type of memory.

Sense of Identity

Presently we experience the sense of identity as our sense of possession, our sense of *"my this" or "my that"*. *"I belong to this or I belong to that."*

Think back in time. You are about five years of age. You are on your way to school for the first day. When you get there, a teacher ask your name.

You reply, "I am Little Rabbit."

The rest goes like this

"Who is your father?"

"My father is Big Rabbit."

"Who is your mother?"

"My Mother is Loving Rabbit."

If you check closely you will find that the word "my" is representative of the sense of identity.

The voice in the head is the internal speaking of the intellect. It acts like a mini microphone. When it is transferred externally through the voice box, it is heard outside the body.

The sense of identity is subtle. It is the subtlest of the components of consciousness besides the coreSelf. It is so close to the core in vibration that the core can hardly distinguish.

One task of a yogi is to keep the intellect in a high state of consciousness, getting energy from a higher level. One other task it to recognize when it is in a lower energy level and when it gives impractical advice.

Take the case of a drunken man. Suppose that despite being intoxicated, he realizes his condition, he may take that into account and behave properly by applying a restraining mental force. Another person who is inebriated and who does not realize the condition may be arrogant. The intellect when it is infused with a low level of energy is terribly flawed.

Cosmic Intellect

There are many lights in the astral existence. One should not be surprised to see aparitions and light during meditation or otherwise. Astral lights are there in the trillions. In fact, in the astral world there are places where everything existing there emits light just as in this world most objects emit none.

For yogis there are four primal lights outside of the individual psyche.

- cosmic lifeForce *(kundalini)*
- cosmic intellect *(buddhi)*
- cosmic sense of identity *(ahankara)*
- cosmic coreSelf *(paramatma)*

One may see a light from the cosmic intellect. When that appears, it has a cooling bliss sensation. It silences everything and demands full attention. It clears the mento-emotional fog in the person's psyche and from the astral atmosphere in which the person finds himself or herself.

It usually strikes the person from the right side about where the right eyebrow is located. The yogi may or may not see its source. He may see a huge ray of light but may not see its source place.

If the origin is seen it will appear to be a vast cosmic reservoir of brightly blinding light. But the origin of it is rarely seen. The yogi has no control over the ray which hits his intellect. It comes and goes of its own accord.

This light has nothing to do with physical vision but it is possible that a yogi may confuse it with that. An advance yogi who shifted most of his attention into the subtle body will not have the confusion with physical vision but if one is not familiar with the subtle body and the higher operations of it, one may confuse it with physical sight.

One should be freed from the reliance on physical vision. If this is done there is the possibility of shifting into the subtle body. Then it will become just as convincing as the physical system.

It does happen that a person who practiced yoga in a previous life and who had success loses his or her grip on the advancement when taking a new body. He becomes lost in the new social identity imposed upon his or her embryo as soon as it is delivered from the mother's womb.

Such persons have sudden spiritual or supernatural experiences which alerts them that they were yogis in the past. They should in earnest, get serious with the practice again. They should curtail social engagements in order to reserve time for spiritual advancement.

The person will have to reduce the social identification of the new life and resists the influence of the material world in order to make progress, even to resume the advancement from the previous life.

Types of Visual Perception

Types of Visual Perception	Components Required							
	physical eyes	subtle eyes	third eye	intellect	pranaVision	sense of identity	coreSelf	spiritual body
physical eyes	✓			✓		✓	✓	
subtle eyes		✓		✓		✓	✓	
third eye uniVision			✓	✓		✓	✓	
intellect uniVision				✓		✓	✓	
pranaVision					✓	✓	✓	
sense of identity vision						✓	✓	
coreSelf direct perception							✓	
spiritual body, spiritual eyes vision							✓	✓

Needing a Guru

It is hardly likely that a person using an adult physical body, will attain third eye in the present life. It is not natural to see through the third eye. What is natural is physical vision.

The fear about developing third eye vision is not warranted. Many people who meditate regularly did not had even one experience of seeing visually through the third eye the way they see visually through the physical eyes. That means that the opening of the third eye is unnatural.

Some people had third eye experiences without a guru. An advanced yogi who practiced for some time can be of help however. There is no doubt about that.

Third Eye Experience

This morning during meditation I had a third eye experience that is quite normal for yogis who retreated away from society and who have a definite kundalini raising process and intellect shut down procedure.

However, this experience is rare for other yogis and meditators since for this to happen the mind must jump to a higher plane and remain there. Usually during meditation, the mind does jump for a split second but then it returns to its usual location of either hashing over thoughts or remaining without psychic or spiritual perception, a sort of void state with no senses except the rudimentary sense of consciousness which cannot distinguish anything clearly.

This morning while I did exercises, Rishi Singh Gherwal was there on the astral side making comments. He gave some rules two months ago. Yogeshwarananda gave a rule about raising kundalini to brahmarandra daily, as a mandatory requirement.

Atmananda (Yogeshwarananda's guru) asked me to reach a brahma level where he and others reside. This is a spiritual plane. It is reached if one energizes kundalini to the crown and then continues practice so that kundalini stays there for some time, at least for about fifteen minutes.

Kundalini's natural way is to get to the crown and then within a split-second collapse through the spine to the base chakra. It is spooked at the crown. It retracts rapidly and leaves the core hanging without the increased spiritual perception.

Think of a long slender glass cylinder which is so long that a man on the top of a three-story building can pour water into it. This tube is narrow about as wide as the middle finger. There is a plug at the bottom. As the man pours the water, it rises in the tube until it reaches the top of the tube. But then a mischievous kid on the ground floor, walks out of the building, sees the tube and pulls the plug. The water instantly flows from the bottom.

Kundalini is like that. After the efforts to get it to the crown, it regards going back to the base as its objective. The self relies on kundalini. What can it do?

Atmananda instructed for the kundalini to stay up longer in the aroused condition. This is achieved by an increase in the breath infusion practice or a continuation of the practice for several more breaths after kundalini rises to the crown chakra.

Rishi Singh Gherwal gave an instruction that once kundalini is curbed and forced to abandon its normal routines, the yogi should focus on the intellect using breath infusion to target that psychic organ. He said that admittedly the intellect is illusive and is involved in a disappearance act, such that the yogi may not find the organ in particular meditations. But he said that after kundalini rises during practice, one should be alert for thoughts. As soon as they burst, one should direct the infused energy to the mental place where the thoughts originate.

This uses the one locational feature of the orb which is that even though the yogi may never see that psychic organ, still he will perceive a thought, idea or image which it creates. That location is itself the invisible orb.

During breath infusion, after kundalini rises to the crown and after the yogi causes it to linger at the crown, the yogi should shift focus to the intellect and infuse the breath energy into it.

The result of this will be experienced in the meditation session as spiritual and psychic perception of the intellect such that it ceases the thinking and imaging and it gives visual perception and other types of subtle insight.

Irregular Third Eye Opening

This morning during meditation, third eye opened. For this to happen the intellect has to be synchronized into the brow chakra, so that both are operational at the same higher frequency.

This opening was an irregular shape like this:

In the *Meditation Pictorial* book, I listed regular shapes like an oval or a round-cornered rectangle, but in this experience the shape was irregular. In addition, the subtle body which was in a lotus posture displaced itself from the physical one. At first when I focused through the third eye opening, it began to close and to sideshift but then it resumed the original shape. I found the subtle body moving to a moving bus which was somewhere in India in the place where Rishi Singh lived while in his last physical body. My subtle body moved. It moved into the side of a moving bus as if to crash into it.

There was no crash as the subtle body moved through the metal casing of the bus as the vehicle moved on a highway. Neither the bus nor the body was damaged. By this time the coreSelf having shifted into the subtle body, perceived that other dimension through the third eye just as one would perceive this dimension through a single eye (as if one eye was closed), except that the vision was from center rather than from the left or right side of the face.

There were eyes on the subtle body but they were not in use.

Rishi Singh then said, "Develop that vision."

Assault on the Intellect

Rishi Singh Gherwal mentioned that day after day and during sessions of breathing exercises and meditation, the yogi must continue the assault on both the kundalini and the intellect. It is a relentless pursuit for autonomy of the coreSelf over the psyche.

Rishi said.

This is not a religious affair. It is a psychological battle to gain control of the components of the psyche. There is a sense of identity which is the main link between the coreSelf and the other components but it is not possible to attack this sense of identity effectively until the kundalini and the intellect are brought under control.

Take notice that the master theoretician of Yoga, Patanjali, did not instruct about conducting a siege of the sense of identity. He levels the main assault at the intellect, because if that is brought under control and if that is incapacitated by the self everything else will fall in line as it should.

The sense of identity may be compared to the personal secretary of a great king. Unfortunately, the king does not know how to procure services directly. He can give orders to the secretary. Then it is up to the secretary to fulfill those desires. The secretary for his part can only procure what is available. If he finds that the king persists with impractical desires, he may stall the king and say, "I may acquire that tomorrow." Or, "Yes, I already requested that even though the manufacturer is stalled in the production due to lack of raw materials."

On and on the secretary may stall the fanciful king.

Ultimately in a moment of soberness or when cornered by pressing circumstances, the king may consider the reality of his helplessness and utter dependence on the sense-of-identity secretary. Then he may realize that he is reliant on the secretary, who in turn is reliance on the Prime Minster and on the Minister of Defense. The Prime Minister who is a great manipulator, is the intellect, while the Minister of Defense is the kundalini energy which is obsessed with protecting the body from moment to moment.

These components of the psyche are inter-related. The king must realize that for quite some time without his supervision the psychic mechanisms were functional.

How then is he to bring this to order in a way whereby the other components do not act to his peril?

Can someone who was never in control, suddenly gain autonomy?

What is the political process through which the king can sit on the throne with the real powers of sovereignty?

Intellect Meditation Control

Rishi Singh Gherwal provided the following remark for arrest of the impulsive mentality and compulsive emotions.

The purpose of the arrest is more than immobilizing the mind. It is also to develop supernatural vision. Most human beings have physical eyes. In dreams, some humans experience subtle eyes. They have vision in imaginative scenes which are created in mind by wish-energy.

Subtle eyes are eyes of the subtle body just as physical eyes are eyes of the physical form which allow the person to visually perceive objects outside the body. This perception is verified by touching objects to gage if the visual information is correct.

For instance, the moon may appear to be about 100 feet across visually but we know for a fact that it cannot be that size, but a ball which is one foot across can be verified easily by touching the object after getting visual information.

In a similar way one can use subtle eyes and subtle touch to verify objects in the subtle world as contrasted to objects which the mind visualizes in its mind-space.

The intellect which is involved in visualizations is capable of supernatural and spiritual perception. The purpose of silencing it is to allow it to shift into its higher modes of perception.

When someone departs from physical existence, physical vision becomes impossible. When someone becomes synchronized into physical existence, subtle vision is lost. But when a person is in meditation the effort to acquire supernatural vision is a daunting task.

Patañjali gave the hint for the development of spiritual vision in his second *sutra* about ceasing the illustrative displays of the mento-emotional energy. The problem with this instruction is that the beginner does not experience the intellect as an object. How many human beings experience intellectual capacity as a psychic organ?

That is the challenge. Based on information from advanced yogis, students must first accept that there is a psychic organ which operates as an intellect. Once this is accepted, one can take advice on how to control the orb.

Will the students accept this as a matter of faith?

The stage of no content of the mind happens haphazardly by the movement of natural energies in the mind but it hardly occurs on command by the self over the mind. In the normal configuration the self does not have that leverage over the mind. It is too bad that it is so but that is the way it is.

To reach the no content stage, a yogi first energizes the mind by infusing it with subtle energies while doing breathing infusion. This lifts the mind to a higher plane, where the trash thoughts from this level do not exist. The evidence of this comes when the yogi's mind becomes de-energized and he/she finds the self again on the normal level of consciousness. Then immediately the thoughts, images and ideas begin churning in the mind and attracting the attention of the self.

The faint images seen in the mind are subtle phenomena except for residual impressions which remained on the retina and subsequently are constructed by the brain as a photocopy of a physical object seen previously.

Plight of the coreSelf

There is a correlation between the kundalini lifeForce mechanism and the intellect checking system. These psychic components have corresponding apparatus which coordinate or oppose each another.

The senses emerged out of the intellect. They are on the surface of the mind, like smaller bubbles rotating on the large bubble of the mind which is the head of the subtle body. However, these senses come under the influence of the kundalini lifeForce. Somehow, they learn to obey the lifeForce for the sake of protecting it from hostile attacks.

Kundalini sees itself as the protector and controller of the psyche. As such it does not have much respect for the coreSelf, which it regards as a necessary tenant in the psyche. When the core becomes determined to control the intellect, the kundalini undermines the core by influencing the senses to ignore the requests that the core relayed through the intellect.

In this interplay there is the sense of identity, which is more or less like a confused secretary who is caught in the power play between her boss, the coreSelf and the powerful building custodian, the kundalini. For its part the sense of identity sides with either the intellect or the kundalini. In some beings it is the kundalini which influences the sense of identity the most. In others it is the intellect. The coreSelf is the least of the influences even though theoretically the self is supposed to be the main controller.

How to bring this psychological disorder into order?

That is a good question. Each person should study the individual psyche. Then one may get a method for order from an advanced yogi.

If the sense of identity is more in love with the kundalini and sensual energies, than it is with the intellect or rationality, that would require a particular solution to the problem.

In the *Bhagavad Gita,* Lord Krishna posted the coreSelf as the ultimate factor in the components of the psyche, but in ordinary life this ultimate self is powerless to control the psyche. Instead the psyche is operated by and exploited by the kundalini lifeForce. The next authority in the psyche is supposed to be the sense of identity, which was tagged by many philosophers as the ego, which they regard as a rogue principle.

Since this ego component usually leads the self through a blind alley, it is rated as a psychic criminal by many meditators who think that their mission is to eliminate it.

The next powerful element is the kundalini for some and the intellect for others. Those who are emotionally inclined, are prejudiced by the kundalini, while those who are rationally motivated are prejudiced by the intellect. In all cases however, both the kundalini and the intellect express influences. There is a mutual interaction between the two powers with some give and take.

In summary, the situation is this: The coreSelf relies on the sense of identity which in turn depends on the intellect, which in turn is influenced by the senses and the kundalini lifeForce. Overall, the kundalini lifeForce wields the most power. It is the custodian of the psyche.

All yogis, once they become proficient in the practice of asana postures, should do whatever is necessary to bring kundalini under control. Breath infusion contributes significantly to this achievement.

The sense of identity is like a nanny escorting the self which is like a kid trailing behind. This nanny is not educated. She relies on a counselor which is the intellect. The nanny is not the mother of the kid. Hence, she lacks confidence.

But there is a wet nurse who lives there. She is kundalini. She suckles the kid. The nanny takes cues from the wet nurse about the needs of the kid. Except that the wet nurse is an aborigine who is expert at jungle survival skills and who has no finesse.

Coma or Sleep: Study of Awareness

In terms of psychic research there is a clear distinction between coma and sleep. Coma means that the intellect is in a state of suspended animation such that the coreSelf cannot use it. The problem with this condition is that currently the coreSelf is so dependent on the intellect for objectivity, that when the connection with the intellect is broken, the core is left in a state of unconscious subjectivity, which means to exist but to be unaware of one's existence.

A rock sits on the ground but it has no idea of itself. Is that pure consciousness? In a way it is, because it is pure consciousness without objectivity. In Sanskrit this is called the sat state or the state of being part of reality. But being part of reality does not mean that one is objectivity aware. Existence is such that one can exist but be totally oblivious of the fact. Thus, there is the *chit* state which means that the rock becomes cognizant of itself. Thus, we get the word *satchit*. Then there is the *ananda* or bliss state, state of assessment of the one's existence as a secured portion of reality. Thus, we get *satchidananda*.

In a coma the coreSelf is in the *sat* state but it has no *chit* or cognizance of itself. This is because it was deriving cognizance through the assistance it was receiving from the intellect psychic organ. When the intellect was suspended the core lost objectivity.

In sleep this does not happen. In sleep, the coreSelf loses awareness of the physical body and the physical world and becomes aware of the subtle body and the subtle world. This is done because even though in sleep the intellect is disconnected from the physical system, it is still connected to the subtle system and to the coreSelf. Hence the coreSelf may become aware of its operations as dream imaginary states or as actual psychic activity in an astral environment.

In general anesthesia a chemical can affect the intellect, in fact shut it down and make it unavailable for use by the core, then it is obvious that the chemical has a subtle counterpart which affects the intellect while the chemical's physical aspect affects the brains and nervous system. Conversely, yogis produce certain effects by doing special pranayama.

Intellect Absolute Control Procedure

Rishi Singh Gherwal Procedure: Dec 16, 2010

This is a procedure for further reduction of the connection between the intellect and the coreSelf. For meditation, *Patañjali* instructed for the complete severance of the connection between those psychic instruments but that is hard to come by. It occurs in stages as one unlinks various component energies.

According to Rishi Singh the last stage of that is taking away a single remaining ray of energy which leaves the coreSelf, travels through the sense of identity which surrounds it and then hits the intellect to energize it.

intellect — coreSelf — focused ray

invisible non-active intellect — coreSelf — retracted ray

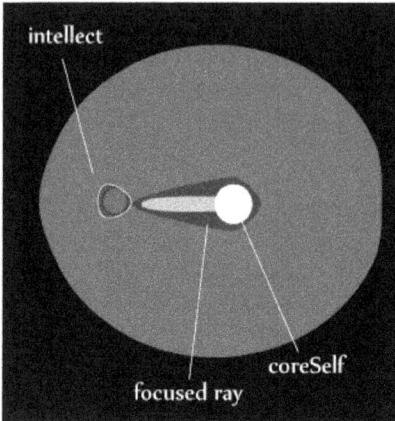

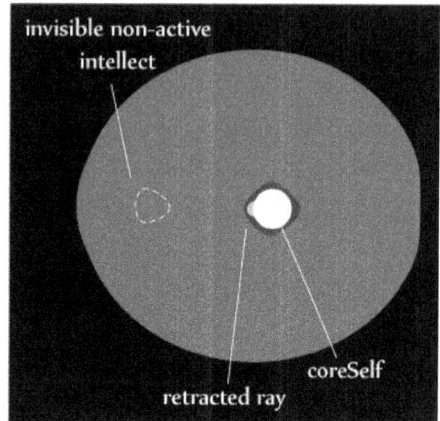

In this practice the withdrawal of that single ray immobilizes the intellect and causes it to seem like an opaque blank space the size of a hen's egg. The yogi should simply hold it there in its position and keep depriving it from the ray of energy which usually leaves the coreSelf and which involuntarily energizes it for the creation of ideas and images.

It must be held in that blank condition for some time during meditation. Then it will convert into a supernatural visionary orb which is desired and which is infused with a divine energy which is not aligned to the physical world or to the lower astral places.

Rishi Singh asked me to write that the *Patañjali* process takes much practice and dedication for its achievement. It cannot be mastered by haphazard, indefinite or whimsical practice. On the high end of the practice, he said that all props like mantras, breath focus and whatever must be abandoned. All by itself, the coreSelf must face the intellect and confront it. But the yogi should be sure to infuse the subtle body with breath energy, raise kundalini and infuse the intellect itself with breath energy before sitting to meditate. Since otherwise the yogi's subtle form will not rise to the required higher plane where this practice can be successful.

The history of the human race is full of incidences where advanced methods were given even though few persons practiced. Take a look at the instructions given to Uddhava by Krishna. It is obvious that advanced instructions were given thousands of years prior, because Krishna mentioned some instruction given by a supernatural swan to the four Kumaras who were yogis using infant-bodies.

One person asked why I bother to record fantastic techniques which no one can practice. The answer is that I must do as I am instructed. The teachers dictate. I publish but my relationship with them is not the kind of relationship where I can say, "This is too advanced. Stop dictating this."

China Visit

When I was in China, I made attempts to consult with the Taoist system but masters were hard to find. Since the Communists take over, all such systems were suppressed. In one semi-remote temple we visited, we spoke to a student of the Taoist system, a young man, via a Chinese friend who served as translator. When I mentioned advanced techniques, the student said that he was not a master and did not get that far in the discipline.

We visited three temples. At one, lay-people were active in ceremonial procedures. But these places are more or less a tourist novelty in China.

After I came back from China, I was in State College, Pennsylvania. There at a used book store I was guided by a transcendental force to a book titled, Taoist Yoga, by Charles Lux. In that book the various advanced practices are described in English. I was surprised though to find diagrams there which I drew from meditation practice in some of my earlier spiral bound books.

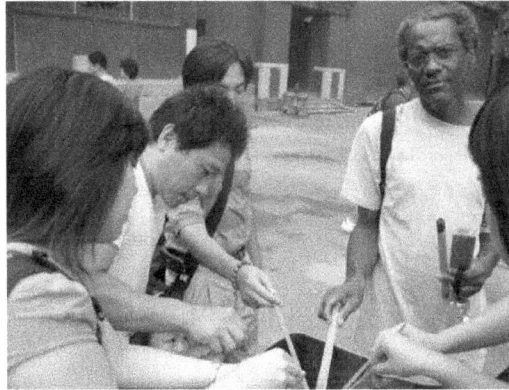

Orb-Kundalini Infusion

Rishi Singh Gherwal explained this morning during the exercise session, that at first one should focus on raising kundalini in any which way. One should do this at least once per day. *Pranayama* breath infusion is the preferred method for yogis but any other effective method may be used.

He said that if kundalini is not mastered, the other parts of spiritual practice will be undermined by kundalini's wayward behavior. Thus, it is absolutely necessary for the yogi to get kundalini out of its residence which is the base chakra, *muladhara*.

He estimated that it would take at least three years of practice minimum, raising kundalini at least once per day.

The next stage is to get kundalini to raise into the trunk of the body. Rishi Singh said that even though one becomes elated with success in raising kundalini into the brain, that accomplishment does not in any way mean that one mastered kundalini. To master it the yogi has to lose interest in getting kundalini into the brain and cause kundalini to rise in the various parts of the trunk of the body where there are many *nadi* tiny subtle tubes which are full of polluted subtle energies. These channels should be blasted by the force of the infused kundalini.

He said further,

Because of the attachment to sexual pleasure, students usually focus on raising kundalini into the head to get the bliss feelings which result from that but eventually one loses interest in this, especially when one realizes that kundalini's vulgar habits continue regardless. To get kundalini to give up the vulgarities one must cause it to rise in all parts of the trunk of the body.

The next stage is to cause the unification of the intellect and kundalini under the supervision of the coreSelf. The two forces, the intellect and kundalini have a relationship which is based on procurement and exploitation of sensual data. This primitive relationship should be upgraded by the yogi.

He can only do this if he infuses the intellect and kundalini with a higher grade of subtle energy. This is done through pranayama *infusion. A yogi who does breath infusion and who was successful in using it to raise kundalini, should use the same method to infuse the intellect. When the infusion is thorough, the yogi can arrest the intellect and hold it in suspension until it develops into spiritual and supernatural insight.*

Religion Dissected

It is a fact that people derive a tangible benefit from religious association but they also derive some psychological satisfaction and sense of security from the dogma of religion. It really does not matter whether a religion will be validated or not after death. Most people cannot remember a past life. As such a validation is not required because death means the inability to verify anything.

Still, a human being likes to know that he is on the right side of fate. Even if his dogma is false, that is of little concern since the immediate gratification from being in the best most superior spiritual group or religion, gives one the confidence that fate will act on one's behalf and put one into a superior position hereafter.

Suppose there is no hereafter. Suppose death is the end of the individual. In that case, it is more the merrier because at least if I believe in a religion which gives full confidence, I will be the happier of the lot of human beings. The fact that my beliefs are ultimately false does not in any way deprive me of enjoying a sense of security while living.

If the congregation I belong to is large, that is all the better because I derive social security from the collective. If we believe in a religion and put full trust in it, it is all the better for our feelings as a group.

But yoga is different. Yoga involves facing cold facts about this existence and finding the underlying basis of reality. Yoga requires individual progression, individual research and individual conquest over the inner nature.

Group consciousness is present in yoga as well but in terms of fellow students comparing notes, and teacher and students relating in terms of the student getting information and techniques to further his or her personal investigation into the construction of the human psyche. With that information, the yogi gets on the inside of the self to discover its core.

When I used a boy's body, I was under the authority of senior relatives. I could not be absent from church services. I was in a Methodist denomination. I had school friends. I had church friends who were children like myself who had no choice in the matter of mandatory church attendance.

I observed then that the group consciousness at church was functional both in the practical and psychological sense. One church member would advise or even assist another upon request. Later I lived in religious communities and saw there also where fellow members associated and found novel ways of assisting one another. There was social cohesion which kept members in mental association. A member would derive confidence and a sense of security from the associations.

Yoga is different because it focuses on the yogi's personal flaws and his or her inability to bring the psyche to order, for spiritual purposes.

In summary, one should take a course which is suited to one's evolutionary level and which gives the satisfaction or dissatisfaction which one seeks. Gautama Buddha for instance, began by identifying dissatisfaction. Instead of carefully avoiding social and bodily hassles, he astutely observed it. Death did not reach him as yet. Old age did not reach him. It was not necessary for him to become a renunciant because he was in no hardship and had conveniences merely because his body was the son of a chieftain. Still, he hounded after the dissatisfaction of the negatives in human life. To know what caused suffering he ceased nature's enjoyments.

Last week I considered my fate which is death of this body. I realized that the arrow of death already departed from the taut bow of fate. There is no way to avoid it. What should I do? Should I ponder? Should I deny it and enjoy myself.

Rishi Singh Gherwal thinks that my yoga practice is not intense enough for me to be liberated in full in this life. I must accept his conclusion. That means that the arrow left the bow which was drawn tight by fate, which never misses its target. But I am not going to contest it. I will endeavor to complete the course after fate kills the body.

I cannot win in the battle with fate. Fate will win because the odds are in its favor. Recognizing the power of fate and accepting it, is the very means for completing the practice in the hereafter.

Once the practice is transferred into the subtle body and once that body identifies with the practice, it can be continued in the hereafter. But if the yogi is unable to transfer that practice habit into the subtle body, he cannot continue the progress hereafter and must acquire another physical body to practice again.

Working with Memory

While meditating this morning, I began to think about a time in this life when I lived at a Hare Krishna farm. I remembered the people, their faces and names, and the circumstances under which I left the farm. In the end, I concluded that the devotees were sincere seekers. I did not judge them or my time there negatively.

While remembering this, I made a conscious decision to let myself reflect on it, rather than squelch the train of thought. Usually the insignificant mental distractions that arise in meditation are not worth noting, but some memories that arise are worth reviewing.

When I was finished reflecting, I was inspired with this method of dealing with arising memories:

- Greet memories of people with a mood of friendliness and compassion.
- Acknowledge both the pain and pleasure that occurred in the remembered circumstance. This neutralizes one's reaction to it. This enables one to look objectively at the memory, and to release it.
- Extract positive and sincere energy from it. Extract and preserve any intensity of motivation.

Third Eye/Intellect Difference

Rishi Singh Gherwal requested that I clarify that the third eye or brow chakra is not the intellect. He said that many yogis get this idea that it is all about the third eye but that in higher yoga, the third eye is not a significant consideration because the problem goes back to the request of *Patañjali* in his second sutra about checking the vrittis and gaining direct control in doing that.

Rishi said this.

People need to understand that the third eye is not the problem. It is the intellect or the jnana-chakshus (jnana-dipah) *which is the problem. This is addressed in chapter two of the* Bhagavad Gita *as buddhi yoga. The* buddhi *or the intellect, the psychic organ used for thinking and imaging, must be curbed. It is not the third eye even though the intellect works in conjunction with the third eye.*

Just as the physical body is not homogenous, the subtle one is not a homogenous psychic organism. In the brain, there are specialized cells which are nowhere else in the body. In the subtle body there are special organs as well.

For success in the Patanjali yoga one must confront and directly curb the intellect. It is not located at the position of the third eye. It is located between the coreSelf and the third eye.

Initially Patanjali recommended kaivalyam as the separation of the seer from its seeing apparatus. The observer is the iSelf, the coreSelf. But if it does not know what it is or if it does not experience itself as separate as he suggested, then the first stage is to achieve this separation.

Intellect is in the front part of the head. It may however move forward towards the third eye on occasion. Usually it is not as close as shown in the diagram.

coreSelf with sense of identity
focused on it

intellect

energy of
third eye

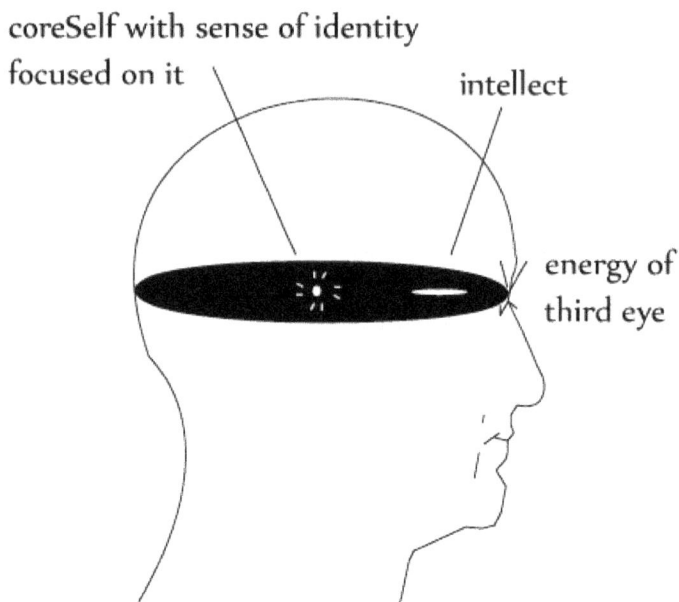

The sense of identity is a subtle organ but it is experienced as an urge to identify with or to not identify with some other thing besides the coreSelf. Only on a very high level of consciousness is it experience as a subtle organ.

There is a distinction between the sense of identity and the intellect, in that the sense of identity surrounds the coreSelf, the way air surrounds the head, or the way glass surrounds the filament of a bulb. If something which is invisible surrounds you it is difficult for you to understand that it is an object. One may think and feel as if it is part of oneself. The other thing is that just like the filament of a bulb the coreSelf has no idea how it can transcend the sense of identity.

Parallel World Problem

When one is mentally tired and when one is at the end of the day, lucid dreaming is still possible if one is proficient at it, otherwise one has better luck when the body and mind are rested, like when you already slept sufficiently and then you rest again. In that case the mental energy is not occupied with fixing the exhausted physical body. It has more sensitivity on the astral side.

Sleep paralysis or cataleptic trance usually occurs when one is about to astral project and when an astral projection is finishing and the mind returns to the physical body. If at that time the astral body and the physical one do not synchronize, one experiences that out-of-sync condition as the inability to move the physical body. It feels as if one is restricted. In that condition one can at least operate the breath and can by holding the breath, make the two bodies go in sync.

Sometimes one can move an arm or leg and that too will jerk the subtle body back into the physical one.

It is possible to get stuck in a parallel dimension or any of the adjacent astral worlds but it is hardly likely that would happen. When one astral-projects, the lifeForce remains in the physical body. So long as it is in the physical body, one must return to this physical existence. Only when the lifeForce permanently leaves the physical body, does one find oneself permanently deprived of physical existence.

If someone is awakened on the physical side, his lucid dream existence is immediately finished. In astral projection experiences that is realized sometimes when one's physical body sleeps and when someone on the physical side shakes or calls the sleeping form.

At that time, instantly, one is yanked into the physical body. One awakens on this side either forgetting or remembering the astral experience.

Sometimes during an astral projection when one finds oneself in an adjacent astral world, the people there may ask one to stay permanently but even though one agrees, one finds that one is drawn back to the physical existence and must continue life here anyway.

Part 5

Rishi Singh Gherwal's Kundalini Yoga Ideas

Yesterday I met Rishi Singh Gherwal who was the teacher of Arthur Beverford. Rishi descended from a siddhaloka place to discuss the practice of kundalini yoga. Some years back during the 1970's I made efforts in the astral regions to meet this yogi. I failed to do so. The reason was that he left the lower astral regions and was no longer available.

While conversing with him this morning during kundalini yoga exercises, I asked about his remoteness. He said that there is no need for a yogi to remain on a lower level if there is another agent stationed there who can explain the practice to students. His stress was that the key issue was the particular process, not the person who teaches it. So long as there is someone who can teach a practice, who is familiar with it, there is no need for another yogi to remain on a lower level to instruct. As soon as a yogi can train someone in a process, and bring that person to a proficient level, there is no need for the teacher to remain on a lower plane.

In any case this yogi's stress is on clearing the tiny *nadi* tubes in the subtle body, especially in the lower part of that body. He feels that to raise kundalini habitually to the crown chakra and even to clear *sushumna nadi* central spinal passage is not enough. One will not permanently relate to a higher plane of existence if one only accomplishes that.

He asked me if I saw the diagram. When I said yes, he said, "What diagram?"

I replied, "Swami Dada's" He said, "Very good, you understand this. Endeavor and complete the practice. Upgrade the psyche." After this he left and went upwards in the dimensions.

Swami *Dada* is Swami Shivananda. *Dada* means grandfather in Sanskrit or it means *old father*, and *great master* from the past. Shivananda guruji gave the world this diagram: (The Sanskrit letters on the top right mean praa-naa-yaa-ma.)

प्राणायाम

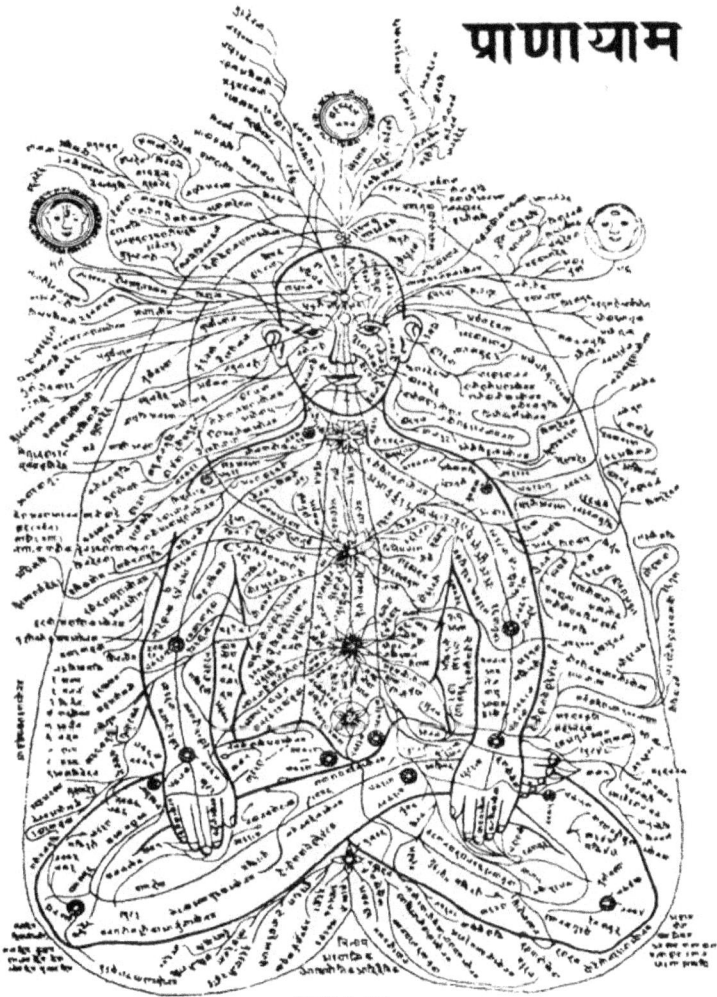

Here is a photo of Rishi Singh Gherwal's last material body (1889-1964):

Association with Yogis and Non-Yogis

We are in a situation of having social relationship on the physical and spiritual levels. Both types should be handled with great care.

Do not think that the association of accomplished yogis is worthless or that since they are advanced, they do not have feelings. They do, even though their feelings are of a different nature to the ones we exchange with worldly people.

Both types of association are necessary. An effective way needs to be initiated for servicing each satisfactorily. Do not neglect spiritual masters and only service social concerns which one has as duties in this current life. This life will wind down to death and then what?

Suppose you cannot get back into this family because no wombs are available, that means you will enter another family. There you will begin a new set of social obligations. This will happen repeatedly. Regardless, one should maintain the relationship with advanced entities. Do not feel that there is no God in control and that this creation is a free for all where one can do as one pleases. Feel that you are accountable to advanced entities, just as one feels accountable to senior relatives.

Infusing the Intellect

Rishi Singh Gherwal gave another kriya that supplements the second sutra of *Patañjali* regarding the stopping of the vrittis. This requires that the intellect be inactive. If one never saw this psychic instrument and therefore have reason to doubt its existence, do this practice. One should at least accept the fact that the mental thought process occurs in a certain location in the mind-brain apparatus.

This is about location. If one cannot perceive the intellect, one should accept my word that it is a subtle object which is used for thought and image making. Once you identity its general or specific location, you can do this instruction.

- Sit to do rapid breathing. Use either posture as shown in the photos below or use just one of those postures. This should be done after one infuses the spinal column with breath energy.
- Place the four fingers over the face as shown and use the thumb to close the ear canal. Mainly the third finger is used to press on the eyes.
- Once you are in that posture, make sure that the thumb closes the ear canal. Begin the rapid breathing but make sure that you find the location of the intellect. Focus your attention on that mental place. Mentally direct the infused breath there. Do this for some time. Then stop and sit to meditate.

If this was done correctly you will find that the mind stopped thought activity or its rapid thought generation impulses slowed noticeably, with thoughts which usually would appear with great rapidity now occuring in slow motion.

Keep the attention on that location. Insist that no thoughts be generated.

If you are successful you comply with Patanjali's instructions. There should be no focus on the breath. No mantra is used. To infuse the intellect location, breath is used for rapid breathing in the first part of this practice. After that there is no more focus on breathing.

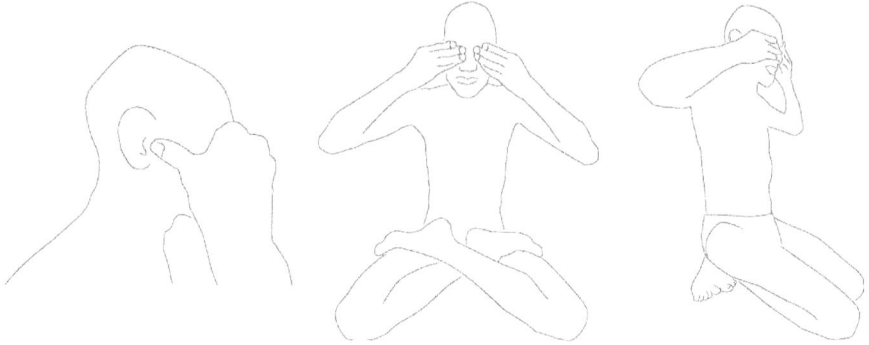

Marcia Beloved's Experience

The description of the intellect as a "thought maker" caused me to wonder if I saw it some months ago. I mentioned to Michael that I figured I had seen the intellect in that experience. He said: "Use the painting program on your computer and draw a sketch and then I will assist further."

The following image is my rough sketch. What I remember clearly is the spinning funnel, which spewed out thoughts, one at a time. As they popped up, I would simultaneously think the thought while I viewed it. I experienced myself as an observer, some distance back, as represented by the black oval blob.

thought packages

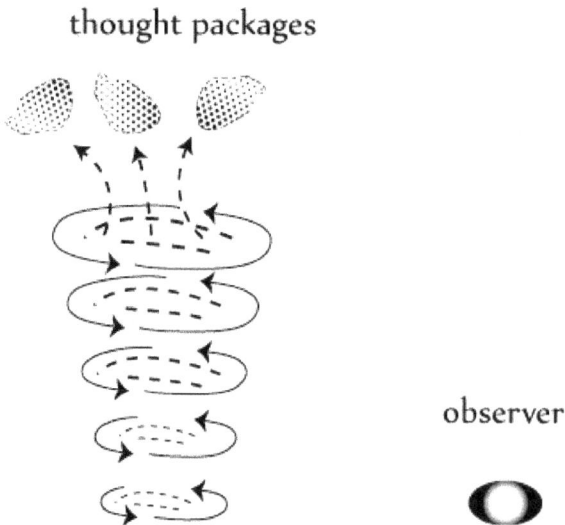

observer

Then Michael did some fancy adjustments with his illustrator program. He asked me to fit the sketch into a head silhouette, and he created the shapes which represent the thoughts.

Here is the final product, showing

- the observer (white sphere in center of head)
- the spinning intellect, throwing out thoughts

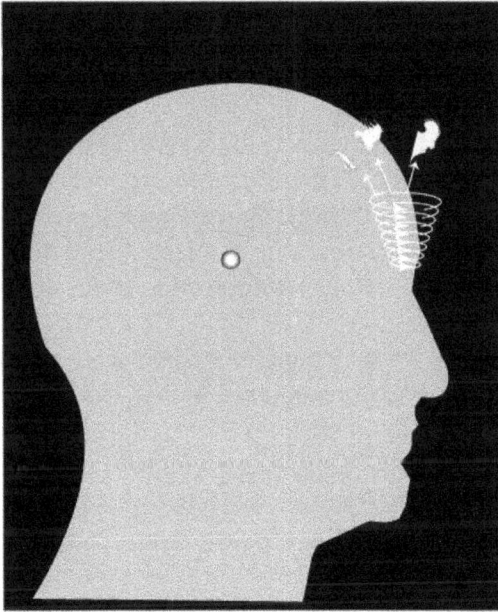

Did I really see the intellect, as defined by Michael? Maybe it was something else. Maybe the drawing misrepresents what I saw.

Overall, I think it was helpful to go through the process and try to make further sense of the experience. Hopefully the effort will help me to have more clarity in the future.

MiBeloved's Response

The intellect is the psychic organ which produces the thoughts and images which are usually seen in the mind space in the frontal part of the head. Its shape varies according to what it does and according to the energy it uses for those productions. There is no doubt that it is the only psychic organ which produces thoughts and images.

Consider your heart, is it a specific organ?

Does it have a specific function?

Suppose someone's heart has an odd shape, as this happens from time to time. Still, a surgeon can identify it by the functions.

One of the most difficult things to get into one's head is that there are psychic organs in a subtle body. People feel that there is no such thing and that there is only a physical body and a void self without individualization but I say that it is not so. There is individualization on the subtle plane and distinctions of specific objects and forms. Since nature is reluctant to award it, the real problem is to develop the psychic sensual perception.

Dreams at the Workplace

A yogi should make efforts to curtail the astral body's tendency to return to a work place when the physical body sleeps. The astral form likes to do that. It does so instinctively but this is counterproductive to yoga attainment.

Keep a close record of the dream experiences. Write them in a journal. If you recall nothing, do not stress over it. Instead write that you remembered nothing. Doing this will eventually get the mind to recall what occurs on the astral planes.

People who have a spiritual discipline and who are physically focused will have difficulty remembering dreams. In fact, that person will more than likely say that there are no dreams.

Actually, it is impossible to not dream. What happens is that the person is unable to transfer the memory and objective consciousness into the subtle body when it separates from the physical form. That lack of observation is interpreted as having no dreams. If someone has no way of objectively having an experience, then for that person, it does not happen, even if the whole world testifies about it.

Those who were physically focused have in-born resistance and blindness to astral experience. That condition can change if such persons adjust their attitudes toward subtle experiences and open their attitudes to the possibility of astral perception.

However, my main point is that one should curb the astral body so that it does not return to the place of employment during the night when the physical form sleeps.

Bodiless State

While doing a kundalini yoga session this morning I had a visit from Swami Shivananda. He used what is called a bodiless form. Some yogis describe this as formlessness but what it really means is that the coreSelf does not have a subtle body nor a causal body with latent desire energies. The self resides in the existential place called *sat* in Sanskrit.

In this place all selves are more or less bare or naked, as compared to when one is on an astral plane and one has a subtle covering or in the physical plane and has a physical body.

Imagine a situation in which everyone in crowded auditorium had clothing. They stood next to each other. Imagine if suddenly all clothing disappeared. Each person would exist individually and would be in contact with each other but without clothing.

Beyond the *sat* level there is a spiritual world where the spirits have spiritual limbs and senses as compared to the *sat brahman* level where the spirits are sparkling dazzling minute specks of light.

Swamiji Shivananda explained this.

A yogi must clear the *nadis*. If the yogi can raise kundalini and bring it to crown chakra (brahmrandra), there is hardly any guarantee that the yogi will go to a higher level after finally leaving the body. To ensure full success a yogi should clear the entire subtle body. Failure to do so will result in a short stay in a higher dimension and then a return to the lower astral places in preparation for another physical body, somewhere somehow.

The yogi must directly attack the intellect in meditation. He should abandon props like mantras, focus on breathing and what not. He should directly curb the thinking imaging mechanism. He practices to such proficiency that he develops supernatural vision.

Shivananda's accomplishment of the bodiless state was described by *Patañjali* in this way:

बहिरकल्पिता वृत्तिर्महाविदेहा ततः प्रकाशावरणक्षयः ॥४४॥

bahiḥ akalpitā vṛttiḥ mahāvidehā tataḥ
prakāśa āvaraṇakṣayaḥ

bahiḥ – outside, external; akalpitā – not manufactured, not artificial, not formed; vṛttiḥ – operation; mahā – great; videhā – bodiless state; tataḥ – thence, from that, resulting from that; prakāśa – light; āvaraṇa – covering, mental darkens; kṣayaḥ – dissipation, removal.

By the complete restraint of the mento-emotional energy which is external, which is not formed, a yogi achieves the great bodiless state. From that the great mental darkness which veils the light, is dissipated. (*Yoga Sutras* 3.44)

Videha in the Sanskrit mean *vi + deha* = without + body

Divine Beings

An astral being may not have to evolve to be superior. There are supernatural beings who are superior because they are, not because they evolved.

Consider that you went to an uninhabited planet, what will you find there? You may find some gold nuggets and then find much dust. But the nuggets are a higher quality of metal.

In existence certain realities happen to be superior just because they are existentially that. Some attained superiority through development. Do not think that every elevated being or every divine being had to go through a learning or purificatory process as others must do.

Clarity comes if one continues to have the experiences. Things clear up as one develops psychic and spiritual perception. One should be persistent and make this the number one priority.

Medical science explains that initially we did not see clearly through the eyes we had as babies. After some time, the infant's eyes come into focus. A similar thing may happen if one persists with these experiences, where overtime one will develop supernatural perception and can distinguish subtle objects.

For divine beings there is no evolution in the way that we must endure for becoming upgraded. Just as there is impure gold ore and sometimes a miner finds a nugget of gold that is pure, so there are beings who do not require evolutionary upliftment.

They are not stuck because their level of existence is the absolute spiritual plane where everything is perfect and complete. From India we benefited from the concept of avatar which means one who descends from a divine world into this human situation on the physical plane and lower astral regions.

But then we should acknowledge people like Charles Darwin who brought to our attention that some beings are moving upwards in the mundane evolutionary cycle. Some beings are being elevated. Others are descending. It seems that the human species is a junction between those who go up and those who come down.

While the evolutionary beings must strive for something better, the divine beings who come to the human world only need to express their divine status when they are done with human incarnations.

Intellect Shut-Down

Rishi Singh Gherwal gave another procedure for those students who hustle to come to terms with Patañjali's no vrittis instruction. *Patañjali* ordered the shutting down of the intellect so that the coreSelf can experience itself in isolation and also so that the coreSelf can consider the possibility of having a new trouble-free non-independent spiritually-infused intellect.

In this practice, infusing the *sushumna* central passage is a preliminary requirement. The yogi must do the exercises, raise kundalini and then blast the *sushumna* passage from the base chakra to the neck.

Once this is achieved, the yogi becomes aware of the *nadis* which run from the spine through the subtle body, the way nerves run from the physical spine through the physical body.

During the exercises the yogi should feel the kundalini coursing through those *nadis*. This feels like the spreading of tiny electrical currents or like a bliss energy going through certain parts of the body according to the posture and quantity of breath infusion.

After the *sushumna* is blasted, the yogi should sit to meditate. He should relocate the coreSelf to the back of the head, so that the core is no longer situated in its default position. This relocation is vital, since if it is done, the yogi will find that the intellect becomes helpless and can no longer influence the mind. It will be unable to produce impressions. It will no longer have the power to influence the core. The pulling action on the core will fail to cause the intellect to move to the back but the intellect's energy field will begin flowing to the back to the core.

The yogi should hold the intellect in that posture for a time and observe that it will make weak attempts to resume its old behavior which is generation of thoughts and images and the accommodation of information gathered by the senses.

The sensual orbs take energy from kundalini. From that they develop resistance to the coreSelf. Hence, when the kundalini central passage is blasted, the sensual orbs become powerless. They lose the power to act on their own. For the time of the meditation, the sensual orbs are deactivated.

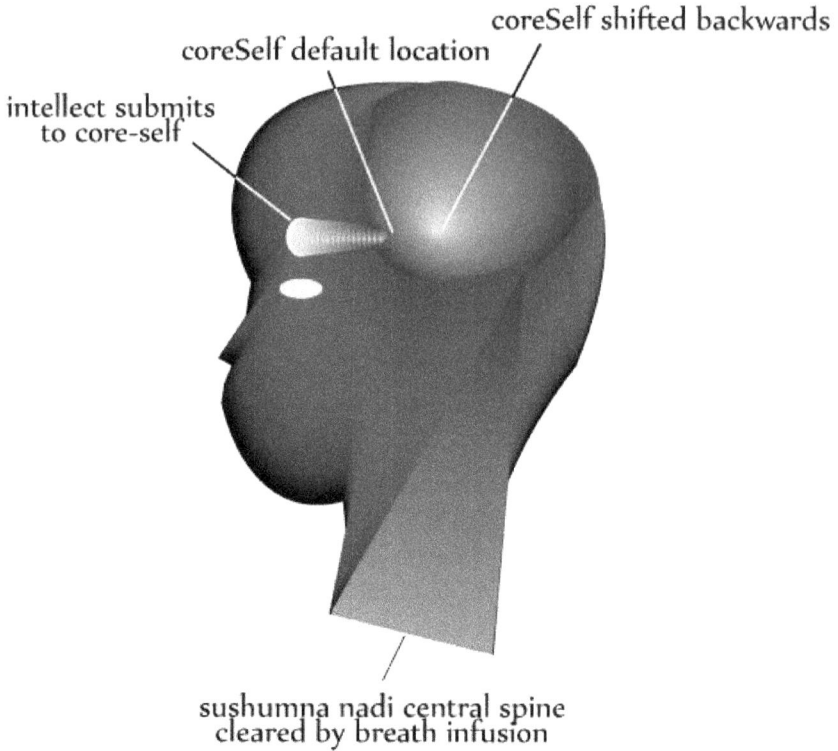

coreSelf shifted backwards

coreSelf default location

intellect submits
to core-self

sushumna nadi central spine
cleared by breath infusion

In Meditation Pictorial, in the first chapter, there are diagrams which instruct on how to discover the position of the coreSelf. This would be its default position. It is rooted there usually. Once one locates that, one can meditate on stationing the awareness there and pulling in the optic energy which is usually focused there for all visual perception.

If one masters that meditation, one can practice moving the coreSelf backwards in the head. This begins with listening to naad sound which is a high-pitched frequency which is heard mostly on the right side near the physical ear. Constant listening to naad sound causes the coreSelf to drift backwards to that sound. After being observed by the coreSelf, that movement gives it a hint on how to pull the core backwards from its default position.

The key is that the coreSelf will notice that when it is withdrawn, the intellect loses its grip on the core. The self is freed from mental dominance and does not have to observe thoughts coming and going. It does not have to be detached from thoughts. It does not have to focus on the breath. It discovers that the intellect is disabled when the core is pulled backwards.

Elimination of Kundalini

When the physical universe is exhausted, when the parallel worlds which use energy of light frequency are retrogressed into dark matter, then the kundalini polarity is finished. Since such an occurrence will happen in billions of years hence, it means that the individual spirits will continue to be tagged with individual kundalinis just as children are tagged with a name by parents when they are born.

The primary information on the tag has to do with the social identity of the mother. The children will grow and go on their own but even then, they cannot deny the tag. Nor can anyone shed the genetic information which runs through his/her body. Even if I do not like my mother, I am still stuck with her genes. I will display the tendencies which those genes sponsor. This is because in the infant stage, I was unable to establish my identity without respect to the mother.

This is similar to our situation, where we feel that we should be free agents and that we can achieve absolute freedom but our desires as such occurred after the fact of our appearance with a kundalini force.

Can anyone remember who he or she was, before discovering the self with a kundalini lifeForce? Can the infant remember his or her life before being part of the mother's body as an embryo? Was the infant in whatever existence it was in prior to that, existing without a lifeForce?

How did this individual spirit become fused to a kundalini lifeForce?

Does the individual spirit have the power to release itself from that fusion?

Can a horse remove its bridle?

If I have no recall of the past, and am only focused on the present, and if I find myself to be in a cabin handcuffed to an iron rail, what would be my idea of freedom?

Since I have no memory of the past and can only know my present condition, it would be almost impossible for me to come to the conclusion that there was some time in the past when I was freed.

It is a rare achievement for a yogi to realize himself or herself without kundalini. Of course, one must first understand what kundalini is, and how it functions to control so many activities.

For the elimination of kundalini however, a yogi must forego his mundane needs, relinquishing every facility which kundalini provides in the physical and astral worlds.

Are we sure that we are ready for this drastic reduction of needs?

Birth Influences

Even though some men failed to respect the mother institution of nature, they are not responsible for the discrepancy, but it so happens that even though they are not liable, they are penalized by the same nature which caused the social situation.

A faulty human being did not create nature, nor himself nor herself, but still human beings, as well as nature itself; holds the individual accountable. Men bear the brunt of the liabilities for their lack of appreciation and the exploitation of the mother institution of nature.

For the most part the father's side of a family takes most of the available new bodies which come as progeny. There are cases of where the mother's side of the family takes the opportunities.

To answer the question as to why this prejudice exists, we should investigate nature to find out. In the human species, the entity taking birth must begin the possession of a sperm body in the father's form. That is nature's situation. Due to this, usually only those ancestors on the father's side can arrest the opportunity. The reason being their familiarity with the father which is due to the pious credits invested in his life.

It does happen however that ancestors on the mother's side penetrate the father's form and commandeer the opportunities. If they are powerful enough or if they get the father to like them enough, they can certainly do this.

For convenience sake, governments usually tag a child to its mother. At least initially no government can tell unless they do DNA testing if a certain male was the father. The midwife certainly knows who the mother is because of the obvious which happens at delivery.

From a biological angle however, the females are predominant by virtue of the fact that the sperm's only food source is the genetic nourishment from the mother.

What happens is this, once I get my sperm body in the father's form, I am more or less stuck, like a passenger at an abandoned airport. He got to the airport but it was closed. His only hope is the resumption of flights.

At that point after the sperm particle is finished as a product in the father's form, the sperm itself gets antsy-pansy to find female accommodation. In that condition, it is eager to get into a woman's body.

Somehow there is attraction between the father and my would-be mother. Intercourse occurrs. In the midst of that sexual clash, I was transferred into the mother's form. I already have a kundalini of my own. In fact, I had that before I entered into my father's emotions. Now that my kundalini is present in the sperm particle, it knows what it has to do and experiences that knowledge as an urge to move up the birth canal and embed itself into an egg.

But the story does not end there because whether I want to be influenced or not, the information in the egg will affect me. Furthermore, after being embedded in the mother's uterine wall, I will take nutrients from her body. With that there will be genetic influence regardless of what I prefer. I must accept those conditions.

Along with that there is the psychic influence of the mother's kundalini which will influence my kundalini to become subjected to it. This will occur even if I do not desire it.

By the time the nine months transpire, I am not longer myself as I was before I entered the father's form. I am now a new somebody, which is the resultant infant as Jim or Mary with a mother and father. I will be molded further as the body develops.

Mind Distinguished

In astral projections, the mind is experienced independently from the thinking brain but this proof of the mind's independent existence is not the type of proof which science accepts. There is also another important hitch in this, which is that the mind which is used when using an aware physical body is a multi-component mind which is partially different from the mind used in astral projection.

To understand this considers the situation of having two power supplies in two separate locations. One is in your home. The other is in your office in another city. The one in your home is designed for 120 volts. The one in the office is for 440 volts.

Your computer has two power supply input jacks. Within the computer there are two hard drives, one which uses 120 volts and another which uses 440 volts. It is the same computer but it has two input circuits, one which is used when you are at home and the other when you are at the office in the other city. The jacks are designed differently such that you cannot accidentally connect the 120-volt plug to the 440-volt system.

What is the point?

It is this: When the mind is connected into the physical brain it operates with one hard drive using a special circuit. When it is connected into the astral body and not connected to a physical brain simultaneously, it operates with the other hard drive and the other input circuit.

In that sense it is the same computer and then again it is not the same because of the differences in the circuits used.

During astral projection some facilities which we use while in a waking physical body become unavailable. These are not turned on and not wired into our perception. As soon as we again become consciously fused into the physical body, some astral facilities shut down and we use the physical system.

Third Eye Meditation Adjustments

This morning, Rishi Singh Gherwal made the following suggestions about the third eye meditation procedure. He made adjustments to some procedures which his disciple Arthur Beverford gave to myself and Sir Paul in the early 1970's.

He said that the subtle body must be energized by doing pranayama, preferably bhastrika or kapalabhati breath infusion. The yogi should make sure that *sushumna nadi* is scrubbed aggressively with new breath energy which is infused into the system by the breathing. Once *sushumna nadi* is cleared to the neck, the yogi should try to move kundalini into the brain.

Then the yogi should sit to meditate, preferably in padmasana or lotus posture. Rishi says that lotus posture is not a necessity but he said that there should be no tension in the spine. The body should be balanced. Pillows or pads can be used to support it. One can sit on a confortable couch.

The yogi should pull the coreSelf to the back of the head so that it is away from its default location which is convenient for thinking and imaging which is undesirable during meditation. As soon as the core moves back the yogi should check to see where the visual interest flows. If it flows forward, the yogi should pull it with a gentle tug.

When the yogi feels that the visual interest flows backwards with ease, he should keep doing that and simultaneously gather before him the third eye energy. He should keep doing this until the third eye opens or until there appears a tiny star in the distance, or until a sparkling star like object appears, or until he perceives divine beings in the divine world.

Rishi showed this practice in my subtle head. He was in a miniature form, showing how this was to be done.

Once someone can identify the visual interest energy, that person will discover it as a singular energy. Normally this energy is in one beam and then it splits and runs through the left and right optic nerves.

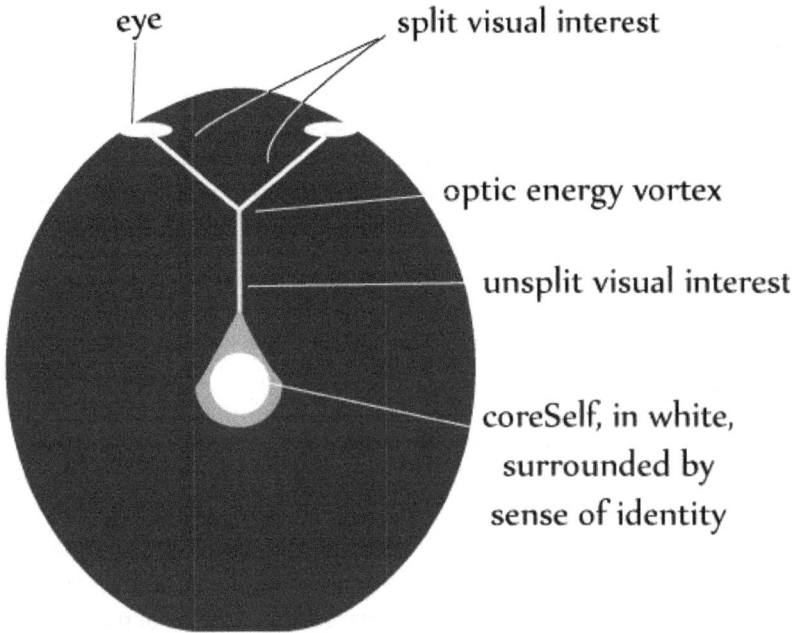

eye

split visual interest

optic energy vortex

unsplit visual interest

coreSelf, in white,
surrounded by
sense of identity

As soon as one gets that energy travelling backwards (usually it travels forwards), one will find that there are other energies rushing forward in streams. If a swimmer moves upstream, he or she will be aware of water flowing in the other direction downstream.

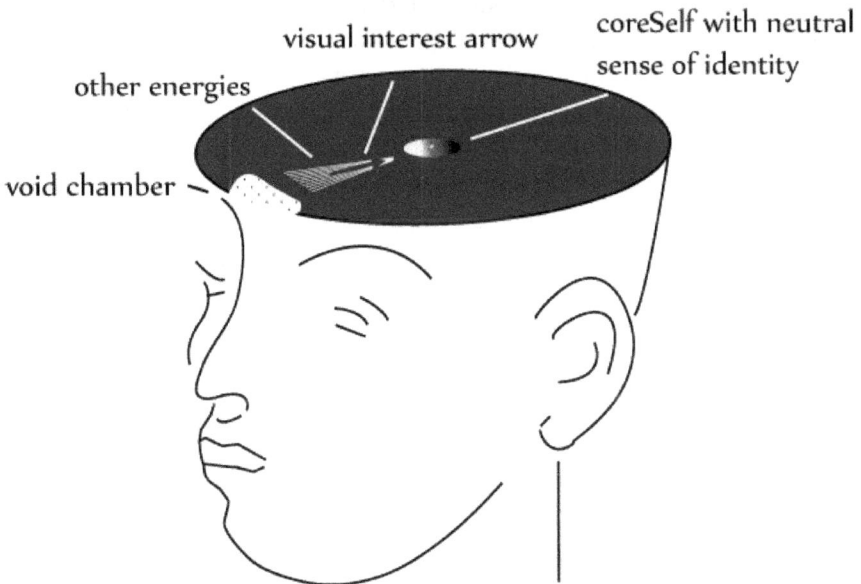

visual interest arrow

coreSelf with neutral
sense of identity

other energies

void chamber

The streams of energy will not enter the coreSelf but will go towards it continuously. Once the yogi is aware of that he will notice that those variant energies move towards the front part of the subtle head or front part of the physical head.

As they flow, they will reach the third eye area and then seem to disappear or dissipate. At that disappearance place where they seem to be nothing, one should gather that void energy mentally. Let it remain there in as a collective.

The coreSelf should not go forward in the head, otherwise the usual mental imaginings will resume.

Morning Meditation

Someone asked about morning meditation, about how to prepare for and conduct it. I explained that the morning session begins the previous night.

If a person wants to do it with quality and attention, meditation like anything else, requires preparation. For morning meditation, one should prepare the night prior by bringing order to the mental activities and the emotional issues at the time of resting. If one fails to do this, some mental and emotional stresses will feed into the morning session. It will not be efficiently done.

Ideally the body should get sufficient rest which means getting to bed early and relaxing the physical, mental and emotional systems. If you rise early and you get this feeling that you did not have enough rest, it means that your meditation will not be as good as if you had rested sufficiently.

Meditation is best done after ample rest.

When meditation takes priority in your life, it will like any other aspect bring your life into order for its convenience, such that you rest early, you eat at a certain time, you do postures and breath infusion before a session, you carefully restrict association with persons who carry a negative impact on meditation and you are attentive during the session.

Kundalini Diverted to Back of Head

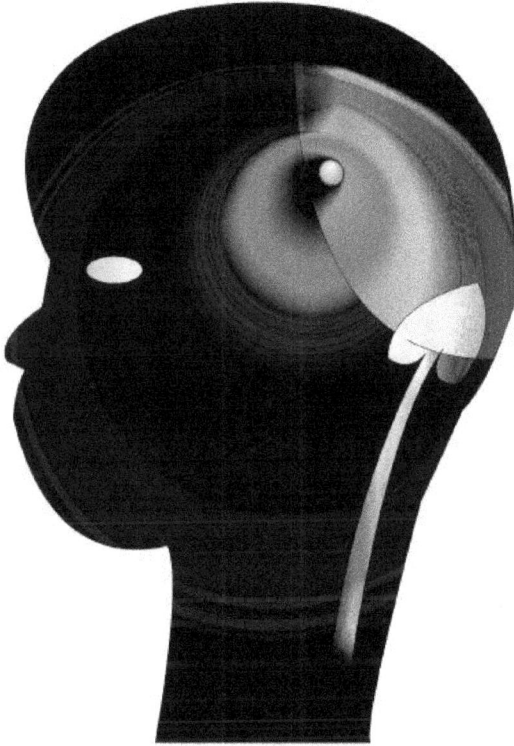

back of the head deep meditation

This meditation is at the back of head, with intentions of diverting kundalini there. Kundalini lost interest in reaching the crown chakra since it is arrested by a strong meditation focus in the back of the subtle head.

Since the coreSelf successfully shifted itself away from the sensual concerns in the front of the head, kundalini became powerless to attack brow chakra or crown chakra. It finds itself being pulled to the back irresistibly. The yogi notices this achievement.

Mind and Brain

The word for mind in Sanskrit is usually manas or manah. It is usually used in two ways:
- mental and/or emotional functions of a person
- analytical functions of a person

When it is used for analysis, the word mind becomes the same as the word *buddhi* or intellect.

I rarely use mind to mean mental analysis. I use the word to mean the psychological collective which houses the following:

- the analytical function
- the sensual investigations
- the sense of identity
- the coreSelf
- the flash memory

Stated in another way, my use of the word mind is to say that it is the head of the subtle body which houses the functions listed above. In my usage the mind is a psychic compartment.

For the purpose of inSelf Yoga™, a meaning other than the one I use would be inadequate since in this yoga, one deals with subtle organs in the subtle head. One must differentiate between one organ and the other, instead of considering the head as an organ.

Patañjali's instruction to stop the vrittis is directed to the analytical functions. Krishna gave instructions in chapter two of *Bhagavad Gita* where he explained a psychological discipline which he termed as *buddhi* yoga. For all practical purposes however control of the *buddhi* or intellect results in control of the entire subtle head or mind. The intellect is the lead advisor of the psychic organs. If a yogi gets that one organ under control, the other components will act favorably.

The sense of identity is another component in the mind but it is a nuisance only when it is subservient to the intellect. As soon as it is detached from the intellect, the sense of identity remains neutral and does not indulge.

On the Difference Between the Brain and Mind

Brain is the physical organ which is well documented in medical books. All activity of the physical brain pertains to it, but its electric activities also pertain to the mind.

The mind is larger than the brain or utilizes more spatial space but so does an electric current which passes through a wire. There is a force field around a wire which an instrument can detect but which the human eyes cannot see. There is also a force field which comes from the subtle head and which extends into the space surrounding the physical head.

Whatever takes place on a psychological level occurs in the mind. Some of it occurs in the brain simultaneously. When the brain dies, the mind continues to exist but without its physical facility. It can no longer use the physical thinking system. Thought continues but they are no longer illustrated in a physical brain.

To understand this, we may consider static electricity and machine generated electricity. Static electricity is a fact. It is in the air at all times, but it cannot function usefully in the physical sense. Machine generated electricity is useful in the physical sense. When the mind has a brain parallelly aligned to it, it is like when we generate electricity by machine, in the sense that the electricity now has a wire to conduit and intensify it. When the mind does not have a brain, it is like when we have static electricity.

Convention says that first there is a brain and then there is mind, but yoga says that first there is mind and then there is brain. It is a perpetual argument that may never be settled until we can detect psychic reality.

Conventional thinking and physical evidence say that first the brain developed and then it produced intelligence. Yoga says that first there was a mind, and then a rudimentary brain started which developed further on the basis of the blueprint of the mind. Those are opposing views.

Convention says that I began as a baby. I went to school, got some learning and then showed some intelligent activity. Yoga says that I was an adult psychic being, I went into a coma in which nature formed for me a material body which was patterned by the blueprint of my psychic being. It took nature about twenty-one years to complete the construction of the adult body, which supports the functions of my psychic being.

Patañjali yoga concerns the segregation, not integration, of the self (core observer) and its perception equipment.

People who translate *Patañjali* with intentions to use him to endorse unity ideas, cry out about *Patañjali* being all about unity. That is a distortion.

The key term of *Patañjali* is *kaivalyam* and even though in the second definition *Patañjali* speaks of the fusion of the self and a perception apparatus, initially this is not the case. In fact, if one does not perform the segregation one cannot go to the final step which is integration.

Patañjali does not deal with the mind as a whole as is used in Western psychology. He splinters the mind into parts and then advises the yogi to identify the coreSelf and isolate it so that it can sever its fusion with the other parts.

When that is achieved to proficiency, the yogi checks to be sure that the troublesome equipment which he was allotted by nature is nowhere in sight. Then there arises a new equipment and the yogi integrates with that. This last action is a new fusion or new unity.

Patañjali does not endorse a void existence as a permanent stage but only as a stage of development when moving from troublesome equipment to a non-troublesome type. There is a blank in the interim. In order to make it safely through the required isolation a yogi takes help from the naad sound which is mentioned by Patanjali.

If a person opens his mind to Patanjali, he has nothing to lose because no one can go beyond Patanjali. This is because the full human potential is laid out by him. If you desire to go further than *Patañjali* then study the *Uddhava Gita Explained*. Beyond that there is nothing more detailed about self-realization.

If you want more education than that you should go to the higher planets on the highest level where celestial people live. Here on earth, *Uddhava Gita* is the highest information.

One important clarification which I should make is this:

In kriya yoga there is the mind and there is the kundalini lifeForce. These two together is the whole being. The kundalini is segregated because it is resistant to the coreSelf and does not have to tally with anything the core says.

Basically, this means there is a head and there is a tail. The tail is like the kundalini. The head is like the mind. These two are fused.

The head itself being mostly an operator cannot function by itself without a machine. A tractor is there, it is running but there is no driver. There is kundalini but it needs a driver. The driver must have training to operate the equipment.

The problem is that as soon as the driver tries to operate the already-started tractor, the machine moves in a contrary direction. The driver is thrown from the seat and is almost crushed to death.

But the machine, for all its energy, cannot function by itself. After it throws the driver it runs into a ditch and is stuck there. The driver must again sit on the machine to control it.

Mind and kundalini make the complete psyche. The coreSelf is in the mind. The core has difficulty controlling the power surges which the kundalini produces.

For instance, during the climax of sex experience, the person is overwhelmed by pleasure. During the rise of kundalini into the head some persons go off into nothingness and have no recall of the experience.

The coreSelf for its part sees itself as a big wig. It surmises many theories about its divinity. Still, it cannot explain why it cannot control kundalini and why it is dominated and kept spell-bound by the thought constructions of the intellect. I vouch for Patanjali. He is correct about everything pertaining to the development of the human psyche from this level to the spiritual plane.

Dark Matter

Dark matter would be the state of matter which was the initial state when matter was in its quiescence. That is a total non-manifested state of matter. It is always non-perceptible except as an indistinguishable reservoir of energy. It cannot be seen by the psychic organs in the subtle body but those organs can divine it or surmise its existence and know that it is in the background.

If you are in a dark cave with a rodent and if you are blind, vision is out of the question. But suppose you are not blind, you were checked and found to have vision. If then you enter the dark cave, then what? Again, it is the same situation in that you cannot see the mouse because your vision cannot function in pitch darkness. But despite that you and a blind man can surmise that the mouse is present.

The causal body has no perception equipment. It is the root sense from which the subtle senses emerged. Hence it can sense but not with distinction.

Imagine if you were blind, deaf, devoid of a membrane, without nostrils and without a tasting sense. That may be compared to what it is like to be the causal body.

But the causal body arises after dark matter is brought into a stage of movement of instability. Therefore, it cannot transcend dark matter, because dark matter is transcendental to it.

Now let us consider something deeper which is the spiritual body. That body is on the other side of dark matter. Even though the spiritual body is beyond dark matter it does not perceive dark matter.

Advanced Withdrawal

Yogeshwarananda requested that I explain an advanced *pratyahar* practice which must be done to complete *Patañjali* yoga. This concerns the retraction of all out-shoot interest which emitted from the causal body and which initially produced the subtle form.

If this is not done, one cannot go to the spiritual universes, to the brahman level. It is more than just retracting one's interest in the social concerns of this world. One has to retract the interest energy which goes out of the psyche into the physical world and into the lower astral regions.

Pratyahar or sensual energy withdrawal is the fifth stage of yoga but it continues in the other stages because one cannot complete it in the fifth stage.

When one reaches the level where the *samadhi* continuous absorption begins, one discovers that unless one is proficient at the pratyahar, the *samadhi* cannot be perfected. It will not last for more than a second or two. It is then that one practices the retraction of interest in earnest.

In the beginning *pratyahar* is retraction of sensual energy but in the advanced stage it changes into being a requirement for retraction of interest-energy. What is this interest energy?

To develop an interest in anything, one must have a corresponding energy in the psyche which is concerned with that pursuit. This refers to objects. Take for example a rock. For it to be useful, one must have an interest in it. But that does not mean that the interest has to be deliberate or has to be under consideration. An aborigine may pick up a rock casually without a definite interest. As soon as he does that his mind will immediately scan itself to see if there is a need for that. If there is no need, the aborigine will drop the rock. We can then safely say that he lacks interest. But wait a minute, are we thinking that the aborigine has all his interest energy in his surface consciousness. Suppose there is interest energy but it is subconscious, then what?

When the aborigine took the rock, his mind filed information about it in memory. That information will be kept until a time when his subconscious interest is released into his conscious mind. Then the aborigine will have an interest.

These are the energies which a yogin must retract in advanced *pratyahar* practice. I hope I clarified this. These interest energies were the causes of us assuming various bodies in various species of life. From these interest energies particular types of bodily forms with particular sensual capabilities were created.

Human Freedom

Throughout the *Mahabharata* there is discourse on destiny as to whether it is caused by personal endeavor or by forces which are beyond the person's control, forces which are labeled as fate. Perhaps the most intense discussions on the subject was between King Dhritarashtra and Vidura.

There was a discussion about it between Sanjaya and Dhritarashtra. In conclusion Sanjaya told Dhritarashtra that what happened was due to the careless acts of Dhritarashtra in siding with his son Duryodhana, the villain of the *Mahabharata*. However, Dhritarashtra for his part, kept insisting that it was destined and that he had little to do with it.

Before the war, when Vidura made efforts to bring peace, he was annoyed with the situation when his reasonable arguments for peace were rejected by Duryodhana. Vidura resigned as an advisor to King Dhritarashtra. He declared that fate was supreme.

Krishna said several times during the war when there were reverses for the Pandavas and also when things went in their favor, that life on earth occurs by the agency of fate as well as by human endeavor. He admitted both realities but he did not give a set percentage of each.

However, in the *Bhagavad Gita,* Krishna listed five factors which he said must be present before any action occurs. On the basis of that verse, my admission is that we are only responsible for the percentage of our contribution in any act.

Unless the percentage the other four factors is zero, our responsibility cannot be 100%. It is not possible for any action to take place with the other factors being zero.

पञ्चैतानि महाबाहो

कारणानि निबोध मे ।

सांख्ये कृतान्ते प्रोक्तानि

सिद्धये सर्वकर्मणाम् ॥१८.१३॥

pañcaitāni mahābāho

kāraṇāni nibodha me

sāṁkhye kṛtānte proktāni

siddhaye sarvakarmaṇām (18.13)

pañcaitāni — pañca — five + tāni — these; mahābāho — O mighty-armed man; kāraṇāni — factors; nibodha — learn; me — from me; sāṁkhye — in Sāṁkhya philosophy; kṛtānte — in conclusion, in doctrine; proktāni — declared; siddhaye — in accomplishment; sarvakarmaṇām — of all actions

Learn from Me, O mighty-armed man, of the five factors declared in the Sāṁkhya doctrine for the accomplishment of all actions. (Bhagavad Gita 18.13)

अधिष्ठानं तथा कर्ता

करणं च पृथग्विधम् ।

विविधाश्च पृथक्चेष्टा

दैवं चैवात्र पञ्चमम् ॥१८.१४॥

adhiṣṭhānaṁ tathā kartā

karaṇaṁ ca pṛthagvidham

vividhāśca pṛthakceṣṭā

daivaṁ caivātra pañcama (18.14)

adhiṣṭhānaṁ — location; tathā — as well as; kartā — the agent; karaṇaṁ — the instrument; ca — and; pṛthagvidham — various kinds; vividhāśca = vividhāḥ — various + ca — and; pṛthakceṣṭā —

movements; daivam — destiny; caivātra — ca — and + eva — indeed + atra — here in this case; pañcamam — the fifth

The location, the agent, the various instruments, the various movements, and destiny, the fifth factor. (Bhagavad Gita 18.14)

शरीरवाङ्‌नोभिर्यत्

कर्म प्रारभते नरः ।

न्याय्यं वा विपरीतं वा

पञ्चैते तस्य हेतवः ॥१८.१५॥

śarīravāṅmanobhiryat

karma prārabhate naraḥ

nyāyyaṁ vā viparītaṁ vā

pañcaite tasya hetavaḥ (18.15)

śarīravāṅmanobhiḥ = śarīra — body + vān(vās) — speech + manobhiḥ — with mind; yat = yad — whatever; karma — project; prārabhate — he undertakes; naraḥ — a human being; nyāyyaṁ — moral; vā — or; viparītam — immoral; vā — or; pañcaite — pañca — five + ete — these; tasya — of it; hetayaḥ — factors

As for whatever project a human being undertakes with body, speech and mind, regardless of it being moral or immoral, these are its five factors. (Bhagavad Gita 18.15)

Meditation Requirements

The minimum requirement for yogis is to practice once daily. On days when practice is not possible because of pressing social commitments or other timely mishaps, a yogi should make a note regarding the upset. He should realize that destiny does not care about his progress.

One should realize that destiny's disregard for one's spiritual welfare in no way diminishes destiny's power in one's life. Hence one should not assume an offensive attitude to fate but should merely comply by it, and wait for it to release one so that one can resume the daily practice.

No good can come to a person through fighting fate but if one is respectful of it and patient with its conclusions, one will find that sooner or later it facilitates. There should be a minimum of one session of meditation per day. This should last for at least twenty minutes. This little investment will bring one to the point of realizing how long it takes to quiet the mind for meditation and meaningful insight.

Twenty minutes is not enough but it is sufficient for a beginner. Through that investment of time, one can form conclusions about the value of meditation and about the preliminary preparation which is required for it. If one does not do pranayama breath infusion, or if one does not do something to calm the mind and energize it before doing meditation, the meditation will consist of a session of fighting undesirable thoughts and ideas in the mind. This fighting habit of the mind may go on for five, ten or fifteen minutes or more.

It is for this reason that a meditator may come to the conclusion that an effective way of silencing the mind is an absolute must as a preliminary procedure before meditation. But what would be that effective method?

Should we argue over it?

Should I say that it is this?

Obviously, arguments will not help. The issue is not the method but the establishment of whatever practice brings the mind into a silent peaceful state.

Since meditation only begins in earnest after the mind is quieted, the procedure for meditation is this.

- use an effective method to bring the mind to silence
- meditate in the silenced mind

One cannot exist without social pressure. It is an all-pervasive reality. From the time one is put into the world from the mother's uterine system, one is under social pressure and its demands. Unless one can blank one's existence or erase it from being a reality here, there is no question of becoming freed from social obligation.

Anytime one cannot do yoga, it is due to a pressing social influence. There is more than one method for breaking one's resolution to be persistent at a spiritual practice.

Some social influences are blatant. Some are sublimal. Some are so subtle that one would never know they were there in the first place, but you can always know that you are under an influence.

Why do I not practice even when the negative influences are subtle?

It is unfair to recommend a method if one did not practice it to proficiency and did not get results from it. The only system that I can recommend is bhastrika breath infusion but that is an aggressive practice. I was introduced to it by Yogi Harbhajan Singh, who is departed. There are other pranayama breath infusions and various yogis recommended those based on their practice.

Even if you do not have an effective method you should practice. Why? Because in this life you cannot always get exactly what you require at all times. It is a shuffle in this existence where today I get what I want and then tomorrow that thing is not available.

Some yoga students spent lifetimes trying to find an effective method. They continue the search because they feel it as a pressing need to gain some spiritual footing.

Patanjali Yoga

To successfully complete Patanjali's ultimatum which is to stop the mento-emotional energy from its normal operations, one must lose interest even in the psychic facilities which are provided by the third eye. This is not an easy achievement and requires extreme detachment.

In any case, I am pleased to announce that the mystic action for the completion of Patanjali's request is the pulling back of the intellect into the sense-of-identity energy. This causes the intellect to stop its normal operations and to become stunned, like a runaway car which stopped and which had its ignition switched off. Even though there is this idea that the mind is a botheration, that mind is a chamber which contains psychic organs. Of these the most useful and the most troublesome is the intellect or *buddhi*, as it is called.

After the yogi lost interest in the advantages for existence which are derived from the brow chakra (third eye), he is freed to pursue the control of the intellect. This orb is a nuisance. It is the root cause of the lack of mind control. Fortunately, even though it is not usually perceived it can still be detected and curbed. The secret to curbing this orb if you cannot perceive it as a psychic object, is to identify its spatial location, or its position in the mind space. Once a yogi knows where it is, he can perform the recommended mental actions on that space. Even though he cannot see it, he will affect it.

It is important that a yogi endeavors to find the location of the intellect. He should find the place where thoughts transpire, where ideas arise, where mental images appear and especially where daydreaming occurs. Spend time in meditation patiently identifying that place. Once you know the location, complete the meditative actions on that intellect with full confidence that you will affect its operations even though you cannot see it.

Here is the technique.

Be sure that your interests in the advantages of the third eye brow chakra are neutralized. Test to see if that is a fact by meditating on the third eye and checking to be sure there is no strong energy-pull from the coreSelf to the brow chakra area. Once you are sure there is no such pull, move from the location of the intellect into the coreSelf. If when you pull back you find that the pull extends to the third eye, that means that the third eye interest is still active. Realizing this you must decide not to complete this meditation.

Whenever you find that the third eye interest is inactive or neutral, keep retracting from the intellect and feel its energy flowing back with force into the coreSelf.

This is the procedure. It is that simple. Note that at this stage the action is that the energy of the intellect goes into the sense-of-identity but it will feel as if it goes directly into the core even though it does not.

The sense of identity surrounds the coreSelf the way light surrounds the filament of a bulb; hence it is not possible for the intellect's energy to reach the coreSelf without passing into the sense of identity.

Do this practice repeatedly. If you find that you usually drift to viewing thoughts and images, do not be disturbed. Ideation is the default operation or natural mode of the intellect. It will always go back into such operations if there is any slack of the pulling influence on it.

Whenever one finds oneself under that influence resume the meditation. From time to time one will find that suddenly there are tiny little lights for a split second. Or one will find that the intellect or its space area has converted into visual perception of another dimension. Or you will find that there is bliss energy in all directions. These are the advanced stages of operation of the intellect. These are the states which one should attain if one successfully completes this practice.

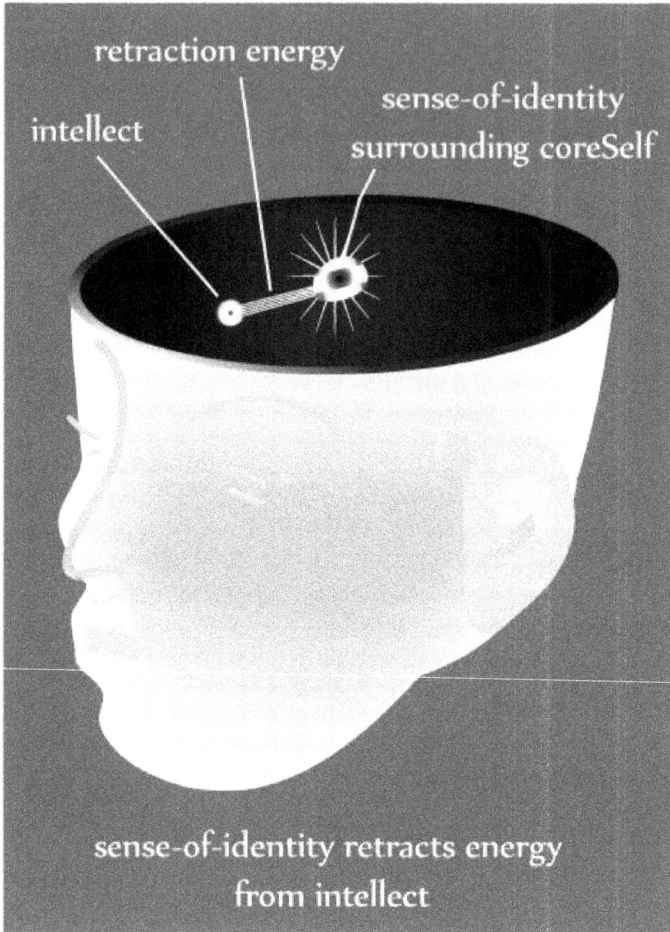

retraction energy

sense-of-identity

intellect

surrounding coreSelf

sense-of-identity retracts energy
from intellect

Part 6

Eating Animals

To survive here, one must be involved directly or indirectly in violence. To sustain a physical body, one must eat. To do so involves digesting other life forms, even vegetation. The only way out of this dilemma is to go to a place where the bodies are sustained without violence.

There is a story in the *Mahabharata*, *Shalya parva*, about the ascetic Asita Devala. He was a family man living at a place called *Surya Tirtha*. Once the great yogi named Jaigeeshavya came there. As custom would have it Asita was glad to be the yogi's host. However, after providing accommodations for that great yogi for years, Asita grew resentful because the only time he would see Jaigeeshavya was when it was time to eat. It got on Asita's nerves that Jaigeeshavya never said a word to him and never shared the secrets of his austerities.

The great yogin for his part knew how Asita felt. After that anywhere that Asita would go, Jaigeeshavya would appear ahead of him, and when Asita returned home he would see that Jaigeeshavya had arrived there as well.

Eventually Jaigee passed on. Asita heard that Jaigee attained the realm of Brahma, a spiritual dimension. Asita realized how great Jaigee was but he regretted his own situation since he knew he could not attain that place. He decided to renounce family life and take up yoga austerities fulltime.

As soon as he made that decision in his mind his relatives and pets lamented that if he did that no one would be there to provide food for them. Subsequently he changed his mind. But as soon as he did that, he heard plants lamenting that he would start cutting them again.

This was when he decided definitely that he wanted nothing to do with encroaching on other life forms to maintain his body. He decided to become a great yogi. He abandoned family life.

This story illustrates that the only way to avoid violence is to attain a level of existence where violence is not necessary. All the same this does not mean that we should make no effort to decrease violence. We should. One of the required behaviors for yogis is ahimsa which is non-violence. All violent behaviors should be reduced as much as possible. One should not continue living under the excuse that violence must be committed.

It does matter. If one is unwilling to eat the flesh of human bodies, then one should extend that dietary attitude to all mammalian forms. This is the least we can do.

There are many things which I did when I was in the care of parents, which I no longer do. I discontinued those habits. One can discontinue some of the dietary means which one acquired from parents. We do not have to continue eating animal bodies.

Those of you, who are interested in kriya yoga practice, may take it from me, that Babaji Mahasaya does not want any practitioners to use knives. Since knives are a prime utensil in any kitchen how practical is that advice? Let me explain. Once when I still had small children, I used to get up around 3 am daily. About 5 am I would be in the kitchen cutting vegetables.

Once Babaji came there. He shouted, "Stop this! Why the knife? What is the necessity? Are you a butcher?" Just as he said this, he left. He was annoyed. I knew it. I paused for a bit. I continued cutting the turnip greens, but when the knife went through the stems and leaves, I felt it as if I cut my body. After that I tried not to use knives as frequently. I tried tearing the leaves instead of using a knife.

Memory Power-Down

I had the opportunity to observe the operation of long-term memory in an elderly lady today. She tried to remember which storage unit belonged to her friend. She said that it looked like this and looked like that.

Peering into her subtle body, I saw the long-term memory storage a little below her throat. As she tried to recall the facts, her intellect reached to get the information from that long-term memory but it could not. It was a dull grey color. Its energy level was low. It could only reach her short-term memory chamber which was much closer to it.

This is an example of the power-down mode of the kundalini life-force in the elderly years of a body. At a certain age, the lifeForce withdraws its power energy from certain subtle organs. This results in a power down even to the corresponding organs in the physical system. The coreSelf is left with barely any memory. Its identity has no anchor, no support. It becomes like a helpless infant.

Should we be Vegetarians?

Regardless of the beliefs about the various species and their relative or absolute values, my intention is to make spiritual progress, to increase psychic perception. That is facilitated by a vegetarian diet.

My senses work in such a way that if I see a chicken thigh in a grocery store it is similar to a human thigh. If I see one fried at a restaurant, that is similar to frying a human one.

Since I see that sensually, I cannot proceed with eating chicken parts. As for fish, I bought live fish, gutted them live and then fried them as a duty when

I lived as a juvenile in Guyana. In the family situation I was in, that was my daily duty. Later however a change occurred. I realized that the fish suffocated when they were removed from water. Once I gutted a pregnant fish. Thousands of eggs came out. Once I gutted a chicken which I was instructed to kill. I saw hundreds of eggs all in different sizes from large in a soft white shell to pin size which were without shell. This caused me not to proceed with poultry in diet.

Paramhansa Yogananda went to visit Luther Burbank a famous botanist who provided evidence to prove that plants have feelings. They react to violence or kindness. However, Paramhansa convinced Gandhi that it was okay to eat eggs if they were not fertilized. I do not accept that idea.

I do not see any difference between a human egg in a woman's ovary and a chicken egg in a chicken body. Both are forms of liquid flesh. Before I eat an egg, I have to think about whether I would eat human menses because I see both as being liquid flesh.

The other thing is astral consciousness of how the various species seem when one passes on and looks back into this world and sees emotional relationships. In that stage one can hardly distinguish between human and animal emotions.

If someone is serious about yoga practice and advanced meditation and ask me for advice, I would suggest forgoing all food which has meat, fish, eggs or any animal matter. But in the case of the cow you can take milk as you would from a mother but not eat the cow just as you would not eat your mother's body.

Ultimately, we make adjustments to achieve what we wish to achieve. If eating animals accelerate spiritual consciousness, go on with it. Personally, I experienced the contrary.

There is another part to this. *That is resentment.*

Anyone who is into advanced meditation should know that resentment is a big minus in spiritual life. This applies both to the yogi's resentment of others and to the resentment the yogi receives, or is targeted for, from others. When it comes to eating animals and fish, a yogi, in the advanced stage is scared about the resentment of these creatures for being killed for the purpose of eating their bodies.

Admittedly however it may be said that this is a moot point since the cycle of this life always involved violence for the most part with the hawk eating the small bird which ate the grasshopper. For a fact it is true that such resentment is an integral part of the world. That is more reason why a yogi should reduce participation to the minimum.

There is a religious group in India known as the Jains. Their teacher, Mahavira, banned violence for the sake of maintaining the body. He filtered water through cloths before drinking. He never walked on any visible insect on the ground. This was years ago when there were no water filters and paved roads, when everywhere the earth had crawling insects.

There is a story in the *Srimad Bhagavatam* of a person named Rishabha (Ri-shab-ha) and a person named Bharat. Bharat used to never step on insects. To walk through the jungle, it took him a long time since before stepping he checked to avoid killing insects. The idea is that creatures are everywhere. One must be careful not to inconvenience them. If the hawk could get out of the habit of eating the swallow, then the hawk should do that. If the swallow could live on grain and fruits, it should do that. But is that possible? Is a hawk body capable of that?

We know that animals like bears can be very gentle at times. Otherwise they are ferocious as lions. Let the bear express the gentle side and suppress the vicious needs. In eating let the bear subsist on berries and decrease its craving for fish and meat.

But how will it survive in the ice lands if it does so? Obviously, this advice is impractical. Let the bear relocate to a place where it is not required to store fat for sleeping through the winter. My idea is to transmigrate to a dimension where viciousness is not a requirement of nature.

Obviously, there is a limit to this advice because a lion for instance is not built for eating grass and fruit. Its mouth design would not facilitate that. To change it would have to cross over into a gentler species like the wildebeest. If in a species one can shift to gentler habits one should do so and forsake the upside of violence which predatory species are equipped for.

There is a folk tale of interest. A lady once had a pig which was her pet. She was invited to a wedding. She was asked to bring the pet. It was well known in the village. Wanting to be sure that the creature would act appropriately, the woman got wedding attire made for the pig by a seamstress. This was in white taffeta and lace. On the day of the wedding with the pig well-dressed, the lady set out. Along the way there was a mud pond. Unfortunately, the pig saw the lake and yanked on the leash with such force, that it was released from the lady's hand. The pig ran into the water and had a good time wallowing. The lady regretted that because she could not take the creature to the wedding in that condition. This is an example of the inability to transcend the lower habits which are permitted in a certain species. For me this story is appropriate.

Growing up in Guyana, I ate several species of fish, crab, and chicken. I even ate iguana. As a boy I heard stories about my father who was a primitive gold and diamond diver in his teen years. It was said that he ate snake, turtle, labba (a large rodent), ant-eaters and anything that dared to move in the jungle. I had my fill of this. Even my embryo was produced from such edibles.

My mother's favorite food was a fish called hassa. It is a small armor-plated river fish. She liked iguana curry.

In that country, British Guiana as it was known, there were descendants of African slaves. A favorite food was black pudding. But what is that? It is boiled rice mixed with condiments and cow blood. Then it is stuffed through a funnel into either pig's or cow's intestines. Then it is tied like the people do in Germany with sausage. Then it is boiled until it is thoroughly cooked. Then it is sliced and eaten. Believe it or not it can be delicious to the human tongue. Of course, if you saw someone purchasing cow blood at a slaughter house, you may not be interested in eating that. But suppose you never saw that, then if you tasted it, you may think it is delicious.

On the other hand, if you are a bushman in an African forest seeing the bloodletting may well entice you to want to eat it since your sense of sight may regard that as appropriate. That is my background or more precisely that is the background of my body. Even in Africa today certain Masai warriors, keep cows and instead of taking milk from udders, they puncture an artery and take blood.

My point is that as humans we should curtail these vicious habits. Decrease the violence. We must realize that eating a vegetable entails much less encroachment on life then killing an animal. We should review this behavior. Sometimes people wonder why I spend so much time meditating and why I am obsessed with the search for another suitable dimension. The reason is given here. I wish to transmigrate to a place which is devoid of this violence for subsistence.

Perception equipment

When the coreSelf is caught off-guard or is unable to direct or influence the flow of risen kundalini, the core floats without a point of reference. It loses objectivity and enters into a subjective state. In that condition it is not aware of itself as an individual self but it is anyway. Sometimes the core remains partially objective in this state. It experiences the energy as sheer white or golden light or as a bliss energy, a bliss enclosure.

It is important when doing breath infusion that one is attentive to how the energy moves within. One should learn how to apply the locks. It is the locks which kundalini responds to. Kundalini does not usually respond to willpower but it will respond to brute force which is the various bodily locks.

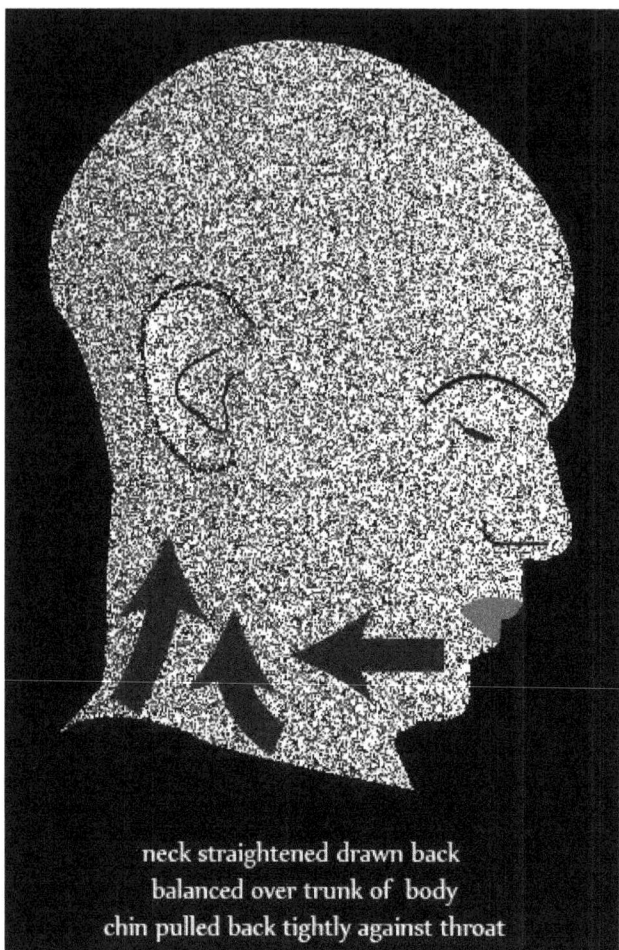

neck straightened drawn back
balanced over trunk of body
chin pulled back tightly against throat

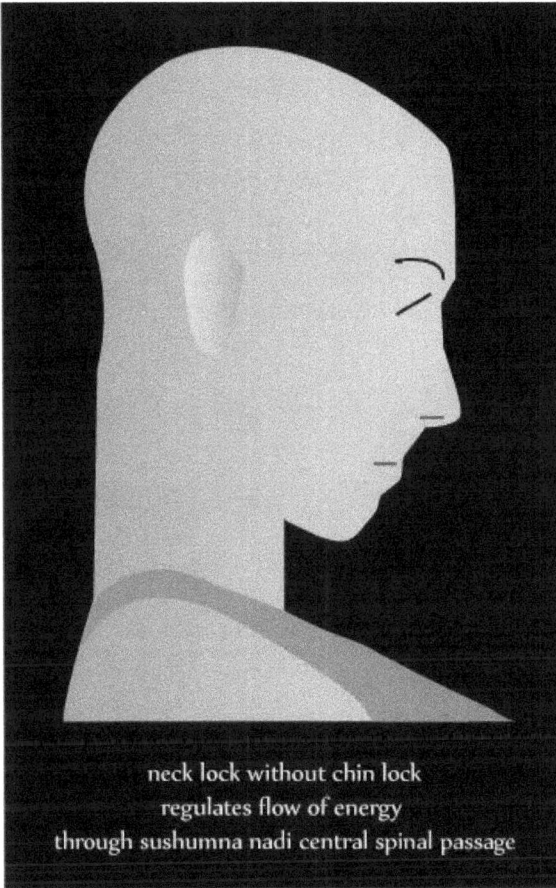

neck lock without chin lock
regulates flow of energy
through sushumna nadi central spinal passage

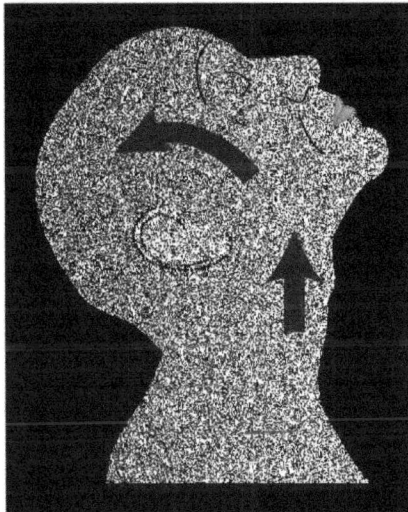

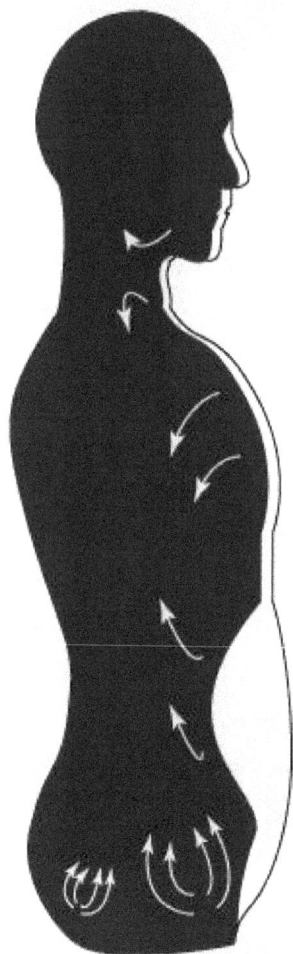

lock pressure (bandhas)   pull back and up higher abdomen

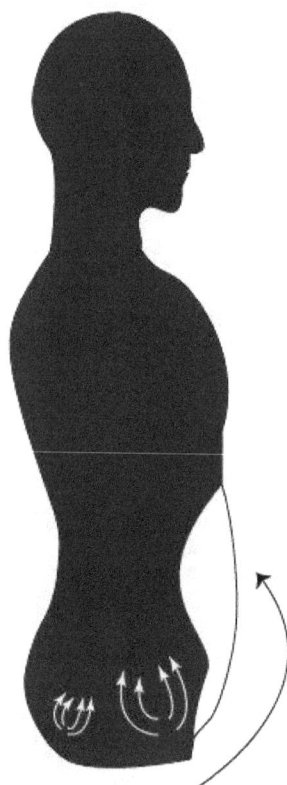

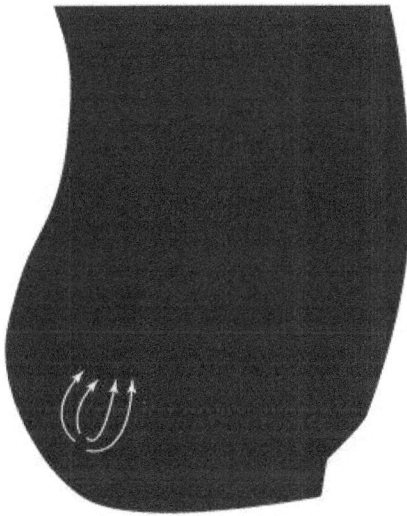

pull-up anal sphincter muscle

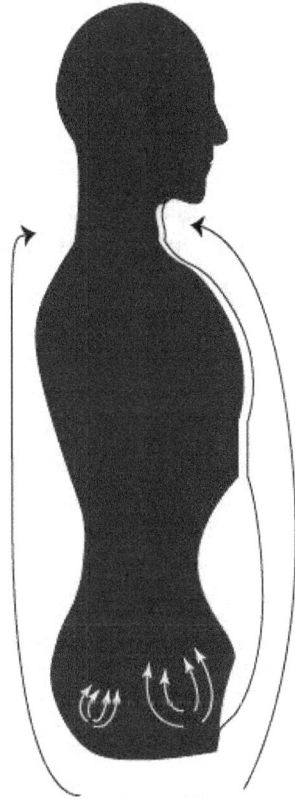

apply neck lock
by firming and straightening
vertebrate in neck

Even though yoga books usually give the third eye *mind focus* lock, the *draw in the chin* neck lock, the *pull up under the rib cage* belly lock, the *pubio coccyx* sex lock and the anal muscles *pull up* lock, there are other locks in the body. As one advances one is taught these.

Always remember that Michael Beloved wrote that kundalini does not care to respond to anyone's willpower. It will have to be forced to change its habits. There will be a power struggle between the coreSelf and kundalini if the core is to be liberated. Those who do not raise kundalini and who cannot bring it under control, cannot attain liberation, no matter what method they use, because they will be pulled to lower planes by kundalini.

If Kundalini strikes the crown then either of these five things listed below may occur. Please note that this does not happen unless it strikes the crown. Other things happen when it strikes the other chakras. Location is important.

There is nothing void. Here are the experiences which occur due to kundalini striking the crown.

- Loss of objective consciousness with no memory after the experience
- Loss of objective consciousness with memory after the experience
- Split-second loss of objective consciousness with memory of what happened before and after the split second

Point of Reference

A person should shift from the physical body importance to the astral body prominence. This is a point of reference shift. Unfortunately, the natural point of reference is the physical body. One should begin higher yoga somewhere. One should work hard day and night to change the point of reference to the subtle body. It is that body which will dictate the next existential location.

The subtle body is temporary but it last for the duration of the universe. When the cosmic gas-out occurs, that body will be finished. Speaking in terms of science, when the visible matter is gased out of existence and only dark matter remains, the subtle body will be annihilated.

That is the reason why yogis endeavor to transit to a place called siddhaloka. Once a yogi achieves that place his practice has to do with relocating to the causal body and abandoning his personal spaceship which is the astral body.

The causal body will be destroyed after the big melt down occurs several times and then the whole system of these universes collapses permanently. That is why yogis go to a place called satyaloka, because from there one abandons the causal body and learns how to allow the coreSelf to expand into itself as a spiritual body.

Considering this, if you accept what I declare, you can surmise that you must strive because you have not transferred the reference even to the subtle body.

Each yogi has the duty to identify whatever sensual hang-ups he or she has. That person should work with psychological disciplines for curbing that addiction. Some persons are addicted to taste more than anything else. Some are addicted to sound; some to sight and so on. Each person needs an individual prescription for sensual conquest. If one does not attain this, yoga practice cannot be successful.

In one person the sensual orbs are biased more to sound than to anything else. But this does not mean that others are the same. It may be that in that instance, it was so. One should meditate, struggle in the psyche to control the various psychic orbs and then locate the various vices one has.

We know for a fact that we are addicted to sound. This is why radio is such a compelling experience. Even today, even when we are exposed to visual media and that became a staple sensual intake, we are still addicted to music. In yoga these addictions are eliminated.

One has to be ruthless in meditation and not allow any sense preference to rule the psyche. This does not mean that one should not use a particular sense in meditation but it means that one should not be ruled by a sense unless its control is in the interest of the objective of meditation.

Brow Chakra Importance

Even though the ultimate objective with kundalini is to relocate it into the crown chakra (brahmrandra), that cannot be attained in full unless the lower chakras are purified.

For instance, celibacy with sexual energy up-flow is necessary for purifying the sex chakra. Vegetarian diet with ridding the self of the need for animal-body protein is required for purifying the navel chakra.

These lower chakras must be purified. It is not sufficient to say that one reaches a higher stage of consciousness while still operating on the physical level in a vicious or vulgar lifestyle. The system of animal existence must be reduced to nil over time by the practice. Progressively, one must work to clear the psyche's need for the lower behaviors.

Yogis who mastered kundalini yoga, to the extent that they can raise kundalini at least once per day with it rising through the spine into the head, will experience various levels of the crown chakra operation but these yogis when they sit to meditate must also struggle with the intellect in the quest to control and cause the brow chakra (third eye) to operate in higher dimensions. The brow chakra is not the intellect but these two organs are intimately related.

There is a serious flaw in the intellect. Each yogi should realize this and find a way to work around it. It is designed in the way it is by the Cosmic God who established the pool of Cosmic Intelligence which we use. There is no point in complaining. At this stage of existence, we cannot change the design. We may find a way to get that organ curbed so that it will do what is beneficial.

As soon as one makes an effort to meditate in the front part of the head, one will find that the intellect becomes empowered to resist one's will and to install for itself its mind games of images, sounds and ideas.

Patañjali, one of our yoga gurus who long passed on, instructed that we put an end to the mind games. That is not an easy achievement. In fact, many people who meditated consistently for years, concluded that some of Patañjali's ideas are idealistic. Some feel that he wrote an interesting but impossible-to-apply thesis on yoga.

Since there is no other way to get the intellect under control, one should stick to Patañjali and find a method which will curtail the independence of the intellect. Those who never saw, nor heard, nor perceived in any way, this orb, should take my word that it exists as a psychic organ. But since one cannot perceive it, one should regard it as a mental location. You should believe that it is present wherever one daydreams and imagines in the mental space.

Instead of pushing forward to concentrate on it, on that mental space, one should retract energy from the space into the coreSelf. This pulling action should be constant.

If this is done correctly, when the subtle body was energized by breath infusion, that mental space will change into a perception orb. One will see into higher dimensions. The usual use of the space for imaginations and ideas from this side of existence will cease, at least for as long as one is permitted to stay in touch with the higher realms.

My Innocence

The reality of time and its choke-hold on life becomes very evident when one can increase psychic sensitivity and track a current event as being a projectile from the past. It is similar to when soldiers go through an enemy territory and commit themselves to complete eradication of the enemy. They very cautiously kill every enemy soldier making sure that none are left with a living body.

But somehow the past comes back to haunt them when suddenly as they move forward, barrages of missiles and bullets come from behind and kill many of their men. It is then that the survivors consider the possibility of having made errors in the clean-up operations. With comrades dead, they regret the carelessness and wish that they were thorough.

Sometimes, something happens and when by the honor of providence, one passes away, one feels free of it. This gives one the allowance of memory deletion. This grand honor which is a boon for all, services the self as innocence in the new life. Innocence is real joy since it free of memories and responsibilities. It allows one to enjoy what seems to be new, beautiful and enjoyable. Innocence is the child of open ignorance.

Without the grim jury of past-life memories one cannot identity a projectile that is hurled from the past or a bullet sent with the speed of resentment-thought to shatter one's innocence-joy. Like that, the past makes its claim on one's life, stating,

"Not one more step will you take, without considering my fate. From the past, I come into your present and future. I weave myself into you. I will choke you. Your innocence is flawed."

External World Within

This is about religion within the psyche but not religion for the self unto itself or the self to become one or to become God. This is about the self objectifying the physical environment and also leaving that inner psyche to go into dimensions which are external to that psyche.

In the physical condition, the self lives in a particular body, which in turns lives in a particular location on a planet called earth. This self ventures into the physical environment but only through moving a physical body. That is similar to a man who uses a submarine to enter the sea. The man is in the sea but he is not in direct contact with the water. He resides in a sealed tubing which is in contact with the water.

In this meditation, the self must first realize that it has a consciousness membrane. Within that there is consciousness floating like air in the submarine. Within that membrane there are objects like the engine in the submarine.

The meditator does not go off with the idea that he or she is the entire psyche but only is a particular spiritual object in the psyche, just as the submariner is a particular object in the submarine. The submariner may as he desires, go out of the submarine and venture into the marine world using a wet-suit and appropriate gear.

These dimensions are not himself or herself. They are environments just as this earthly planet and its atmosphere is a habitat.

In meditation, the meditator goes outside the psyche into other environments. When he or she does that, the person uses a higher psyche, one with the appropriate higher sensual perception. If there is no visual perception, the meditator must interpret the environment as a level of consciousness with certain feelings of pervasiveness or bliss consciousness.

Mobility Split-Energy Retraction

In brahma yoga practice, there is a stage where one is required to retract the mobility split-energy. This is based on the evolutionary development of mobility in creature forms. At first most of the unicellular forms remain in one place. As they evolve there is a need to move from place to place. This occurs due to the need to feed at leisure.

If one remains in one location, one must wait for food sources to develop at or drift to that place. Therefore, at first, the unicellular organisms develop mobility as a way of getting food at leisure by moving to food sources.

Spirits who enter the physical world and who take unicellular forms, at first use such forms until they realize that they can develop mobility. At first some of this comes about by forms which can use ingestion and expulsion of liquids because the first forms are in water.

Later, other types of propulsion develop like fins in fish and limbs in tortoises. However, our concern in brahma yoga is the root cause which is the need for nutrition.

The key issue is that it originated from an internal energy. The yogi should locate that energy and curb it. This internal energy begins in the causal body which is out of reach. When it surfaces in the subtle body, it takes a two-part configuration, one which produces the limbs for mobility and one which sends out feelers for locating the food sources. Thus, the energy which is singular in the subtle body develops or evolves into two rays, one for creating suitable limbs and one which develops eyes or feelers. Once you get on the move to find food, you need a way to see and feel it.

What does this have to do with brahma yoga?

In brahma yoga, the yogi must discover incomplete areas of proficiency which make the yoga efforts fail to come to fruition. One such area is the fifth stage of yoga called *pratyahara* which is sensual energy withdrawal from this physical world and from the lower astral domains.

However, advance meditation is not easy. It entails the complete withdrawal of evolutionary interest which we developed transmigrating for millions of years.

Asana practice helps to locate some of the primeval urges and bring them under control. In this case when doing stretches which concern the thigh and leg, a yogi can locate the ray energy which came out of the coreSelf for developing survival mobility. He can retract it. As this is done, he will find that a vision energy is also retracted. This is the other part of the energy which protruded to provide sight or feeler capacity to recognize food.

A thigh stretch can cause the yogi to recognize a causal energy which operates mobility. The yogi can retract that energy. As he/she does this, a vision-feeler energy in the frontal part of the brain will be retracted.

Sensual Procurement Operations

A yogi has the extra chore to train the mind to develop an interest in internalization, internal research into mental, emotional and psychic objects. People usually feel that there are physical objects and everything else is a figment of imagination and is based on the self's imaginary powers. However, in yoga there is a requirement to become aware of subtle objects which are not manifest physically but which should be brought into purview and brought under control.

This is an example of how to bring the mind into internal interest, substituting that for the mind's instinctive interest in external concerns in the physical world. The mind has a research and curiosity feature which can be used to advance meditation practice but it has to be diverted to the internal parts of the psyche.

This morning I am in Chicago. With a small mat, I went through the front door of a building to do kundalini yoga exercises. There was a large plant-pot with some dried and some fresh marigold flowers. Some were yellow marigolds. Some were orange. As soon as the eye informed the intellect, that there were flowers ahead on concrete walk, the intellect gave the feet an instruction to go closer to the flower pot. It directed the hands to take an orange flower to compare it with a yellow one.

Wherefrom does the intellect have the power to command the body to do this? Where does the coreSelf fit in? Should the core claim itself as one with the intellect in order to not cause disharmony in the psyche?

In any case, as soon as I, the coreSelf, perceived that the intellect ordered the body to move towards the flower pot, I instructed the body to stay on the mat and to begin the exercise session.

The intellect immediately noticed that there was a veto order by the core. It complied without complaint. I then reviewed what happened and found some details as follows:

When the body stepped out of the building, the senses which are by nature extrovert and which are mostly concerned to hunt for commodities in the physical world, perceived the marigold flowers. This perception caused happiness energy to be released in the mind. This happiness energy reached the intellect, which immediately sent a message-energy to get information about the cause of the happiness from the senses.

The senses for their part hurried along the communication channel to bring the good news to the intellect that there were some bright colors which should be investigated and which had the potential for yielding pleasure.

The intellect for its part, decided that this may be yet another opportunity to procure enjoyment. It sent an order into the body for the feet to quicken their steps and reach the flower pot so that the hands could pick the flowers and put them to the nose for fragrance. Along with this order, the intellect created an imagination plan for how the fragrance and color of the flowers would be procured for enjoyment.

The intellect was not concerned as to how the mobility information would reach the feet. It usually gives an order and the body complies.

What actually took place however was that the order of the intellect was received gratefully by the kundalini energy. It made a rapid check with the senses to pin-point the flowers? The kundalini did not give an order to the feet immediately. There was a pause. In that delay I saw that the kundalini decided to send the body towards the flower pot but only after it got some more information from the senses as to the exact location of the pot.

As soon as I saw this, I ordered the intellect to cease all interest in the flowers and to be attentive to the exercise session. The three aspects of the psyche, namely the senses, which initiated the interest in the flowers, the intellect which wanted to commandeer the body, and the kundalini lifeForce which intended to endorse the interest in the flowers, stopped the activity and were attentive to the task of raising kundalini into the brain.

This is an example of training the mind in the fifth stage of yoga which is *pratyahara* or sensual energy withdrawal.

Believe it or not, in the Yoga Sutras, *Patañjali* said that one transfers into a higher dimension as soon as one's psyche becomes saturated with the energy from that higher realm. Much of what *Patañjali* said may seem to be idealistic at first reading but his philosophy is sound.

Most of our bad attitude and self-destructive habits have to do with the kind of energy we ingest into our individual psyches. As soon as a higher grade of energy displaces the lower energy, our outlook improves. The stage of yoga known as breath infusion *(pranayama)* concerns just that displacement of negative energies with positive promotional types.

Each person should practice and make the effort to slip away from lower energies and enter zones of higher energy or to invite or infuse higher energy into the psyche.

Thinking / Observing

What distinguishes thinking from observing?

Thinking usually involves involvement while observing requires neutrality.

If, however one observes a thought and then is drawn into it, it means that one observed it with some interest. If there is interest, thoughts will fire one after the other.

A lack of interest shuts down the thought process just as water would put out a fire.

When someone says that he sits to meditate and observe the thoughts coming and going, it means that he observed in part and fed energy to the thought mechanism. The person should be given credit for limiting the amount of energy given to the thought. As soon as one gives much energy one stops being an observer and becomes an indulger or participant.

If there is no interest in a thought process it ceases. It gets no power to reinforce it. A thought needs mental power to be illustrated.

Relationship with a Yoga-guru

This is an example of how one may have a relationship with a yoga guru. For about one year now, Yogeshwarananda restricted my relationship. It used to be that he came frequently or infrequently and did not make stipulations. He would offer advisories and show techniques.

About a year ago this stopped. The relationship changed where it hinged on my reaching a certain level before he would appear. This requires that I raise kundalini before seeing him.

Since kundalini is disinclined from remaining at the crown chakra, and always makes successful efforts to fall back to the base after it is raised, I am compelled to raise it daily if I want to get his association. Our relation hinges on my reaching a certain level. If I fail to get there, the relationship is nil.

When I was in the Hare Krishna Movement, there was a requirement for 1728 (16 X 108) rounds of chanting the Hare Krishna Mahamantra. If one failed to do so or even if one did so but did not associate in the group in a certain way, one was severely criticized. They said that everything hinged on association with them.

In yoga practice however everything hinges on practice. It is not group dependent organization like the Hare Krishna Movement. There are only three factors to take into consideration:

- oneself
- one's practice
- association with advanced teachers for direction and higher instruction

Yogis are required to use the kundalini-elevator method when leaving the body for good but they cannot be successful at this if they have not mastered it while using the body, way before the body's death. While in traditional religious process, the follower hopes to go to heaven or to a spiritual world to meet the cherished deity; in yoga, the idea is to ascend the kundalini elevator shaft in the subtle body and escape through the sixth or seventh chakra to a higher world.

Yoga gurus give senior students, methods for routing kundalini to the crown chakra long before the time of death, such that kundalini knows that passage, is familiar with it and is inclined to using it.

Sound for Meditation

In a discussion, I explained that ultimately all props used in meditation must be abandoned. The yogi must face the problems in the mind head on. One person asked about sound in meditation.

Sound can be used to induce a meditative state or to change the stubborn attitude of the mind. We find that if someone is sad, listening to certain music lifts the person out of depression. The person may even assume happiness which is converse to a sad mood.

Chanting *om* is a valid method. If done correctly, it can take one to a spiritual plane either where there is no distinguishing sense perception or where there is that. Yogis in the past used *om* sound chanting extensively. They reached the Supreme Reality. It was possible then. It is possible now.

In the final analysis, one should control the mind. One must get the kundalini lifeForce to be cooperative and obedient to the coreSelf.

In higher yoga, the *om* sound which resonates in the universe of its own accord, is used. This is better since the yogi is not required to generate the sound. He/she can focus on the sound fully and reach a spiritual plane.

It is preferred that while listening to unuttered *om* sound (naad) one should be in a quiet place. Some of us live in a humbug city which has noises. In the buildings motors and compressors operate to keep the temperature at a desirable degree for human beings. Below the roadway in some cities, trains travel which cause the earth to vibrate. These sounds upset the listening capability of a meditator.

If one practiced extensively, one can locate naad sound and listen to it even in humbug city but that is not the same as hearing it in a quiet environment. Noisy urban areas are not as conducive to meditation practice.

This morning while I meditated, Yogeshwarananda observed the session. At the end he said this.

They want full success without mastering the preliminary stages. They do not want to do asanas. They do not want to do pranayamas. They demand assistance with the higher stages of meditation. How is that possible? Everything has its preliminary stage, even secular education.

He made this remark because it is not possible to raise kundalini consistently without doing the asana postures and the breath infusion methods. Kundalini remains unresponsive to a person's imagination and will-power unless it is energized to a higher energy level. In its dense survival condition, it has no interest in higher yoga. If one does not infuse it, one will make little progress.

My original point had to do with the use of sound. Do I approve its use?

Yes, I do approve its use but keep in mind that in the final analysis one has to battle the mind directly without props. Use sound and let it help to observe the passage from a lower state of mind to a higher one. Then try to find your way through to that higher level without the use of sound.

Location Situation Move

One meditation habit I have tried to introduce is the location-situation move. This is when a person finds himself or herself fighting the mind and getting nowhere, stalled as it were in the chaos of the mind and not being able to silence it to enter a meditative stage.

This method consists of taking refuge in a location in which the mind is unable to dominate the self. It seems however that this method is not practical for some persons. I wish to introduce this as a standard procedure.

First one should discover if there is any part of the mind in which, thoughts and images do not occur. One should also observe in which parts of the mind thoughts and images always occur. Lastly one should identify parts of the mind in which thought and images may or may not occur.

Let me list this:

- Locations where thoughts do not occur
- Locations where thoughts always occur
- Locations where thoughts may or may not occur

Why do this research?

By doing this one can take refuge in the no-thought zone when one finds the self helplessly besieged by images and thoughts. One could enter the location where there may or may not be thoughts and observe how the control of the mind fluctuates according to the force and rapidity of thoughts. If one could map these locations, one could easily adjust the relationship with thoughts and images by moving to the thought free location when the ideas are resistant to one's willpower.

Five Senses – Five Vrittis?

I was questioned about the correlation between the five senses and the five vrittis.

Actually, there is no correlation. Unfortunately, Patañjali is high-end yoga which hardly deals with the preliminary stages. Someone read my second translation and commentary of the *Yoga Sutras* which is titled *Meditation Expertise*. He inquired of the correlation between the senses and the vrittis which are listed by Patañjali as correct perception, incorrect perception, imagination, memory and sleep. However, the vrittis in that listing are not related to the five senses.

To understand Patañjali, we may consider an automobile. Usually a consumer is interested in driving the vehicle and wants it to be in a good condition with an automatic transmission.

But Patañjali discussed the components under the hood. Like the human body, we may posit that a car has five sensing mechanisms:

- lights instead of eyes
- carburetor and exhaust instead of nostrils
- metallic outer body instead of skin for touching
- rare view mirror instead of ears for hearing
- combustion cylinder instead of mouth and tongue for tasting.

But Patañjali is interested in what is under the hood of the car. He claims that there are five types of operations which the car performs under the hood.

In modern cars there is an automatic transmission. Patañjali's is more like a manual shift gear system which the driver will have to operate deliberately.

Patañjali listed four forward gears and one reverse.

The reverse is memory.

The forward gears are correct perception, incorrect perception, imagination and sleep. But Patañjali requested that the driver find the neutral position in the gear box and remain in idle there.

Lotus Posture

To have persons with a western body sit in lotus is questionable. Their limbs are not used to that. I find that it is best to allow people who are used to sitting on couches to use that when meditating. In that way their minds are not stressed over the aches and pains of postures.

Reclining is great for those who are uncomfortable sitting. When I first entered Yogi Bhajan's ashram in Denver in 1973, the ashram senior would instruct us to do various postures with breath infusion. This was done for about 30 minutes to 40 minutes. It was intense. A student went from one posture to the next and in each he did aggressive breathing. In some he did breathing as he said the Sikh mantra, Sat Nam. By the time he got to the last posture kundalini would rise. For beginners that meant that their bodies dropped to the floor.

Those who were advanced could control the risen kundalini and continue. As soon as the exercises stopped, one was told to lie on one's back with palms up.

The ashram leader would hit a large gong at intervals. The sound would cause the astral body to separate from the physical one. The astral form was highly charged by the postures and rapid breathing.

The ashram leader would sit in lotus giving the instructions but all others would lie during the meditation. This was done at 5 am each morning.

Using the lotus posture while meditating, if that posture is painful or unnatural, is counterproductive. Generally speaking, a Western body cannot do the lotus posture without pain and stress. I began doing yoga postures around 1966 by intuition alone. In 1969 in the Philippines I practiced under the instruction of Arthur Beverford, who was trained by Rishi Singh Gherwal. I could not do lotus posture at that time. I forced my body into it and sat up in a metal locker hidden away from others who did not understand what I did. I forced myself to stay in the posture for about 20 minutes. It was 20 minutes of sheer pain and cramps.

Later I invented some exercises which loosed the ligaments and muscles which needed to be stretched for lotus sitting. In addition, I adopted vegetarian diet. That helped considerably.

Just about three months ago something happened that relates to this. I travelled and was not sitting in lotus to meditate. For that matter for five years now, I relaxed my disciplines for lotus sitting. I sat in easy pose or on a couch depending on where I was located. But three months ago, after Atmananda give me a procedure to reach him on the brahma level of existence, Yogeshwarananda came. He was annoyed.

I did not know the reason but I could sense something was amiss. I got the feeling that he wanted to say that at the rate I practice, I would not achieve the brahma level when I leave this body. However, he said nothing. I did not ask him because one should not challenge a yoga teacher. One wrong question could rupture the association.

After a week he released an energy and in it there was a warning like this:

If you do not sit in lotus, do not consider yourself to be a disciple. A yogi has to practice brahmrandra meditation in lotus. There is no exception nor exemption for this. This is the last time that I will explain this.

Still I would not recommend it to someone who cannot sit in it without aches and pains.

I did yoga for many lives. For me there is no excuse. For me it is required. For others, it may cause them not to meditate since their minds will dwell on the aches and pains.

When to meditate?

I suggest a minimum of two sessions per day: One soon after rising. The other just before resting. Consider the second period to be a mind re-order process and the meditation soon after rising to be meditation.

Mind re-order is part of the preparation for meditation. It is not meditation. Usually at the end of the day, it is difficult to assume a state of deep meditation but one should take time then to catalog the impressions in the mind and set those in order.

For example, something that could be done before resting should be done. Something that must be postponed for the next day should be released from the attention for the time being. It should become dormant until the next day. Something that should be regarded before resting should be considered. In this way the mind will be set for resting, for relaxing.

As soon as one retires, one should check the mind to see if it is quieted or if some ideas persist and utilize the attention. If it happens that you are forcibly compelled to see anxiety pictures and ideas, you should retreat to the back of the head.

Retreat to the back of the head. Use whatever mental force is required to disempower compulsive ideas. If the yogi is successful with this the mind will cease its ideas and picture show. But even if you are successful doing this do not expect that the mind will permanently give in. It will again attempt to resume the slide slow. You will again be focused into the frontal part of the head to see the mind's video.

Eventually, you will drift off to sleep but then you should find yourself awake from time to time in dreams. When you first rise in the morning, do so gradually. Recall dreams. Jot down the ones you should make a note off.

Do postures and breath infusion if that is your routine. Sit to meditate immediately after. If you do not have an exercise procedure, sit to meditate. Do not remain lying in bed since you may drift to sleep. Sit in bed or sit somewhere else and meditate.

Meditation Tip

Check on the time you usually rest. Rising early before daybreak to meditate hinges on the time one rested the previous night.

The early morning meditation begins when one goes to bed. Be your own watchman to be sure that you rest early enough to make it convenient and pleasant to rise early for meditation.

Not motivated?

That is a problem.

Make a commitment to a yoga teacher. Report regularly on your efforts.

Since it hinges on you, it is reliant on your self-control. Analyze that and come to a decision on how you could increase self-discipline.

In this life I meditated consistently for forty plus years. In all cases I reported to teachers. There were times when I pushed myself on the basis of past life advancement which I tried to recover but overall, I always relied on a connection to a teacher.

Is a teacher necessary?

Of course not! But if you cannot move forward and motivate yourself without one, you would be fool number one not to adopt one. Because you are person, pretending that you do not believe in any other superior person is absurd. Your person-self needs to be in relation to other person-selves.

Since you are not absolute, you will need to rely on other persons from time to time for various things which are not your natural possession or skill. Do not deprive yourself of the reliance needed for a meditation practice.

Outsmarting and Manipulating Nature

A yogi has to constantly review his behavior in terms of outsmarting and manipulating nature. There is a pleasure in outwitting the laws of nature which place limitations on the forms we use. A yogi should review habits and curtail if not eliminate totally the tendency to outwit nature. The part of the psyche why sneers at and which enjoys when a yogi does something to circumvent a law of nature, should be squelched.

Most scientific discoveries, even the simple ones like the washing machine, and the internal combustion engine, are feats of humanity which laugh at the restrictions which nature placed on human beings for millions of years.

At least within the past 200 years, humanity leaped away from many inconveniences but the tendency to snicker at nature and to enjoy these aspects may well hurt the advancement of a yogi. It may cause nature to upset the progress by causing the yogi to become attracted to some lower species of life in another birth. In such a lower species, how will the yogi gain the upper hand again. Will he languish in disappointment because the form of another species has no potential for inventing conveniences?

Can it be said that the washing machine and the internal combustion engine give us more time for spiritual practice? Are there more successful yogis on the planet today because of the technological gadgets which are time saving?

I wonder!

Nature sponsors the technological development. For that matter everything we create scientifically is being done in imitation to nature. There is not one invention which was not patterned after something we observed conscious or subconsciously from nature. It has imprinted itself permanently in the mento-emotional energy. There is no escaping its influence if we are in touch with it even in the slightest possible most detached way.

That is more the reason why we should not try to enjoy the manipulation of nature. In the end the laugh will be on us. The trick is to do whatever one must but to be sure not to be proud nor take credit. Superficially one should take credit on occasion but in all seriousness, one should not crave credit.

For instance, I write books. It crosses my mind as to the proprietorship of this literature. Sometimes I get a feeling that something erases my claim as the proprietor. Something usurps my right as the author. The proper attitude in that case is merely to observe the confiscation of those rights and go on without being a claimant like a man whose bank balance was taken by the government. Usually you expect a tax law would only take a fractional percentage, but in some cases, the government takes everything and then threatens to arrest the citizen if he or she does not pay interest.

There is a verse in the Gita, where Krishna says that the supreme reality develops and devours everything. How is that? Am I not the developer of my books? How it is that reality claims the publications? How should I take it when time devour what I created?

Part 7

Respecting Providence

The use of the computer in my case is an imposition on my normal way of doing things. For me it is a force activity which was applied by destiny and time. In such situations, one had better go along with the force but that does not mean that one should think that it is under one's control. Many people think that the internet and computers are here as a great convenience. I see that in some cases, one identifies positively with an enforcement and at other times, one becomes negative about it.

That was like the guy who was arrested on an outstanding warrant and who smiled when the judge said that his sentence was ten years. Usually people regret a jail term but this fellow was happy. He thought that it was his good luck because his gangster friends wanted to kill him at the time of the arrest. He felt that he was safer in prison.

This type of thinking should be avoided by a yogi. He should indifferently observe the facilities and obstructions of nature. If one enjoys the computer and if one becomes reliant on it, one will enter a depression when one is deprived of its use. It is providence's facility. Providence is designed to humble the limited entities. It has this idea that its duty is to frustrate plans.

A yogi should respect providence because otherwise he will have problems when providence applies obstructions. But even while respecting providence one should respect it by not getting into the habit of enjoying it and thinking that it is here merely for one's convenience.

Providence is contrary and paradoxical. No sane person will trust that. At any moment, providence may promote someone and establish that person as the greatest human being. At any movement, fate could ruin the opportunity. Recognizing this one should not feel at any stage that this creation is centered on one's interest or that this creation is in need of a master and one could be that individual.

Working for liberation is a direct assault on providence. This should be done carefully so as to encourage providence to give the least resistance. A slave is useful to the master, only if the slave cooperates. The master will never say, "You are free. By my grace, you can go away." That will not happen. The slave should act in such a way as to encourage the master to release him even though the master is forever disinclined from that.

Computers are used by me but not because it is what I want and not because it is a facility, and not because of this or that, but only because providence made it a necessity at this time.

For me, not using technology at this stage, would be an offence to providence. In compliance I use it but I know that it is based on the desire of providence (the master) and not on my wish (the slave).

Thus, when it is no longer in use by me, I lost nothing, nor would I gain anything for myself personally, even though providence which is like a python will surely enjoy, digest and excrete the history of the incidence.

Patañjali put it in a nice way when he said that in terms of the liberation of a living entity, material nature is more like a farmer, which is a superficial agent of the sprouting of seeds. The farmer is not the seed. The seed will never get the growing impulse from the farmer. The farmer does help facilitate the growth of the seed, but still he is not the cause of the seed. He surely has no interest in any independent ideas about the seed being in absolute control of itself.

Therefore, if a seed wants freedom, it must find the motive and intelligence for that from within itself. There is no point in befriending the farmer in the hope that he will tell the seed that it can grow in the wild, where the farmer cannot reap its ripened state.

निमित्तमप्रयोजकं प्रकृतीनां

वरणभेदस्तु ततः क्षेत्रिकवत् ॥३॥

nimittaṁ aprayojakaṁ prakṛtīnām

varaṇabhedaḥ tu tataḥ kṣetrikavat

nimittaṁ – cause, motive, apparent cause; aprayojakaṁ – not used, not employed, not causing; prakṛtīnām – of the subtle material energy; varaṇa – impediments, obstacles; bhedaḥ – splitting, removing, disintegrating; tu – but, except; tataḥ – hence; kṣetrikavat – like a farmer.

The motivating force of the subtle material energy is not used except for the disintegration of impediments, hence it is compared to a farmer. (Yoga Sutras 3.3)

Nature does want us to blossom and produce fruit but not for our benefit, only in order to further the interest of nature. Since right now we are captives bound by chains of cultural activities, which is the real master, we must work for liberation quietly without allowing the master to divine our intentions.

When my subtle body is at last freed from having to use this physical body, I have no intentions of going where there are computers. The people I hope to stay with have no technology. It would do me well to remain detached and to know that it is not mine and is not produced for my pleasure.

Higher Levels of Awareness

The main thing is to deal with the components of consciousness on the gut level. Going to a higher level is only useful in so far as it gives clarity and sorts the components.

Waiting for death to banish the lower levels is a sham. If they are not banished now, if they assert themselves now, it is illogical to think that they will run for cover and leave the self alone to enjoy a higher plane after death.

Components of Consciousness

The components of consciousness which must be objectified and realized are listed in order from the easiest to realize to the most abstract. Sanskrit terms are in parenthesis.

- lifeForce *(kundalini)*
- sensual energy *(indriyas)*
- intellect *(buddhi)*
- plural memory *(smrti)*
- sense of identity *(ahankara)*
- coreSelf (atma)

The sense of identity is the most abstract adjunct. It is near impossible to realize because its frequency is near to the frequency of the coreSelf.

The first achievement is to locate each component. Students usually want to know if there is a standard location which we can agree on. It is not important that we find the locations to be the same. But it is important that each find a recurring location for a particular psychic component.

Once when I discussed human anatomy with a surgeon, I asked if there was any difference in locations of the organs in various human patients whom he examined. He said that sometimes there are anomalies.

For instance, a person's heart was found to be on the right side even though most human bodies have the heart tilted to the left. A person's spleen was found to be in an unusual place. From that it is probable that one person's mind may be in the fingers. We should not argue about the varying locations discovered.

Each student should research the adjuncts. Physically we assume that the sexual function is located in the groin. We agree that there is an anus near that area. In the same way with the same interest and curiosity, we should catalog the parts of the subtle body.

My Method of Meditation

I suggest that before meditation there should be a pre-session of some type of breath infusion. It is a procedure of ashtanga yoga (ashtanga means 8) that there be breath infusion before a yogi meditates. It is not compulsory but the ancient yogis did that for a reason. The subtle body should be surcharged, or else it will only go so far during meditation.

Each yogi should have an effective way of surcharging the subtle body and raising kundalini before meditation. I feel that meditation without raising kundalini is mediocre.

One should find a system for raising kundalini through the spine into the head before one meditates. That means one should feel it rise with a definite sensation and go into the head. Once it is aroused, then meditate.

It does not matter to me which pranayama or mantra method a person uses to raise kundalini. My point is that by any effective means, it should rise before meditating. But I feel that unless that is done, the meditation will be low quality.

Each person should have a method of raising kundalini into the head at least once, if not twice per day and then meditate. It is absolutely essential in my view. For that matter kundalini refuses to remain in the aroused condition. Therefore, one should make a repeated daily effort to get it to enter the head. Once it is there one should sit quickly before it subsides again to *muladhara* chakra. One should take advantage of the increased psychic consciousness which is made available because kundalini rushed into the head and became directly linked with the intellect in the head of the subtle body.

I cannot overstress this. These spiritual paths and methods of liberation are worthless if kundalini is allowed to remain at *muladhara* chakra during meditation.

In my psyche, the idea of kundalini staying in the head or moving into the head by virtue of a willpower command and by visualization is a farce. This does not mean that it did not or does not do so in the psyche of others. My experience in this present psyche is that it does not stay up or move up unless it is first energized by breath infusion.

Currently in my practice it moves up much quicker than before but the effort must be made. I learnt how to accelerate the infusion by doing certain postures which cause the *nadi*s to be more receptive to the infused breath.

I could sit and meditate without doing pranayama. The question is why do I do it, when I can sit and meditate? Why make the effort to raise kundalini. It is because I find that I reach a much higher plane with kundalini raised.

Yogeshwarananda gave orders to keep doing the practice until this body drops dead or is incapacitated. The person who taught me a specific type of breath infusion, who is Yogi Bhajan, expects that I will continue the practice. In addition, in the astral world, there are yoga masters who do the practice in their subtle bodies.

Help from Gurus

One should have confidence in yoga teachers because without that one will not get far in meditation. It is just the way it is. Even Buddha, who bypassed his initial meditation teachers, had full confidence in them. He used their systems to the max until he exhausted the benefits of those practices.

This confidence in the teacher never ends. It continues onwards into the advanced stages. People who have no confidence in teachers and who specialize in ridiculing, censoring and resisting the teacher can only get so far. To go higher one must be assisted by someone.

A person on this level of existence cannot get to the spiritual plane with only tools from this side of existence. It is not possible. Even if that person gets to a high level, he or she will not stay there unless there is affinity and relationship with someone who permanently resides on that higher plane.

About a month ago, Yogeshwarananda gave some procedures which I am to master. He said that I would reach the plane of existence which is just above the astral heavens. But then after he did that, his teacher, Swami Atmananda, came. He gave a process which he said would allow me to go to a place which is called Satyaloka in the Indian yoga books.

In both cases, I took help from other persons. I could find my way there all by myself. And yet I take assistance and follow instructions.

When Atmananda gave the techniques, it was like handing a person a package. He said, "Hold this for a while. Use it to follow me higher. I will send a message when you should share this with others."

There was a time some years ago when Yogeshwarananda came into my subtle head in a miniature form and showed the intellect organ. It looked like a jelly-fish with a milky yellow-white color.

I saw it before and after without his assistance. Why do I have to deal with him? Yogeshwarananda is one of the persons in the Indian Yoga books who are titled as the Vedas Personified. These are super-people, divine beings. Can they be ignored?

Many people go to Buddhism because they do not want to take anyone as an authority. The idea is to follow Buddha who discovered everything by himself. When I was in South Korea some years ago at a temple, a lady said that she wanted to establish her Buddha nature. She had the opinion that since we are potential Buddhas there is no teacher or god to deal with.

Some persons are agnostics and are disinclined to submit to anyone. Still Buddha himself submitted and then went further after he extracted the benefits of the systems of his initial teachers.

Furthermore, if one reads about the life of Buddha one will see that he maintained a strict system of discipleship once he was recognized as a master. For that matter he made it clear that there would not be a buddha like him for thousands of years to come.

Everyone can be buddha?

I associate with Gautama Buddha from time to time. I never saw anyone near him who did not have a disciple attitude. If you do not see him as God then you will not be confidential with him.

In my relationship with him, I am a son. It is similar to my relationship with Shiva. With Buddha though, I am like a son of concubine. That means an illegitimate son. Does he give me meditation procedures? He does not care if I do meditation. He does not want to be pestered. I am not important. I am insignificant.

The lady I spoke to in South Korea years ago, prayed to Buddha for help to become enlightened. When I was there, I went into the temple and a large icon of Buddha instructed me to teach her. He said, "Get her started. She should be given the preliminary instructions about transmigrations and continuity of the person after death."

When I spoke to the lady, she already had this idea that she was like Buddha. Because of her attitude I could not instruct her.

There are different grades of selves. One self even in the enlightened state of itself cannot become another grade. Gautama Buddha is a certain grade.

The other side, the bliss energy side, is there but only if such beings are in the bliss world alone. As soon as they make contact with the massive ignorance which is humanity in its present condition, that bliss vanishes, even for them.

There is no question of approaching Buddha as a buddha. Nobody among his disciples when he was alive did that successfully. No one will do it now in the astral existence where he can be reached. If you really want to get his help you must take a subordinate position and not because he is divine which he certainly is, but due to your actual position.

When the publication of my books was first stalled when a friend endeavored to put them into computer files, I did not care about it. Sir Paul pressed the issue for their completion. As it turned out I got involved. At the time I visited a Buddha deity in China Town, Manhattan. The deity was irritable about the books but he avoided speaking of it.

I then took a liberty and peered into his mind. I realized that he wanted to talk to me but that he was occupied with some problems in the East, political concerns which was upsetting the practice of Buddhism for many people in places like Thailand, India, Burma and China (including Tibet). Seeing that he was occupied, I mentioned nothing.

That was a mental intrusion on my part but some of that is permitted. I had to do so to realize what I should do about the books because a decision was to be made. He would not take his attention away from the political issues to advice on it. I either had to stay and do the books or return to Guyana and continue my austerities which were suspended.

In any case after I left the temple, he sent energy which was a message saying that my friend should not edit the material.

When I got that message energy, I check on it by sending a loop energy. Then I saw that he did not want my friend to be involved in the work because that friend procrastinated with the practice. Buddha did not want that energy in the books. He felt that the books would fail if that energy was used in their production.

The other part of this is that Buddha was concerned only with the parts of my writings which have to do with what I wrote in the *sex you!* book. That publication is a continuation of the *Bardo Thodol (Tibetan Book of the Dead),* a set of verses which I co-authored in Tibet in a past life.

At the time the *sex you!* book was not composed but some of its information was in the books which I already published. Lord Buddha wanted that *Bardo Thodol* work continued and made relevant to modern times and in modern terminology.

The reason why he does not care if I get this done, is this: It was assigned to me from many past lives. It is an ongoing duty that stretches over many lives. If I do not do it, that is my problem. I alone will face the consequences of not getting it done. If I do not care about myself in association with divine people. I will be the one who will slide down.

He is somewhat indifferent because I am a servant who was sent on a mission thousands of years ago. If I do not publish the information there is no need for me to return home. If you send someone on a mission and the person returns home before completing it, you are not mindful of him.

If I want to return home I must endeavor and get the work done with or without the assistance of others. For one reason or the other many people refused to assist me during this life and in previous lives. As it is one becomes stymied in material existence by the social entanglements of each life. It is just the way it is. One gets confused and becomes involved in nonsensical projects. One avoids the real duty which is assigned by the superior beings.

Worse still is when one gets this idea that there is no God or there is no Person Deity, there is no accountability and that one is God. Down here nonsense enters the mind. One takes spiritually-suicidal liberties.

Intellect Orb Locator

Yogeshwarananda gave a reply to a recent question about the practicality of finding the intellect which is an invisible psychic adjunct in the head of the subtle body. He replied to a query about knowing for sure that this thing exists.

Early this morning while meditating he show me a procedure.

- Do an intense session of rapid breathing. When you feel that kundalini stirred and ascended the spine sufficiently, sit to meditate.
- Check to see where kundalini is located and how its energy flows. Resituate yourself in the iSelf's default location in the central head.
- Focus forward but not outside the head. Keep the focus in the head but forward. As soon as there is any image, idea or picture, note the location. Note the location not the idea or thought which is at that location.
- As soon as the thought vanishes and there is silence with no image or idea, make a soft non-forceful contact with the location. Try to hold it in focus as if it were a floating cloud which was barely visible.
- In a short time, another image or idea will pop up. It will do so at the same location. Again, note the location. Again, hold it as if you hold a mist or fog.
- Keep your soft focus at that place.

There is a related verse in the Yoga Sutras.

$$देशबन्धश्चित्तस्य धारणा ॥१॥$$

deśa bandhaḥ cittasya dhāraṇā

deśa – location; bandhaḥ – confinement, restriction; cittasya – of the mento-emotional energy; dhāraṇā – linking of the attention to a concentration force or person.

Linking of the attention to a concentration force or person, involves a restricted location in the mento-emotional energy. (Yoga Sutras 3.1)

A person's attention is an auxiliary power supply for the intellect faculty. In the default circuit configuration, this power goes to that faculty automatically. Normally it is not controlled by the coreSelf. The intellect also takes power from the kundalini lifeForce. It is more submissive to that than to the iSelf.

If someone is successful at focusing on in and out breaths, then anytime that focus slackens, the attention energy will take its default route which is to give energy to the intellect. That would cause thoughts, ideas, images to arise spontaneously.

Since it is the default configuration of the system, a meditator should expect that this will happen. One should accept it as the natural way. Patañjali instructed yogis, in fact, it is his order that yogis upset the natural way of mental operations. Buddha also instructed his followers to curb the system. However as soon as one relaxes the hold, the system resumes its default operations.

This is why it will be necessary to transit into other dimensions where the default is set up in a desirable way.

If in any meditation a yogi finds that he can stop the appearance thoughts and images, it means that he is in a leverage position. There are three ways of knowing that you are there:

- Thoughts come in slow motion.
- Thoughts are suddenly absent. There is a blank mind only. The place at which thoughts usually arise is vacant.
- There are no thoughts. One is focused into bliss energy or to a powerful flow of energy which pulls the core to the top of the head.

Sense of Identity Loses Track of Intellect

When meditating if one reaches a stage where there is nothing but awareness, do not be fooled into feeling that nothing is present. There is no void. If something is not perceptible to a person, for someone that is void. Stated precisely, that person interprets that as a void.

There was a time when humans felt that besides a moon, the twinkling stars and a bright sun, there was nothing in outer space. Now we know different. This is due only to taking assistance from telescopes and satellites.

There comes a time in meditation when one perceives psychic objects in the so-called void. The best thing is not to rush to conclusions after meditating for a few weeks or years. Better to stick it out, be open-minded and develop psychic perception so that one can see what exists in inner space.

When one meditates and reaches a stage where the images and thoughts stop, one should relax and be ready for the development of supernatural and spiritual perception of objects which are not made of the materials one is familiar with in physical or even in lower astral existence.

Do not condemn yourself to eternal blindness by holding yourself up in the prison of ignorance about voids.

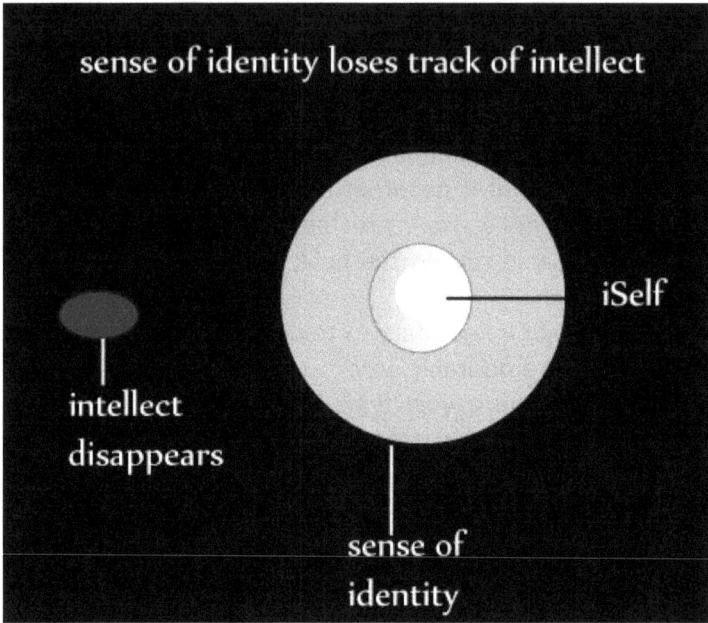

iSelf and sense of identity escaped from influence of intellect, which disappears due to lack of energy supply from sense of identity. Sense of identity is centralized on iSelf which achieves first stage of self realization. In that condition the iSelf is unaware of the intellect but it is fused with the sense of identity, misidentifying that sense as its spirit force.

See the diagram above where the buddhi organ, the intellect fades away just as if there is nothing there. My friend, Sir Paul, said that there is no intellect; there is just what it does which are the manufacture of images and thoughts.

Yes, nothing is there if you cannot see it, just as space is void because we can only see the sun in the day and the stars at night.

My advice is to always remain in reservation when you are confronted by or find yourself in a void. Always have an open mind because void really means that one fails to detect something. Only in arrogance and in assumption of omniscience can a human being say for sure that there is void here or there. It is better to say, I did not perceive anything but I also know that my perception is limited. Hence there may be something.

The organ of discrimination is separate from discrimination but only in the sense that a product is different from its producer. Evidence that the organ of discrimination is different comes when we can discern if the place where discrimination occurs produces other types of mental phenomena. For instance, there may be a neutral image in the mind where the image is there and there is no accompanying discrimination. The question is: Does that image appear at the place where the discrimination occurs or does it appear at another place?

The iSelf is distinct from its sense of identity and from the psychic organ which discriminates for it. But that statement is in a way meaningless because the character of the self is such that it seems to be nothing and lacks status without its identification with the said organs.

In this sense, *Value is Relative*.

Yes, the self is different to the discrimination-organ but that self is embarrassed to be found without the organ. In that sense, the self is the organ or more precisely the self is so reliant on the organ, that if the organ does not function, the self feels as if it is nothing. When the organ functions, the self feels that it is active and useful.

Ramana Maharshi established that the self can exist without psychic adjuncts. To an extend Krishnamurti established that but these persons did not clarify the issue of how the self first was connected to the adjuncts. Some teachers pretend that one can transcend the adjuncts just by accepting the premise that the self should be independent. That is absurd because if the self does not understand how it is fused with these abstract organs, it is not possible for it to renounce the adjuncts. If you cannot see something which is attached to you, it is hardly likely that you could segregate yourself from it.

The proof that the self is different to the discrimination organ is there when the self exists and is unaware of the discrimination, when the self is there and the discrimination ceases. If at any time the discrimination ceases and the self still remains aware, we can safely assume that it is not one and the same as the organ.

More concrete evidence is provided for the self when it studies the locations of the various psychic functions occurring in the mind space. The self, if it can move from one location to another in the mind space and if when doing so has varied relationships with the psychic faculties, can conclude that it is different to those other realities. This may be compared to being in a dark room where no light is present. If there are objects in the room even though they cannot be visually perceived, they can be sorted as being different to the human in the room.

The iSelf has a history but it is a virtual history. The history of the self accompanies the self wherever it may roam in these transmigrations. That history does so in a psychic compartment which we know as the subconscious.

Still the fact remains that the self does not have the power to relieve itself of the influence and impositions of the subconscious. Yes, a horse is not the bit in its mouth but that does not mean that the horse will experience itself without the bit attached. It has intelligence but still it cannot remove the bit and is condemned to be with the bit indefinitely.

The average human being cannot be freed from the psychic adjuncts. He is under the influence of the adjuncts as if he/she is the adjuncts.

The self is conditioned by time and experience but these are virtual realities. Unfortunately for us their virtual-ness does not deny their effective influence.

In the immediate sense a person who strives for liberation is thinking of freedom from time and mundane experience. Liberation means freedom from the link between the self and this time and experience. The link must be broken, and the specific freed self should mark this existence in such a way as to never again by unfavorable forces, be induced to accept the link.

The way nature operates is not a matter of justice or fairness. It is a matter of laws of nature as we are being advised by the physicists. Hence the system is that the iSelf is made to be responsible for the actions of his psyche even in cases where he was under an influence from within his psyche or from outside of it.

Once this is understood all cynicism about a deity or about no deity or about nature in control, goes away. One begins the effort at reform of the psyche so as to save the iSelf from haphazard liabilities.

Complaining about a chaotic system of liabilities, and unfair situations does nothing to change the situation. It does not give a specific iSelf the upper hand. The iSelf will be faulted for the actions of the various psychic adjuncts which are fused to it. To save itself from the trauma in the virtual reality world, it must get some grip on the faculties.

When one reaches a stage where there are no images and ideas in the mind, when the awareness is there without it being formed into mental constructions, then the iSelf is there being aware without mental constructions and without focusing into the physical world or focusing on mental and emotional constructions. Its attention energy is relaxed. As soon as the self goes again into sensual focus either in the mind or out of it, it feels the focusing power. This power is a mixture of the attention energy and the discrimination faculty. Those energies inextricably combine. It is difficult to distinguish them.

If a yogi does enough hours of meditation, over time he can sort it. This theoretical explanation explains the achievement of this sorting ability, but only meditation can provide the experience.

Interest in yoga

Recently a person asked about yoga practice and stated that he does stretches while playing golf. In other words, his interest in yoga has to do with athletics and also with counteracting the advance of old age. Can one learn yoga on that premise? Can one continue the practice with that motive?

The answer lies in the definition used for yoga. If we reference to Patañjali yoga, the answer is no. If we go to the Bhagavad Gita, and find the reason for practicing yoga, the answer will also be no.

In fact, in the Bhagavad Gita, the statement in chapter 6 verse 12 about the purpose of yoga does not include even Krishna Consciousness. In other words when talking about the reason for yoga, Krishna, who claimed himself as the Supreme Being, does not mention himself, even though some followers put him as the reason for yoga or anything else in human endeavor.

Still one may ask as to why a teacher should object if someone comes to learn yoga and has other motives besides the ones listed by Patañjali and Krishna. Why not give a person a chance to begin where he is with athletic or health reasons? Why not allow him to proceed and then as he advances, he may change the motive. The answer is that before you can teach yoga, you require permission from the teacher.

Even in cases where one learnt yoga in a past life and then proceeded to do it in a new life without being instructed, by predisposition or instinct alone, even then one is obligated to the teacher from the past life. There is no such thing as self-discovery in yoga. There is ignorance in the neophyte yogin about his dream and astral encounters with teachers. That passes as self-discovery.

In my case, I was never instructed in any life to teach yoga to anyone for athletic or health reasons. The motive for learning yoga is important because the learning of it is handled by the motive. It changes or remains with its original impetus accordingly. There is another major hitch in yoga practice which is that if I teach someone yoga and then I tell him to teach someone else he can either teach or lose some advancement.

There are instances where I requested teaching services from someone in that manner and the person refused to do it or did not have the energy to execute it. In all such cases, the person unknown to himself or herself, suffered a lapse in practice. But it has nothing to do with me. It has to do with the practice itself.

In Patañjali Yoga Sutras, there is a verse which I bring to your attention:

स तु दीर्घकालनैरन्तर्य

सत्कारासेवितो दृढभूमिः ॥१४॥

sa tu dīrghakāla nairantarya

satkāra āsevitaḥ dṛḍhabhūmiḥ

sa = sah – that; tu – but; dīrgha – long; kāla – time; nairantarya – uninterrupted, continuous; satkāra – reverence, care, attention; āsevitaḥ – sustained practice, aggressive interest; dṛḍha – firm; bhūmiḥ – ground, foundation, basis.

But that (persistent endeavor) is attained on the firm basis of a continuous reverential sustained practice which is executed for a long time. (Yoga Sutras 1.14)

The key word is reverential. The Sanskrit is satkara which means honor, high regard. Unless one has high regard for the practice, one cannot get anywhere with it. People come to yoga practice with queer motives. Some expect that they will get instant results, although they are not cleared of contrary motives and although they will not respect the teacher and will treat him inappropriately.

Another problem is that some students are critical of both yoga and yoga teachers. Some have an inborn distrust of anything which is religious. People feel that religion is exploitive and perhaps it is. But still if you go to a teacher who professes a certain faith and if he requires you at adopt that faith why object to it if you really want to learn from him.

Yoga has requirements and demands adjustments from the students. I learnt yoga from many teachers. To progress in any discipline, I was reverential to the practice and respectful of the teacher.

Reading People's Minds

Some people after hearing about yoga and mystic powers get the idea that a yogi can and does read minds. They feel however that they should check the yogi, so as know if he actually can do this. But that silly game gets nowhere. In yoga the purpose of telepathy, clairvoyance and related mystic powers is to give the yogi access to other levels of existence from which he can absolve his complications of destiny and get out of this mire of the physical world. It is not for reading minds and such curiosities and adventures.

Mystic powers are a serious part of a yogi's development since without that ability he could not side step obstacles which are thrown before him by destiny and which would otherwise set him on a course of haphazard transmigrations.

It has little to do with reading someone's mind. Even if a yogi knows what is in someone's mind still that does not mean that the yogi can abuse that information without consequence.

A yogi does on occasion become aware of what others think but that information can only be used by him constructively if he wishes to transit from this physical world, not otherwise.

Kundalini Cap-back

This was a procedure shown by Swami Atmananda. This was shown in my subtle head. He took a miniature form and demonstrated how this is done.

Little is known about Atmananda except that he was a Vaishnava practicing Tibetan yoga in the Himalayas. He freed Yogeshwarananda from having to struggle with lower meditation practices.

Atmananda cannot be found by a neophyte yogi. If one advances sufficiently, he appears in one's head during meditation. He shows special techniques.

Atmananda's Kriya: July 23th 2010
Kundalini cap-back to back-of-head

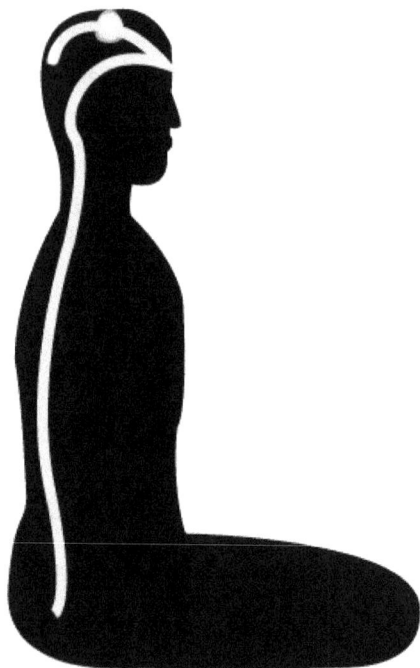

Practice:

Raise Kundalini to brow chakra.

Do bhastrika breath infusion for at least 50 counts.

Hold energy at brow chakra while drawing it back to crown.

Energy will try to disappate through brow chakra.

Mentally prevent it from doing so.

Be sure to hold the core-self in naad sound

while this happens. Naad is the anchor zone.

How to do this:

This is an advanced practice but it is a very simple practice nevertheless.

To do this one must first raise kundalini. How to do that? Use which ever method give results. When kundalini comes into the head and one can feel its bright influence there, check to see what its objective is. Capture it from this objective and pull it back from the brow chakra. Take it to brahmrandra.

If kundalini refuses to do this, make an effort to raise kundalini again.

Begin again. Once it rises into the head, if there is resistance of kundalini to your will, that means it ascended with impurities. Repeat the effort. Pull kundalini into the head.

Once kundalini ascends it will do one of two things; go to brow chakra and then go through the brow chakra into the subtle environments or it will burst into the middle of the head.

Direct kundalini to go from the brow chakra to the crown. Pull kundalini to the back of the head. If you do not keep connection with naad sound you may be distracted as you do this.

A question may be asked as to why Swami Atmananda showed this procedure. The answer is that he thinks that I will honor a pledge to give instructions to people whom he sends. He does not give these techniques whimsically.

Sources of Reactions

A serious mistake religious people make, is to become hung up on the idea that people are punished personally for their miscalculations in performances. Even if we were to solve every problem we could encounter running against social authorities and supernatural people, we will still be left with environmental challenges.

The environment itself is hostile so that it allows us to do certain things which it is offended by. It takes its time subjecting us with the backlash.

Many religious people go tooting about hell and God as if that is the worse event in the life of a living entity. Actually, that is nothing compared to the reactions from the environment.

In the Vedic lay out about reactions, we are said to be confronted by *adhyatmic, adhibhautic* and *adhidaivic* realities.

Here is the break down:

adhyatmic = adhi + atmic = overhanging self afflictions

*adhibhautic = adhi + bhautic =*environmental disagreements with a person's actions

adhidaivic = adhi + daivic = supernatural objections to a person's actions

Hell imposed by a supernatural being is only covered as adhidaivic reality. There are also our subconscious and kundalini attacks. Finally, there is the environment of other individuals and nature at large.

Religious people want to reduce this to God or agents of God. That is adhidaivic. But that is no surprise. You go before the judge. He sends you to the prison. At least you know who sent you, what laws were cited and what evidence they presented.

But how can you trace other afflictions?

What about the time I lost my body when the boat suddenly capsized?

What about that time when a volcano exploded as I walked on a mountain slope? It scaled my body. I was left to die.

God is the least of a person's concern. If there is such a God and one could confront the deity and give him or her the grievance, one would have the satisfaction for having confronted him.

How will one settle with nature and those other limited entities who are appear in these creations?

Our actions themselves seek us, keep us targeted and dish to us reactions which are sensible or insensible.

Naad Brahma

If one feels he cannot tolerate total silence in the mind during meditation, one should become absorbed in naad sound. Naad will give a resonance. It does not have images. It is an audio vibration. When absorbed in naad, one may find that one is tempted to return to the frontal part of the brain. In some cases, one will be drawn there forcibly by impressions which are illustrated in the mind, especially those which came in through video media. When one finds the self drawn forward into those images one should resume listening to naad.

Realize that media, which was viewed previously, serves to sabotage current meditation. However, one should look forward when one feels that the front part of the head is no longer absorbed with the lower vibrations, images and sound of this physical world. From time to time there will be light in the front or an opening or movements of energy in and out. When one sees this, look forward but keep the coreSelf in naad as one does so.

Video images from screen display media ruin deep meditation practice, but it is up to the yogi to realize this. Patañjali instructed the termination of the vrittis but many neophytes do not take the instruction seriously. The higher levels of meditation are not attained by them.

Pranayama Bhastrika Breath Infusion

Bhastrika is one type of pranayama breath infusion. The purpose of pranayama is to target the subtle body for purification of the substances within it. According to yogic lore, there are no other procedures for that purpose which is as effective and rapid as pranayama practice.

None of this is a matter of proof. It is a matter of what an individual should do for success. According to what a person needs at a particular time, he should acquire that skill and practice it. Yoga hinges on what is required. One practices to fulfill the need. A yogi may try a method.

A person who feels a need should inquire for a method from a teacher. If after learning one finds that the practice does not fulfill the need one should learn another process.

Hatha yoga as it is defined in the West means the third stage of yoga which is asana physical postures. Originally hatha yoga meant the complete yoga process with stress on purification of the physical and subtle bodies with the used of musculars contractions, compression of subtle energy and mystic movements.

These were introduced by Gorakshnath, who was a leading teacher in the Nath succession which began with Lord Shiva and was first taught to Gauri, Shiva's wife. Legend has it that while Shiva taught the goddess, Devi, a fish listened but Devi was inattentive. The fish later because the famous yogi by the name of Matsyendranath *(matsya is fish)*. He taught Gorakshnath whatever he learnt from what was told to Devi. Thus, the Nath lineage began. Gorakshnath did write books.

Technically speaking hatha yoga is the same as the ashtanga yoga which was given by Patañjali, except that Gorakshnath give six stages instead of eight which were given by Patañjali. Gorakshnath did not mention the first two stages which are *yama* and *niyama*.

The use of fresh air is only an external manifestation of something that happens internally in terms of the subtle body. When fresh air is infused into the physical system, subtle fresh energy is infused into the subtle form. That is the objective of the practice. That infusion of energy, if done correctly, causes the subtle body to experience a frequency increase, which causes the perception to shift to higher dimensions.

Diversity is Infinite

Right now, there is no evidence that a time will come when all beings will be enlightened. The only place where that happens is in the minds of idealists. What we see is endless disparity, between and within the various species.

Even though we make generalizations about equality and strive to produce it in an endless losing battle with nature, which insists on diversity and inequality, nothing is equal to anything else anywhere. To deal with the issue head on, it seems that there are always those ahead and those behind, those superior and those inferior.

As one becomes enlightened and moves up, what is ahead moves even further. What is behind moves to where one was while nature produces a new batch of primitive organisms.

The diversity is infinite. The disparities and differences are also infinite. What appears to be enlightenment at one stage may turn out to be less than that as one progresses into it, like an ever-present but receding horizon.

lifeForce is Necessity

For all it is, the self cannot produce a physical body. It can speak of enlightenment and perhaps even attain it, but it can neither manufacture or maintain a body.

The factor which creates and maintains the body is the lifeForce. Most human beings mistake this lifeForce as the self. Normal personality is a combination of several psychic components, one of which is the coreSelf.

Does the importance of the lifeForce totally screen out the integrity of the core? In part it does. In part it does not. The lifeForce needs the energy of the self for functioning, but the interference of the self is only tolerated to an extent by the lifeForce, which is in a position to deprive that self of services.

Meditation and Sound

For meditation one should learn how to become oriented to the inner vibration. To find form in the world which is outside the physical body, the mind has a tendency of running away from internal sound. By constant practice, one can break this need of the mind and cause it to be introspectively appreciative of the inner mental environment.

Intelligence

Is it possible to go beyond the rational mind?

I am still waiting for someone to convince me that there is no such thing as emotional intelligence. I have the evidence about rational intelligence but where is the proof that there is no emotional intelligence? I feel that we need to take stock of the benefits we continuously receive from emotional intelligence. I would agree that both rational and emotional intelligence mislead us on occasion. If we did research, we may find that emotional intelligence errs much more than rational sense. Still we cannot live without emotional intelligence.

For the purpose of yoga, emotional intelligence is subdued in kundalini yoga. Rational intelligence is subdued in *buddhi* yoga which is the system *Patañjali* hints at when he speaks of *chitta vritti nirodhah* or shutting down the operations of the mind. If these two faculties are brought under control and are energized so that they move into higher dimensions and function from there, the yogi accesses supernatural perception. That takes him out of the realm of the lower conclusions drawn by the same organs when they derive their energies from lower planes.

When we take into consideration the biology of the body and the individual actions of cells, we should recognize instinctual intelligence. Until Darwin made his *Origin of the Species* presentation, instinct was berated but since then, there is a revision. We no longer see instinct as being something which is not an expression of intelligence. But the second leap in this affair came about with the work of Gregor Mendel who lay out the foundation for genetic observation. When the genes are considered, intelligence begins on the cellular level and decision making though rudimentary takes place there. In fact, the sum of the parts of the human body is more than the individual parts working in isolation. That says much for intelligence. If you can get millions of cells to function together to keep a complex system, a body, alive, that requires intelligence.

Cooperation takes intelligence. When that breaks down, the body dies. The problem with intelligence is solved very quickly as soon as each of us can distant ourselves from claiming it for ourselves.

Then we understand that we live and move in intelligence itself. Our individual and collective decision making on the basis of intelligence, functions because of the substrata of primitive intelligence, instinct and cellular cooperative intelligence.

My experience is that one can draw conclusions through meditative experiences even when those experiences transcend or occur with disconnection from the intellect. But I see a difficulty presenting that idea in scientific circles, because the proof of it is hard to come by. Science succeeds and gets its credibility because in the final analysis it gives physical proof, while with meditation physical proof is a scarce commodity. Spirituality, I am not so sure about, since the definition of that varies. Musing is in question since it implies subjective considerations. It goes back to proof and verification. If there is an experience which is out of this world, the proof will be hard in coming. Doubts will remain. In that sense the intellect will rule the day and will surpass every other means of verification, except of course, just plain instinct which is so blatantly displayed by nature, that even science cannot deny it.

Meditation or quiet time?

Meditation is not quiet time but it is related to that and can develop out of that practice, if one takes just one step further.

Usually quiet time means a quiet external environment. For instance, while going to college, one may leave an apartment or noisy dorm and go to the library to get peace and quiet for serious study.

This is the method of escaping from noises in the external environment. One may go to a Park in the city or to the countryside to get away from the hustle and bustle of a metropolitan area.

For meditation however the quiet place required is psychological not physical. For meditation both the external and internal quietude is required. The mental chatter and emotional illustrations should be stopped for successful meditation.

Most people who do meditation usually spend their half or three-fourths of an hour fighting the mind to quiet it. On some days they are unsuccessful because the mind puts a prize fighter's defense to any effort to silence it.

Sense of Identity Repels the Intellect

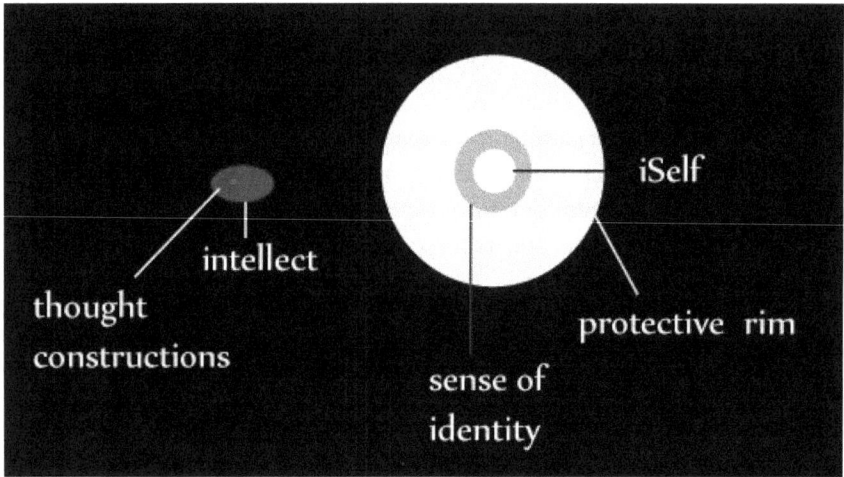

iSelf and sense of identity escaped from influence of intellect, which shrinks due to lack of energy supply from sense of identity. The identity is centralized on iSelf. It has an expanded protective rim. It is focused on iSelf.

When the sense of identity focuses on the iSelf it eventually develops an interest in that. The iSelf in turn being freed from the mental dominance of the intellect, considers its existence in fusion with the sense of identity.

It tries to rationalize this new development but it finds that without the intellect, its rationalization faculties operate in an entirely different way.

In the meantime, the sense of identity expands and puts out a repulsion energy which causes the intellect to shrink even more and to be disempowered so much as to appear to be fading. This fading process is termed "no mind" in some meditation practices.

Isolated Intellect

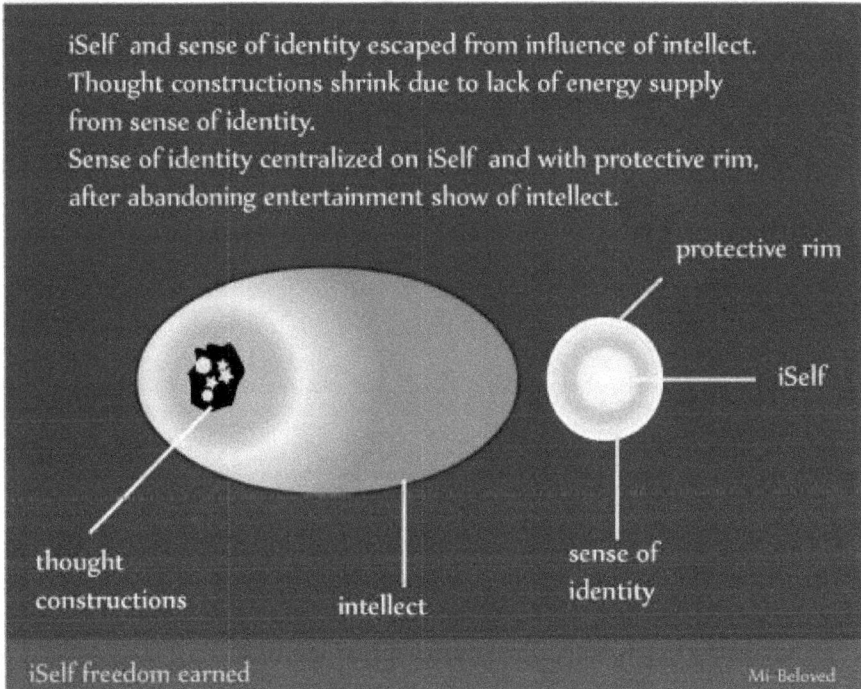

iSelf and sense of identity escaped from influence of intellect.
Thought constructions shrink due to lack of energy supply from sense of identity.
Sense of identity centralized on iSelf and with protective rim, after abandoning entertainment show of intellect.

protective rim

iSelf

thought constructions

intellect

sense of identity

iSelf freedom earned   Mi-Beloved

In order to remain in isolation from its lover which is the intellect, the sense of identity coats itself with a protective rim. This allows the identity to focus on its relationship to the iSelf.

If during the separation the identity fails to maintain this protective rim or membrane, it will be forced by an irresistible urge to be influenced by the intellect. Its detachment from that subtle object will be compromised.

The intellect for its part, suffers in such isolation and begins to feel that its grasp on the situation decreases drastically as the power to maintain its thought constructions is greatly reduced. It develops a fear of becoming non-existent.

During meditation, this fear may affect the iSelf which would in response to it, relax the concentration and isolation and return to become dominated by the intellect.

Reducing Thought Construction

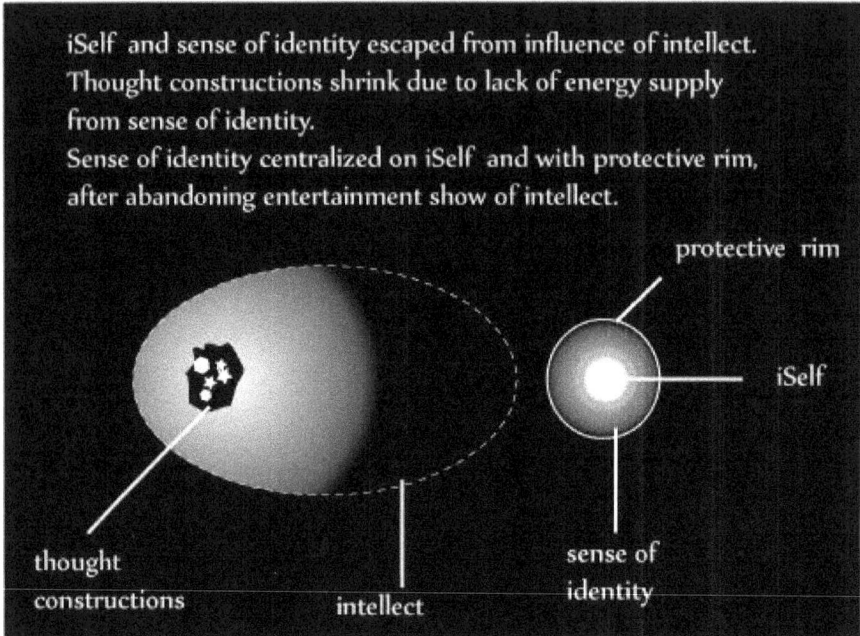

iSelf and sense of identity escaped from influence of intellect. Thought constructions shrink due to lack of energy supply from sense of identity.
Sense of identity centralized on iSelf and with protective rim, after abandoning entertainment show of intellect.

protective rim

iSelf

thought constructions

intellect

sense of identity

This shows a technique for training the mind to reduce thought construction. This is a direct attack. It involves no props like mantras or focus points.

The key to this is to control the sense of identity. As it is, it desires to associate with the intellect. That is its singular tendency. If it is deprived of this association it assumes a dryish non-enjoying mood, which causes the iSelf to release it for indulgence in the fantasies which are created by the intellect.

The yogi must decide to suffer through that drying phase of the sense of identity. If he cannot endure that, this practice cannot be achieved.

At first when the iSelf tries to withdraw the sense of identity from viewing the displays of the intellect, the identity will sulk like a spoilt child. At that point, the iSelf should ignore the negative feeling and proceed to the back of the head. As it does so it will find that the power of the intellect is decreased considerably. The sense of identity will lose interest in the theatrical presentations of the intellect. That in turn will cause the intellect to be de-energized which will slacken its power grasp on the self.

This concerns mystic practice. It has little to do with external social behavior. This means internal behavior in the social world of the iSelf and the other psychological factors which are in the psyche of a person. Meditation is not concerned with external social behavior. The two components in question are the sense of identity and the intellect. These two operate like lovers. Lovers do not like to be separated for any reason. Hence if any action is taken to cause a rupture in their emotional interplay, either of the organs gets upset and reacts internally in the presence of the iSelf. In the internal world where these psychic components interact, they do so just as if they were persons in fact.

The iSelf is sometimes caught in the hassles between these energies. See the iSelf as an expense account. Suppose two lovers have credit cards which are tied to an expense account which is called the iSelf Credit Union. The lovers plan to meet in Tahiti to have a good time with all expenses paid. They fly to the resort and begin enjoying themselves at a luxurious hotel. Superficially they book private rooms but they were sure to secretly book adjacent rooms which have a common inner door. The idea was to be together for sexual purposes. In the middle of the holiday, they return to their rooms one night to find that the common door is sealed. They cannot get to each other. They each make phone calls and decide to complain to the management. Calls are made to the hotel desk. They are informed that an official at the iSelf Credit Union suspended the expense accounts and reduced the financial privileges. This means that they can only remain in the luxurious hotel for one more day. They cannot have the privilege of a common inner entrance to the adjacent rooms. You can imagine what will happen to their attitudes after that.

Thus, when the iSelf takes an action to either reduce or rupture the communication between the sense of identity and the intellect, these components enter into a depressed state. Since the iSelf is surrounded by the sense of identity, that self notices and even feels the mood of the identity, but it is unaware of the depression of the intellect. The question is: Can the iSelf tolerate that? Some authorities seem to think that the iSelf cannot endure that. They give mantras and other props to keep the situation under control with the least possible negativity, but I recommend that the student faces the disharmony. He should reorder the components, causing them to abandon their depressed states.

Influence of intellect

In this diagram there is the influence of the intellect surrounding the sense of identity and the iSelf:

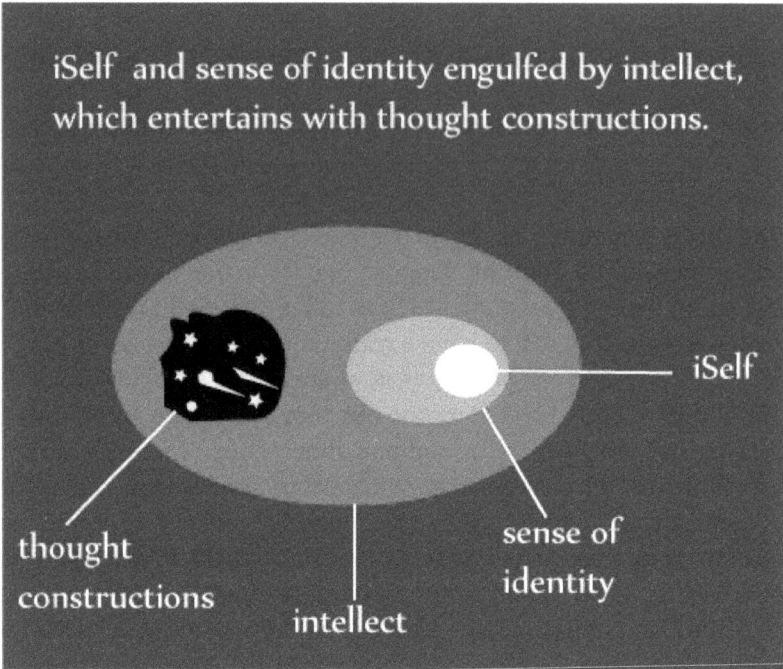

iSelf and sense of identity engulfed by intellect, which entertains with thought constructions.

iSelf

thought constructions

sense of identity

intellect

Some meditators set out with the idea that the sense of identity or ego is a danger to the self and should be eliminated. This caused a cult of *getting rid of ego*. So far however I found no evidence to support the idea that the ego can be abolished.

People retreat from the ego in meditation. They declare its death but what really takes place is that the ego goes dormant and then is reestablished with ease through the subjective energies of the iSelf, thus making a fool of many no-ego advocates.

Many yogis who abandoned physical existence and who retreated to higher levels are still to be related to if one can go to those levels. Their respective iSelves and senses of identity remain intact. Yogis who entered the causal level of existence have no ego identity there but even these persons resumed the sense of identity as soon as they leave the causal plane and come in this direction.

One reason for the inability to eliminate the sense of identity is this:

It was not deliberately created by the iSelf. It is not that the iSelf existed and then the sense of identity was produced by that self. It is rather that when the iSelf is on a certain level of existence, which is the location of where the causal plane meets the subtle levels of mundane existence, it finds itself in possession with the sense of identity.

Something supernatural that was not created by an iSelf cannot be eliminated by that self because the thing is out of the range of proprietorship control of the self. The self can control its relationship to the sense of identity however.

Look at this diagram again:

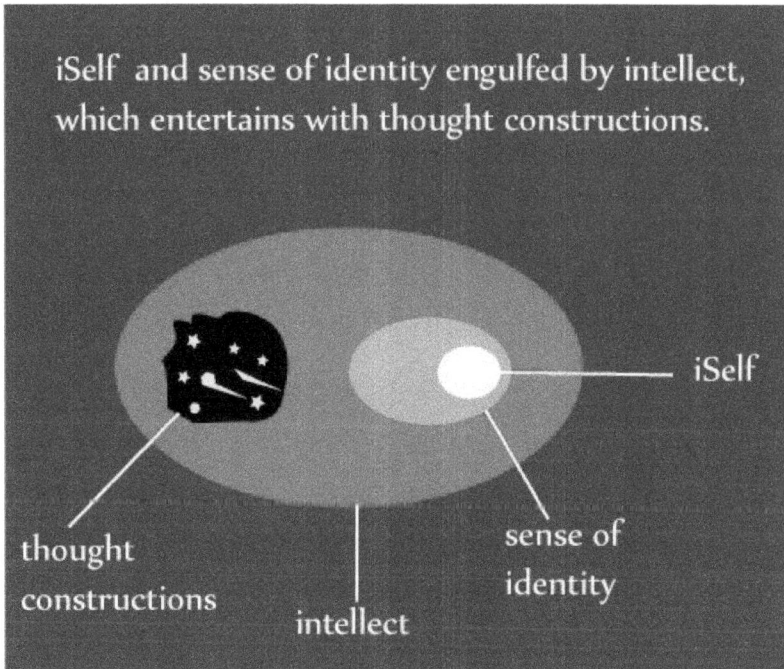

iSelf and sense of identity engulfed by intellect, which entertains with thought constructions.

iSelf

thought constructions

intellect

sense of identity

The iSelf is in white on the right as the smallest circle, with the sense of identity surrounding it. Both are in turn surrounded by the intellect which is the largest circle. By revealing various thoughts, the intellect holds both the iSelf and the sense of identity in a hypnotic trance.

Patañjali instructed that these thought constructions and any other machinations of the intellect be banished. He gave that as the foundation of a meditation practice. For Patanjali, the talk about meditation only begins after the intellect is silenced.

Astral Authority

The astral world is not free of authority. Deity simply means a person in the astral world who has jurisdiction which regulates behavior in the particular place. As in this world if you relocate to one country you may find that a law there which permits a man to have up to four wives, while in another place it is against the law to have more than one wife. These laws are made and enforced by human beings. It is a coincidence that many ancient cultures had laws which some chieftain or king attributed to divine command, because elsewhere in places where people did not feel inspired in that way, other social laws were also in place. In Russian during the Stalin era, there were very harsh laws. Stalin and many of his compatriots were avowed atheists. His laws were enforced. There was no God there to enforce anything or to agree or disagree with anything and still laws were enforced. In that situation Stalin was the law. When laws run parallel with religious stipulations, we may feel that the religion has something to do with it, but on close inspection, it only has that connation superficially. But in the astral world it is not a free for all. Just as in this world you can escape into your mind or I can escape into my mind and avoid considering an inconvenient law, in the astral world also there is such escape but still that does not remove the deities who have jurisdiction over those places.

Psychic Form

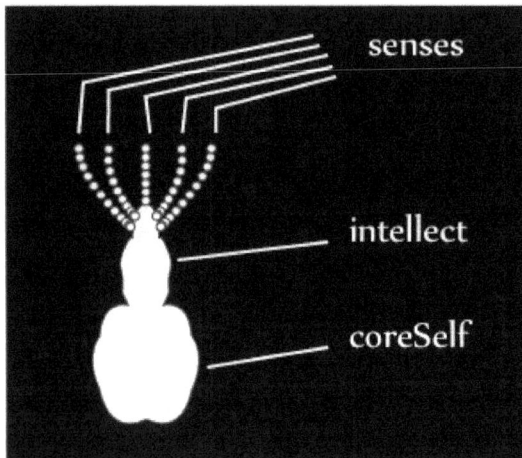

This diagram is a depiction of what it looks like inside a human head, when the human being pursues objects of the senses. It does not matter what kind of object it is, whether it is good or bad, religious or irreligious, the profile will be same.

For instance, if a human being perceives a cloud, or a speck of dirt, the same sensual motions take place. Internally the same psychological forces go into play.

Dark Mind

One reason for a lack of interest in meditation, is the mind's dark energy. Astronomers bring to our attention also that most of the universe consist of an energy which we cannot see and which is called dark matter. So it is, that there is darkness everywhere we turn in the universe except for the suns and stars which shine due to their glitter.

Most of the light in the night sky comes from super-large explosions, violence, but to us it is starlight. We live in the fantasy of its beauty.

This diagram shows the darkness in the mind but with a sudden break in that darkness and with light being seen from the other side of reality.

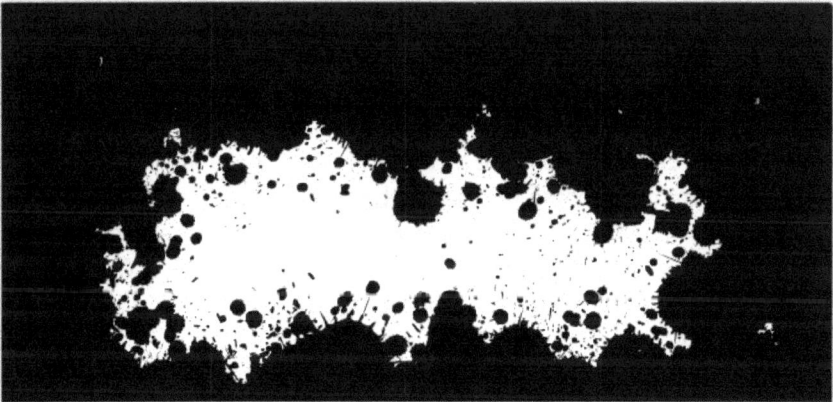

The darkness of the mind is mental dust but to the average person it is not worth the bother. In fact, people escape from this darkness by two methods which are a preoccupation with materialism or a preoccupation with material spirituality which is a focus on spiritually-related objects in the physical world.

However sooner or later one should face this mental darkness and do something to dissipate it. Perchance sometimes in meditation one gets this clarity where the dark cloud of mental energy clears and one sees into the fourth dimension. Then the huge charade of materialism and material spirituality loses its grip on the psyche.

Evolving Selves

The selves evolved through the life forms. It so happens that overall, the human has the best facility because of a well-developed brain. In the other forms one is restricted to a greater degree in regarding to thinking construction, merely because the brain in those forms is not as versatile as the one developed in a human embryo. Of course, this is a generalization since particular superior functions are found in the other life forms, like heat sensors which give a snake precise information about the location of a rodent in total darkness.

One way to look at this is that there are two ends to the spectrum; the low end which leads down to vegetative forms and the high end which leads to celestial subtle forms. We are attracted to the downward levels and the higher ones where one can assume a celestial or divine form. Religion aside, in nature there is pushing and pulling, where each self finds itself being urged into different species of life by evolutionary pressures. These forces are inherent in both the subtle body of the individual and in the environments where the body is manifested.

The need for advancement motivates all selves using these forms, the human beings included. Misbehaviors or adaptation to lower behaviors may cause any spirit to assume a lower life form. A spirit using a human form may descend to take the form of a dog in the next life. To the contrary the spirit using a dog's form may graduate to the human species.

As human children are more attracted to their parents than to any other people and humans become familiar with the environment, all other species are bogged down with particular ideas which limit the subtle body's ability to move into other species. Choices are made on the basis of exposure to particular species in particular environments.

Part 8

Front Kundalini Details

Breath infusion practice this morning was good overall with some highlights which I feel should be described. Front kundalini came up. This is when there are bliss pixels of energy moving up the front of the body rather than through the central spine into the head.

I made observations which I did not and perhaps could not make before. Just as when a person comes out of a dark cave, he cannot focus on a brilliant light, so a yogi may not have clear perception of super-subtle events which occur in meditation or otherwise. Initially in these experiences because the lack of subtle perception, one may adopt the wrong idea. However as one continues the practice day after day, one develops the perception required.

I saw front kundalini strike from two locations.

One is the pudenda-perineum nerve circuitry

The other is from a bulb-like place which keeps reserve sexual energy in the subtle body. This is called a kanda.

If the infused energy goes down through the navel region, through the pubic area, and then strikes the base chakra, what usually happens is that the kundalini will rise through the spine. This is provided the locks are held and especially if the base chakra is restricted so that kundalini cannot express itself downwards through that terminal.

Front kundalini is routed differently. In front kundalini the energy at the pubic area comes up the front of the body and does not hit the base chakra.

Front kundalini may or may not involve the base chakra. It may be that the infused energy mixes with reserve sexual energy, which ignites into a flash force which moves up the front of the body.

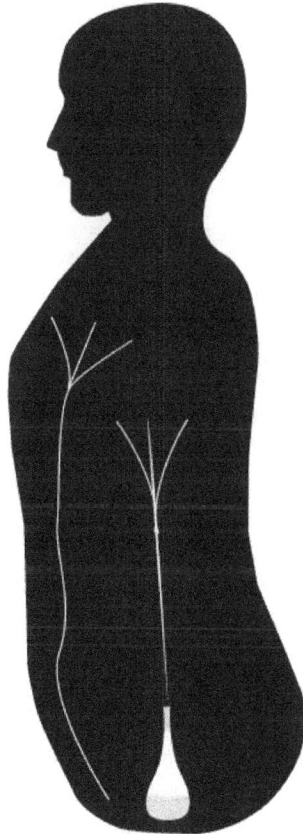

What does this feel like?

This feels like millions of pixels of bliss force or as electrical force broken into micro-bits which spread in a flash up the front of the body and may even reach as far as the shoulders or even pass through the neck into the jaws and cheeks.

Breath Infusion in Winter

Students doing breath infusion in winter should take precautions to avoid influenza.

Cold air might be laden with viruses which come alive as soon as they enter the human body and are warmed. This could result in colds, flu and the like which in turn put a damper on practice.

If you can, do the exercises indoor in a location where cold air from outdoors mixes with warm air from indoors. This may disable some viruses before they enter the lungs.

If you practice outdoors in cold weather be dressed for the occasion. Protect the throat by using a turtle neck sweater or dickey.

Locks and Compression

There is a difference between a lock and compression of infused breath energy. The locks keep the infused energy and the infused mixed energy from escaping the psyche. Once the locks are secured, one can work on the mixed infused energy to direct it here or there or even to compress or diffuse it. The pressure or attention which is applied to do this is not the locks. It is the internal focus into the psyche.

Except for the third eye and the crown chakra, the yogi uses locks to close the passages where energy leaks. With the locks you want to close all passages where energy leaks. Once everything is sealed one is not concerned with leaks. One switches focus to the accumulated energy. One can observe the nature of the infused energy, its movement, expansion or contraction.

Some days, during a session, one will feel as if one cannot absorb more breath. This may happen due to the attitude and health condition of the blood corpuscles where they do not absorb oxygen fully. Or they are unable to completely assimilate the oxygen which they are exposed to in the lungs.

Some of this is due to the chemical composition of the blood on a particular day.

When it seems that the lungs no longer absorb fresh air during a session, I stop the rapid breathing for a bit. I do some slower deep breathing for about 15 breaths or more. This is when I inhale through the nostrils deliberately and bring the air down into the lowest part of the lung, then I exhale through the mouth. I am attentive internally. I direct the air to the bottom of the lungs.

Evacuation Sitting

One posture for evacuation is squatting. This pose is not suitable for the design of Western commodes. In addition, Western bodies are not as flexible since from infancy people use chairs and rarely sit on the floor.

I discovered one posture in variations which can be used to help with evacuation, especially as the body gets older and the waste moves sluggishly through the large intestines and rectum.

It is worth the while to study the design of the intestines and rectum to get some understanding of what the kundalini does to process food from the stomach through the small intestine coiled system into the large intestine which move food up the right side of the body, then across the chest, then down the left side then into the rectum where at last it is evacuated.

The posture below in its variations show a pose in which one may exert the required pressure to move waste which lingers above the inner valve in the rectum.

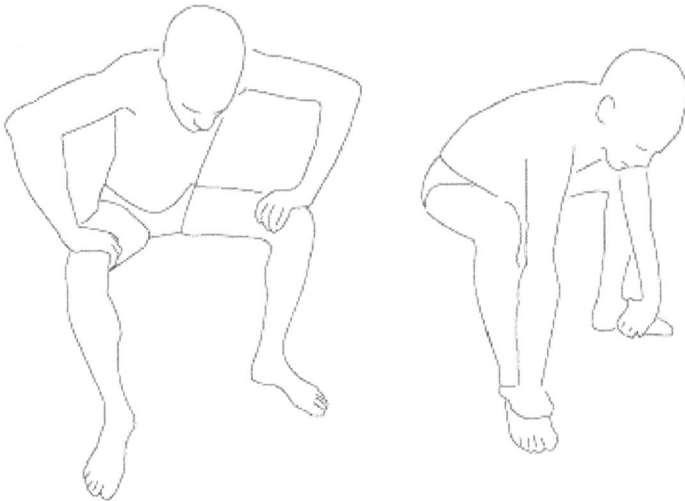

squating over a commode

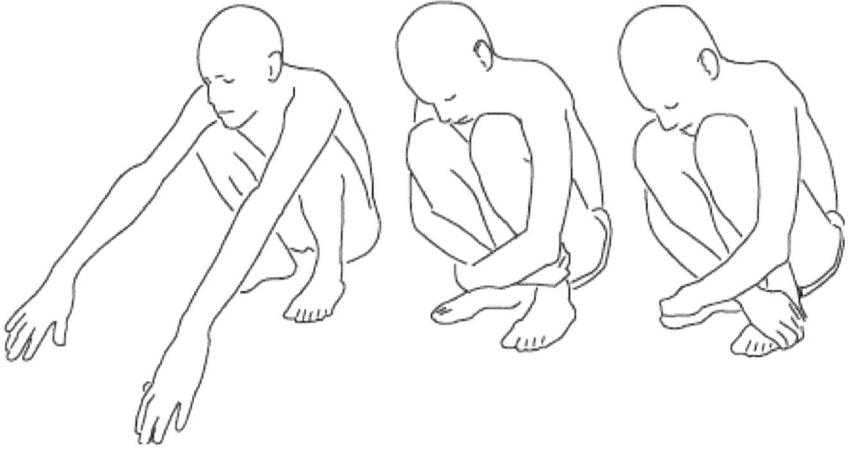

It is important for those doing hatha yoga to have the most efficient processing of food through the intestines and the rapid removal of waste once nutrients are extracted. As it is the system lingers which results in holding waste in the body for longer than necessary which contributes to increased pollution energy and decreased positively charged energy which in turn has a dulling effect on meditation.

Arousing Kundalini

During some sessions when kundalini is raised more than once in the practice, it becomes more difficult to arouse it after the first time, or it does not rise with the same force. This holds true for a period of practice, perhaps for about a period of two to six years. After that the natural configuration of the kundalini and sex hormone system will be disrupted. Kundalini will no longer store energy below the small of the back with intentions of releasing this energy in one burst and then storing energy again and then releasing it again.

Kundalini developed the habit of storing sex hormones in the male bodies and then releasing that in one orgasm after which the body enters a stupor state, takes rest, eats food, accumulates more hormone energy and has another orgasm of this energy.

Since that is its habit, it takes time to change this. The yogi should be pleased that for him, the energy bursts through the spine rather than through the sex organ chakra.

The accomplishment at this stage is that the yogi observes how kundalini operates. He can study it further and endeavor to change it. In that challenge he confronts millions of years of evolutionary development. He cannot change this overnight. Even great yogis are challenged by this.

Besides, the ancestors are against the adjustments. A yogi may not successfully deny the ancestors their claim on his body. They desire to use the body in the evolutionary way for production of embryos which they so badly desire? A yogi should not disenfranchise souls on the astral planes who have rights to use his body to get embryos for themselves.

Kundalini has an addiction to the rush of pleasure. It will influence the psyche, not necessarily the core self, but the psyche and even the cells in the physical body to focus on the rush. This habit of kundalini must be reformed and then something else will happen during practice or better, there will be a change of attitude of the coreSelf because then kundalini will present the infusion of breath energy and the response it makes to that in a different way.

Ancestors have an impact due to their innate rights to use the forms of their descendants. In some cases, with these people; one will lose a battle or two.

Kundalini Rise Formula

- Beginner breath energy + sex hormone concentrate + kundalini
- Intermediate   breath energy + partially distributed sex hormone + kundalini
- Advanced breath energy + fully distributed sex hormone + kundalini

Special Notes:

Breath Energy

Breath energy means breath energy which is accumulated in the psyche by using a method such as bhastrika, kapalabhati or anuloma/viloma pranayama. This must be an efficient infusion so that each in-draw of breath is compressed into the previous one, with none of it being released back through the lungs. It is similar to compressing air into a tire which has an efficiency valve which does not allow air which is put into the tire to escape. The tire must have no puncture holes and that is achieved by doing the locks. The basic body-locks are the anus lock, the sex lock, the navel draw back lock, the stomach pull up under the rib cage lock and the neck lock. These are the basic ones. There are others.

There must also be the mind lock which is to lock the attention mentally so that it does not drift to external objects and thoughts. The yogi should focus the mind on the breathing and the accumulation of the breath energy and any other psychic developments which occur during practice.

Sex Hormone Concentrate:

This is the hormone energy which is produced and conserved in the body for use in sexual indulgence. At the beginner's level this energy provides one or more kundalini rises during practice and then the student finds that there is no more charge. This is because this sex energy was consumed, just as it would be in one grand orgasmic climax experience during sexual intercourse and then the system collapses and becomes reluctant to continue because the energy was exhausted.

On the next day, after this energy has accumulated again, the system will again discharge that energy and the same exhaustion of its supply occurs again.

Partially-distributed Sex Hormone

This is in the intermediate stage. In that state because of having done the breath infusion for some time the attitude of the cells in the sexual reproduction system changes so that there is a reluctance to store so much of the sex hormones. Thus, some of this energy is distributed in the blood stream and only some of it is stored for sexual expression.

This means that the yogi finds that when he or she does the exercises, there are charges of energy as if kundalini is rising in other parts of the body and also the charge of energy up the spine may not be as intense.

Fully-distributed Sex Hormone

This is in the advanced stage. What happens here is the sex hormone accumulation system is disrupted so that the body no longer holds a reservoir of sex energy for use in sexual climax expression.

Hence when the yogi does the practice, he finds that the infused breath energy locates the charge hormone energy anywhere and everywhere within the psyche. There is no primary focus on the spine *sushumna nadi* system. There is no longer that one rush of energy or two rushes of energy, but instead even from the very start of practice, there are kundalini strikes here and there because the energy is distributed throughout the psyche and not just in the sex organs and the spine.

Precaution:

Students who use the anuloma/viloma pranayama method of alternate breathing should note that this does not work if one does not persist with it for about at least 45 minutes. One must keep a tight count and must not allow the air which is drawn in to escape. If this practice is not done efficiently nothing will happen because that would be like inflating a tire and having a leaky valve or having no valve. In that case, the tire will not retain the air.

Why do I list this method if I have little confidence in it?

The reason is that it is a valid method. If one does not have patience to keep the count, if one is incapable of the required concentration, this method will not work.

In this method one must first close the right nostril with the right thumb

- Then inhale through the left nostril
- Then close that nostril with the little finger
- Then hold the air in the lungs while directing the lungs to absorb it.
- Once the air is absorbed release the thumb from the right nostril.
- Exhale through that nostril.
- As soon as the exhale is finished inhale through that same right nostril
- When sufficient air entered close that right nostril with the right thumb
- When that inhaled air is absorbed, release the little finger from the left nostril
- Exhale the air through that left nostril
- Inhale air into that nostril and close it with the little finger.
- When that air is absorbed release the thumb again from the right nostril. Exhale that air.

This is repeated again and again in sequence.

The yogi must control the mind and keep it tied so that it keeps track of the absorption and expulsion of the air.

Knee Caps / Ankles

During breath infusion practice, I had some fascinating releases of the generated infused energy down into the thighs, legs and feet, particularly a release through the knee caps and ankles.

The knee caps and ankles are hard-to-reach areas to target. Some years now I worked on various postures which stretch and release these areas in the physical body, while doing breath infusion. The energy sparkled in the knee caps and then flashed in the ankles. It was like electricity in the form of released springs moving from the knees through the thighs.

I stood up with feet about 12 inches apart, back slightly arched forward and lifted and dropped the ankles several time to assist the energy in penetrating any areas which were not saturated with the infused energy.

Chakras as Bodies?

Each psyche has a coreSelf, which is surrounded on all sides spherically by a sense of identity *(ahamkara/ego)*. This in turn is restricted by an intellect psychic organ which in turn is harnessed to the five sensual orbs *(indriyas)*. These exist in the head of the subtle body, in the mind. However, besides these there is the kundalini which exists mostly not in the head but in the spine of the subtle body, near the bottom of it at the place known in yoga as *muladhara* (root/*mula* - station anchor/*dhara*).

Because of the prevalence of the influence of this kundalini, the coreSelf even though it is not that power, feels as though it is that. Therefore, the situation of kundalini is assumed to be the situation of the self.

When kundalini expresses itself in base chakra (*muladhara*), the person excretes or enjoys sex pleasure during anal penetration.

When kundalini expresses itself through the sex chakra on the spine and when that energy reaches the sex organ chakras which is it offshoots, the person experiences genital pleasure.

When kundalini expresses itself through the navel chakra on the spine a desire to eat and drink is felt. One feels that one must fill the stomach and intestines.

When kundalini expresses itself through the heart chakra, the person becomes emotional, He feels affection or conversely, he hates someone. He may embrace others and becomes happy doing so or feels satisfied being hostile to others.

When kundalini expresses itself though the throat chakra, he desires to speak either harshly or pleasantly. Talking gives him pleasure. This chakra also works with the navel chakra to coordinate getting food into the stomach.

When kundalini expresses itself though the third eye chakra, a person may focus on ambitions and accomplishments. Though possible he rarely become inclined to psychic development.

When kundalini expresses itself through the brahmrandra crown chakra the person becomes spaced-out and cannot focus on anything. He loses the grasping tendency. He feels relieved of responsibilities.

This has nothing to do with the coreSelf except that in the present configuration the core relies on kundalini. As a man in a dark cave must rely on a flashlight, so the self must rely on the kundalini. If the flashlight is dull the man is limited in what he sees.

When kundalini reaches the crown chakra, the coreSelf may or may not get an increase in psyche perception. It can experience a *black out*, a *white out* or a *gold out*. Presence of kundalini at crown chakra is not necessarily a guarantee for a *gold out*.

There is *jada samadhi* and it means *samadhi* with ignorance, with the person having no idea of anything during that state, a total void out with no information, no perception, nothing. That is stupor absorption. It is not enlightenment.

The chakras should be regarded as an elevator system in the building of the subtle body. It is one subtle body which has these chakras. There are more than seven. That is given because seven are the most important ones. It would be ridiculous if we were to name the other chakras and then say that each is a body. No, these chakras are simply like the nerve ganglion in a physical body. Those are part of a system.

One could regard each chakra as access to various levels of consciousness and also various species of life. For instance, let us look at the form of pig. If I am evicted from this body and somehow by bad luck, I become attracted to a pig parent, I may emerge in the next life as a little piggy. In that format, the predominant chakra will be in the mouth which is the throat chakra. It will be so predominant in the form, that the entire body will be geared to finding things to devour. A predominant throat chakra could result in passage to the lower species which has that as the most demanding sense.

The most forceful chakra causes the chakra system to transmigrate with the kundalini into a species or existential niche in which that compelling chakra is the main operation in the chakra system.

Kundalini is anchored at the base chakra. That is its normal attachment. From there its primary interest is survival. This means that if I am unable to unearth kundalini from there, I will have to keep coming back into a species of life, in a world in which survival has all importance.

In this existence the form of the soul is like a shining light which radiates in a spherical way. It shines in all directions. Its shape is spherical. The core is not a chakra but that relies on the services of the kundalini which is the system which operates the chakras as its expression vortexes.

In a city there are roads. Buses travel on the roads. People use the buses to move from one place to another. The coreSelf uses the kundalini like a bus to move through the *nadi*-chakra system of psychic roads.

At some junctions it is dark because for some reason nature is unconcerned about getting its information. That is similar to the base *muladhara* chakra. If one goes there one will find it to be dark, brown-blackish. But at other junctions where nature considered it to be important to have illumination, there is conscious information.

The fact that the soul is not the crown chakra and that the chakra is not a body of the soul or the inner level of the soul is proven by the fact that unless the kundalini rises to a particular chakra, that chakra does not exist even if the soul is present there. In other words, if you go to the brightest part of the city but if the city engineer turned off the lights you can see nothing.

In kundalini yoga we inspire kundalini to energize all parts of the psyche. However, it is reluctant to do so. Because of the pleasure afforded, it wants to energize the sex chakra. It wants to energize the lights at the sex chakra because that is the way it gets the energy to generate sex pleasure. It wants to energize the navel chakra because it likes to eat sweet foods and harsh condiments.

However, it is reluctant to energize the third eye and crown chakra because these operations take energy which it prefers to use for sex enjoyment.

The potential for using all chakras is there but a self can or cannot utilize the higher ones because of its evolution and because of where the soul is located on the tree of life. Everyone has the seven chakras but in some of us, only some are fully activated. The potential is there but it can only be exploited according to our developed interest.

Yogi Bhajan Complains

This morning on the astral side during practice, I got assistance from Yogi Bhajan and from Yogeshwarananda.

Yogi Bhajan expressed disappointment because many students discontinued practice through the years since the 1970s. He said that if they continued, by now he would have several siddha students to his credit.

There are so many distractions and inefficiencies during practice. These serve to slow the progress. Plain determination is not enough. Even living in an ashram is not enough. One has to realize, challenge and eventually obliterate the forces which negatively impact the progression.

Yogesh said that I should be sure to complete Tibeti Yogi's process before doing the head infusion.

Tibeti's process is the one of first making sure that the trunk, thighs, legs and feet are filled with fresh subtle energy by breath infusion. He demands a full focus on this in the first part of a session. It means total neglect of the head of the subtle body during the first part of a kundalini yoga session with full focus down in the trunk of the subtle body and using a blind fold if possible, to keep the mind from visual objects outside the physical body.

Over time, the frequency and intensity of practice accumulates. *Patañjali* wrote this.

तीव्रसंवेगानामासन्नः ॥२१॥

tīvrasaṁvegānām āsannaḥ

tīvra – very intense; saṁvegānām – regarding those who practice forcibly; āsannaḥ – whatever is very near, what will occur soon.

For those who practice forcefully in a very intense way, the skill of yoga will be achieved very soon. (Yoga Sutra 1.21)

Commentary:

Even though Śrī Patañjali stated that yoga is attained after a long time, he qualified that statement by saying that it is achieved shortly by those who have intense speedy practice. In fact, one cannot conclude yoga practice in any life without intensity and persistence. It is impossible otherwise.

मृदुमध्याधिमात्रत्वात्ततोऽपि विशेषः ॥२२॥

mṛdu madhya adhimātratvāt tataḥ api viśeṣaḥ

mṛdu – slight; madhya – mediocre; adhimātratvāt – from intense; tataḥ – then; api – even; viśeṣaḥ – rating.

Then there are even more ratings, according to intense, mediocre, or slight practice. (Yoga Sutra 1.22)

Commentary:

Yoga practice yields results according to the intensity of correct practice. One person might practice intensely with the wrong methods. His result will be the realization of the incorrect practice. Another person might practice very little with the correct method but he too might not get the results because his practice does not have much forcefulness.

Śrī Patañjali Maharshi gave four rates. Very intense *(tīvra saṁvega)*, intense *(adhimātratvā)*, mediocre *(madhya)*, and slight *(mṛdu)*.

Neck Penetration (2012)

Breath infusion and meditation this morning was productive. The first twenty minutes consisted of several releases of compacted breath energy mixed with energy which was stored here and there in the psyche. I completed a bliss effect shock treatment of the neck to be sure that energy passed freely through the neck into the brain, even through the flesh part of the neck.

In the subtle body the fleshy part of the neck is experienced as compacted pixel energy, subtle force which is either in the form of a dark cluster of crystals or a multicolored cluster or preferably when it is energized, a white-golden glow cluster.

After twenty minutes, I did some sex-energy release stretches and did the infusion during those postures reaching down into the thighs, knees, legs, ankle, foot and toes. I targeted the knees and the ankles. Various stretch and pulls with the breath infusion result in penetrating these areas of the subtle body.

Naad Meditation

Meditation began with a special very tight lotus posture which was insisted on by Yogesh, whose astral form left as soon as I sat to meditate and assumed that posture. With this a pillow was used to keep the sacral area of the spine supported. This also helps to keep the rest of the spine upright, otherwise the body flops forward and collapses or one has to give it attention during meditation which is a distraction.

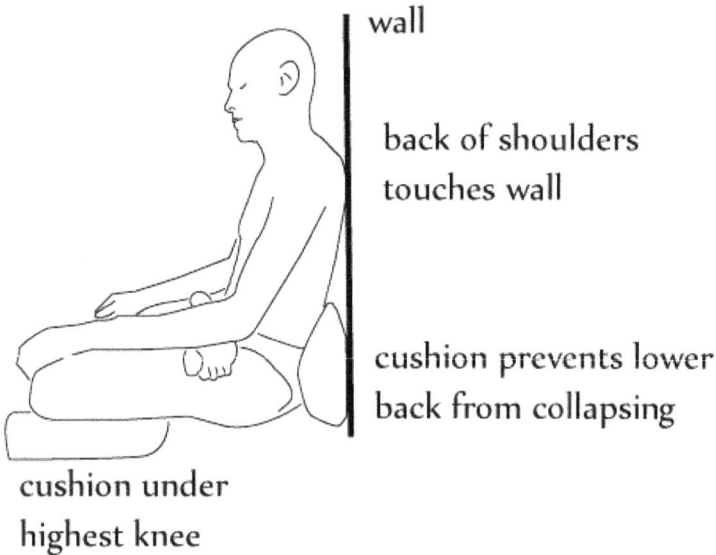

wall

back of shoulders
touches wall

cushion prevents lower
back from collapsing

cushion under
highest knee

I also used a pillow to support the highest knee during this posture. This eases aches and pains from the thigh, legs and feet.

At first there was a loud naad sound to the right back of the subtle head. There was an inverted naad sound which was emitting no sound into my dimension but I could see that it emited a sound in another dimension which I could not reach. I adhered to the loud naad sound because that was the cosmic naad as compared to the no-sound naad which was generated in my individual psyche from down in the trunk of the subtle body.

Staying pinned to this naad sound like someone whose back was glued to a wall, I still looked at the other sound which was to my left. It came through the shoulder and neck into the head.

After about fifteen minutes that naad sound disappeared. There was only the cosmic naad. I moved my attention to the frontal part of the subtle head towards the third eye. It did not reach as far as the third eye but was about two inches short of reaching it.

I kept my attention from spreading and did not allow it to make contact with the intellect organ. The idea is to use the soul force alone without assistance from the usual adjuncts which engage with it and direct it to various sensual objectives.

After thirty minutes, I crossed into an astral place and was in a miniature body, so small that an adult human form would tower over it. I passed between the legs of a woman in that dimension. Then I resumed the place where my physical body sat in the lotus posture. I got no hint of how I wandered over to that astral realm.

Hyperventilation

Hyperventilation means that there is excess oxygen in the blood stream. This may be regarded negatively by medical professionals. Do not confuse this with increased oxygen in the blood cells which float in the blood stream. Even though people confuse it, there is a difference between breath infusion and hyperventilation.

For breath infusion you have to influence the red blood cells to absorb the infused air. If the infused air just lingers in the blood stream one will not get the full result of pranayama practice.

The loose air in the plasma may cause dizziness when it enters the brain.

The blood cells float in a liquid as they are transported through the body. As a general term that fluid is called plasma or the blood stream (river).

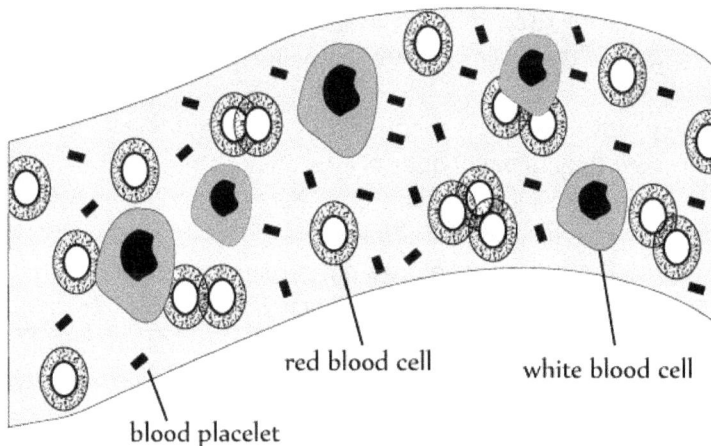

red blood cell   white blood cell

blood placelet

The Neck and Meditation

One area that should be addressed in posture and breath infusion practice is the neck, not just the spine in the neck but the fleshy parts as well. Energy should pass freely through the neck.

In the elderly years the neck is clogged. Because the veins and arteries passing through the neck become inflexible and stiff, the brain is starved for oxygen. This results in mild or severe dementia as more brain cells malfunction. However, that is the physical body.

What about the subtle form?

Does this happen in the subtle body where subtle energy cannot pass freely through the neck?

How does this affect the relationship between the kundalini at *muladhara* chakra and the consciousness in the subtle head?

Does it matter if the subtle neck is blocked and only a trickle of energy passes between the trunk and the head?

Kundalini Rise Frequency

Question:

In a pranayama session of thirty to forty-five minutes, if one can raise kundalini through the *sushumna* more than once, is that recommended? Is it better to do it just once and concentrate on infusing breath in other parts of the body, such as the thighs?

Author's Response:

Both methods have application. A yogi should raise kundalini through *sushumna* and do that more than once if one can. This clears the low vibration energy.

Once kundalini rises through *sushumna* it immediately descends to *muladhara* base chakra. As it does low vibration energy is reestablished immediately.

The elephant does like a fresh water bath but it also likes mud pools. Until one is sure the kundalini does not reestablish the dark astral energy in the *sushumna* after rising and falling, one should repeatedly rise it during the daily practice in the morning and afternoon.

For most people *sushumna* does not remain open by chanting mantras or by visualization. It remains open by blasting it with kundalini which is infused by breath energy. A time will come when this is no longer an issue. Then one can make the rest of the psyche the target and leave aside *sushumna nadi* clearing as the objective.

I worked on *sushumna nadi* cleansing from around 1973 to about 2008. That is over 30 years before I got any hint about dealing with the rest of the psyche. Yogeshwarananda and Tibeti Yogi were the ones who got me to focus on the psyche. From that one can estimate of how long it will take to clear *sushumna nadi* permanently.

Eventually when the yogi is proficient in this practice, kundalini remains hanging from the lower back brain as a short stub of light. It does this when it no longer has an interest in *muladhara* chakra, when that place no longer attracts it.

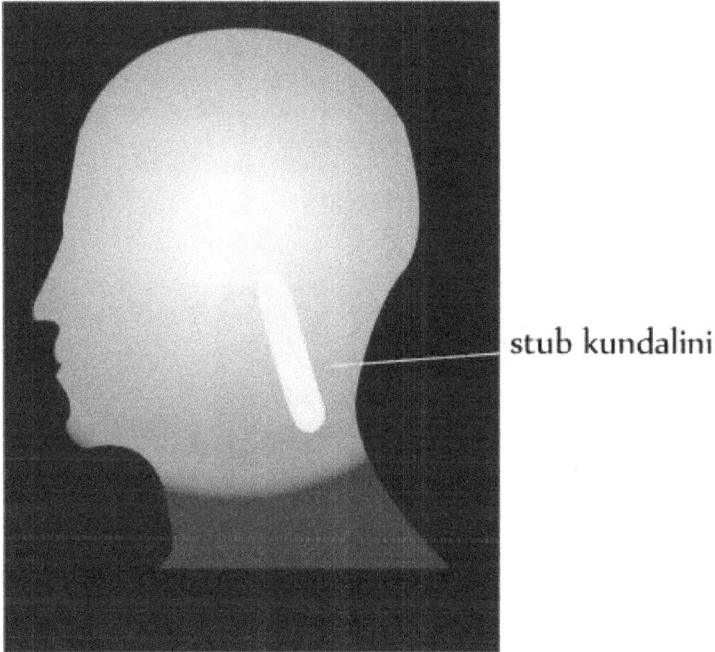

stub kundalini

Small Intestines Attack

This morning during breath infusion I did a procedure which involved energizing the small intestines in the physical body. This in turn affects the spread of energy in the same area of the subtle body which does not have intestinal tubes but which has a centralize energy distribution system.

I am not sure if every subtle body is configured with the centralize energy distribution as per the diagram below. It may be that my subtle body has this configuration presently only because of transformations which occurred during years of bhastrika pranayama practice and daily rising of kundalini.

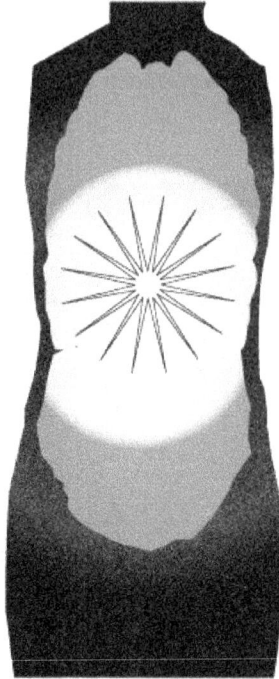

In the configuration subtle air enters a central stub tube area from the back of the body and that energy is distributed in a radial way outwards from the center into the area in which the small intestines are spread. The infusion caused by the rapid breathing, causes this area to turn white like white heat of hot metal, so that all low vibration energy is no longer present.

There is a side effect physically where one notices that digestion gets accelerated so that all matter which passes through the small intestines do so quickly and efficiently.

Breath Energy into the Intestines

There is a claim in the *Hatha Yoga Pradipika* that one should do both hatha yoga and raj yoga. At the time when that book was written hatha yoga was not asana postures. Hatha yoga was what is called kundalini yoga today which is a mixture of asanas, pranayama, mudras and verifiable mystic action.

Raj yoga then was what is termed as samyama in *Patañjali Yoga Sutras* which is a three sequential practice of linking one's attention to a higher concentration force or person, and then doing so effortlessly and then doing so continuously and spontaneously.

Preliminary to this samyama, is *pratyahar* which is sensual energy withdrawal and conservation of existential expressive powers.

Today most people who meditate have no idea about kundalini yoga. They do not practice it. They do not miss the practice of it because they do not know its benefits. There is also a disinclination to do anything but to sit and meditate.

In yoga someone may progress to an advanced stage in a huff and puff and then realizes that the progress keeps slipping, that the consolidation of practice is not happening, after even years of daily efforts.

What to do?

The student consults with a teacher and gets the bad news that some elementary process was not heeded and that unless it is completed, progress will be inconsistent.

There is also the case where the student could not locate a more advanced person or that there is such a person but he or she cannot provide a solution. Then the student is left baffled in a mire, disappointed, with no one to turn to, sad, depressed, because of not resisting negative influences.

During practice a few days ago, I realized that I neglected an elementary part of hatha yoga practice. This has to do with the intestines. These are physical for sure but their condition affects the energy in the subtle body, which in turn affects how far one will go in meditation.

In yoga there is information which is valid but which is stressed as a standard procedure when in fact it is only a routine check and nothing else. For instance, there are the stomach churns and stomach locks, the churning of the stomach so as to use the diaphragm to stimulate organs which one cannot move by any muscle in the body except for the diaphragm.

But these stomach-churning procedures are preliminary only. One should get the quantity of food and the time of eating under control. Once that is achieved, one should find a way to infuse breath energy into the intestines and the other organs in the abdomen and rib cage.

How does one get air infused into cell structures of the intestines?

Today I did the up-the-right-side, across-the-top, down-the-left-side then down-through-the-rectum breath infusion. I worked on the central-push-out breath infusion where from the center of the mass of the higher intestines (small intestines before the appendix), one infuses breath energy into the cells of that system while doing rapid breathing in bhastrika pranayama.

This is physical practice but it has a powerful effect on the psychic components of the subtle body. It enhances meditation if that is done immediately after.

Initially when one is introduced to breath infusion, one cannot direct the infused energy to go in a particular direction or to a particular location in the body. This is because the cells are non-responsive to the will power of the beginner yogi.

This is like when an infant tries to move his left foot but then the right one moves. When this happens, some children cry while some others smile. But then over time, the limbs of the body obey the infant's will power. It takes time.

As a child about 7 years of age, I once saw a boy of about fourteen years of age jump cross a concrete drain with ease. I thought that I should do it but I waited until the elder boy was out of sight. I was afraid that if I failed, he would ridicule me.

By and by, I jumped and barely made it and almost fell into the dirty ditch. I did not have the control over the limbs of my body as the elder boy did. The willpower may not always command the body to do a task. It is an achievement to command breath energy to infuse into the intestinal system.

Looking Down During Breath Infusion

Initially looking down into the body during breath infusion in various postures, does not show anything because there is no developed sensual perception. Vision in a physical body means perception of shape and color outside of the body. This is the expectation when one looks down into the body. One wants to see through the physical vision process just as one normally does.

However, if a student persists, that will change over time. The first part of that change is when the vision interest is separated from the optical nerves. Naturally, it is channeled through the physical optic system but if one keeps looking into the body during practice, the vision interest will eventually retract itself from the optic system.

When this occurs, one will find that the focus during the practice becomes sharper, as if one turns away from the frontal part of the head and faces down through the neck and trunk. Over time, one will develop various types of psychic perception.

Dealing with the Bliss Aspect

During breath infusion with an inspiration from Yogeshwarananda, I studied the mirror effect of the spiritual body into the subtle body which is used in astral adventures.

The astral body is not a spiritual form. During the use of the astral body, the limited self, uses a spherical form like a speck of starlight but this form is indistinct as far as gross and subtle consciousness are concerned. The result of this is the concept of formlessness which really means a lack of detection of the said spiritual form.

The consequence of that lack of detection is an inevitable attachment to the vision which is yielded in the physical world either though a physical system or through the dream-astral casing.

In the spiritual body every part of it is infused with bliss energy to the same absolute degree. No part is better than any other part as in the physical body where we find that the loss of a finger is of little consequence as compared to the loss of an eye.

But the physical system is manufactured by the subtle body on the basis of whatever physical species is available as provided by physical nature. In the subtle body there is super-sensitivity in one area and little sensitivity in another. The result of this is the realization of the kundalini which is energized in the *sushumna* central passage, brain or sexual organs.

It will become necessary as one advances in meditation to transfer from the subtle body into the spiritual form of the self.

Question is: How to do that?

People avoid this by just thinking that the matter may be simplified by having no body, by being bodiless and mostly by oneness or mergence into an absolute sphere or energy.

This morning on an inspiration from Yogesh, I worked on a breath infusion method which causes the chit objectively accurate aspect of consciousness to control the ananda bliss aspect of the infused compressed energy.

There are two ways for the bliss aspect to operate. One is the way where it takes over the psyche partially or completely, where the psyche is dominated by the bliss feelings. This might be understood by studying what happens in sexual climax, where the whole system is overtaken by a pleasure aspect. The entire body is invaded by it in acute feelings which are beyond compare.

When the bliss aspect takes over, the chit objective accurate consciousness surrenders its control of the psyche, gives in, and is overcome completely by the bliss force, at least until that force subsides, then the chit objective accurate consciousness gradually takes control.

In the sexual experience, something similar happens where after the pleasure runs into every part of the psyche and dominates it, gradually over time that pleasure recedes and things get back to normal. The various cells throughout the body resume their normal operations but with a depressed feeling.

To change the subtle body's kundalini configuration, one must use the chit objectively accurate consciousness to control the bliss aspect, so that this aspect is equally distributed through the subtle body and is not just in the *sushumna nadi* or head of the form. During breath infusion practice, when kundalini rises, one should take the upper hand and direct it into the polluted heavy parts of the subtle body, places where it will normally avoid. One should compress it into the extremities, so that every part is infused equally. Of course, one must gain detachment from the bliss aspect of chakras before one can sincerely do this.

Joy is distinguished from pleasure because pleasure has the extra component of passion.

Pleasure if it is hampered uses aggression to secure itself, while joy is easy-going and will not become aggressive if hampered. Bliss is not joy. Bliss is the emotional content of the divine world.

In the highest of the astral regions (heavens/celestial worlds) and in the divine world, the energy content of the psyche of the individual is bliss energy. Imagine if you were always in full sexual climax experience. Being in those higher planes, the body one acts as, has only bliss energy as the content. It has no dulling force.

Brahmachari Upgrade

Brahmachari means decreasing interest in sexual union with a corresponding increasing interest in whatever is spiritual. This is an open-ended approach to brahman, rather than the hard and fast opposing concepts of brahman as Oneness or brahman as a Supreme Person.

The two groups fight it out; the Advaita Vedantists and the Dvaita Bhaktas. One claims that the Supreme is One (advaita). The other says that the Supreme is a Person Deity (adipurusha). For this statement we leave the two groups aside and forge ahead on our own. What is brahman? We will meet it if we forge ahead.

The main attraction in physical existence is sexual union. Inevitably it is reduced to that. Nature is so designed that there is no choice in this matter, as many of the sannyasis sex-renunciants of both the Advaitists and Dvaitists proved with their deviations. Since this is a fact, we begin this quest by moving away from sexual union.

This does not mean that there is no spiritual energy in sexual union. There is but it is the kind of spiritual energy which causes one to resume a life form in the physical world repeatedly. That is undesirable. If I want to complete the research into *brahma (athato brahma jijnasa),* it is necessary to travel away from the direction of sexual union.

Sometimes it happens that when an ascetic tries to get away from sexual union, the reverse takes place where he comes to it with a greater impetus, such that his renunciant vows, his reputation as a spiritual leader, everything, is destroyed in one flash descent back to sexual union. Sex union is so natural that it is laughable when someone says that he is a sannyasi. People grin behind his back, thinking,

"This monk is a fool. We will laugh when he breaches the vows."

The method we will discuss is not the sannyasi ceremonial renunciation vow but rather studying the psyche as it is and finding is a way to redesign it. Psyche in this usage means the subtle body, which means an existential container which has for its contents the psychological energies and components which make up what we call the person.

Since the lifeForce wields the most control over what the subtle body does we should research its design and operation. This life force, has its default location at the base of the spinal column, the sacrum-coccyx area. This design is nature's way but it is unacceptable because it favors the self being irresistibly attached to physical existence.

However, this realization does nothing to change the format. It remains in place even if one realizes that it works against one's ultimate interest. One finds that even after years of posture and breath infusion practice, plus years of meditation, still the psyche retains its creature concerns which oppose travel in the direction of brahman exclusive spiritual existence. There still remains that attraction to sexual union even after years of practice. Why is it that the system cannot be redesigned?

The first thing one should do is to focus on the psychic system which operates sexual attraction. That is the kundalini. Is it possible to redesign or even to eliminate it? At least one should change the tendencies of the system, otherwise what is the use of yoga, meditation or whatever spiritual practice one does?

This morning based on an energy which was left in my psyche by Yogesh, I saw something rather strange which was that the kundalini can be made to abandon *muladhara* base chakra. It can come above the small of the back and establish that as its base.

If that happens, kundalini will no longer use *muladhara* as its anchor. It will instead take a position above the small of the back?

The small of the back is the place on the spine right behind the navel. If one bends backward the back will curve the most at that place. This is the place which acts as a constriction point to hold energy in the lower trunk of the body and to stop energy from going any higher.

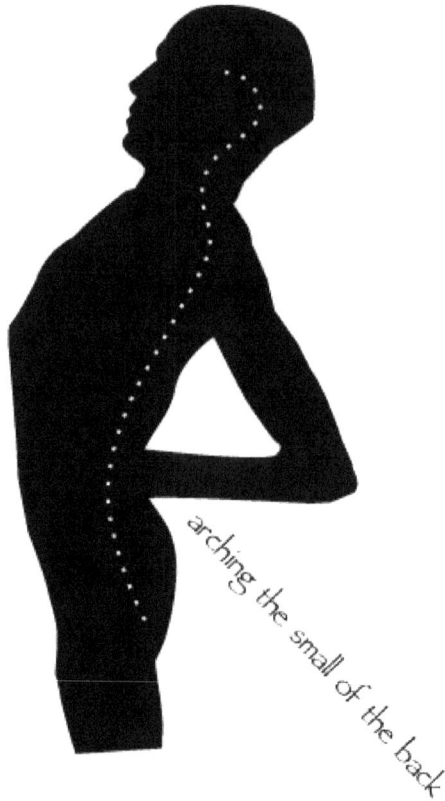

arching the small of the back

To have kundalini ascend permanently and to abandon its primeval cove is a fantastic accomplishment for any yogi. It would mean that kundalini's attitude changes. It would mean that the strong attraction to sexual union would decrease from the individual's psyche. This is possible after years and years of practice, raising kundalini at least once per day, guiding kundalini through the spine into the head away from its base hang-out. But wait! Be sure that kundalini does this new configuration permanently since there is every chance it may return to its old habits. If it did it before, it can do it again. Do not be overconfident.

Bliss Energy / Pranayama Yoga

When pranayama practice begins in earnest, there arises in the psyche a bliss force. This involves the kundalini lifeForce but it also does not involve that. When kundalini is involved, the kundalini controls the flow of and direction of the bliss force, with the coreSelf as a bystander which may perceive the bliss force and experience it depending on where that force travels in the psyche.

In the beginning stages of pranayama practice, the student may be hustling to accumulate the breath energy but once he or she can do that, it is a matter of targeting *muladhara* base chakra so that the energy generated during the breathing session, fuses into the kundalini and causes its arousal up the spine. That is the sum and substance of elementary kundalini yoga.

Doing this once, or doing this once in a while, does not cause a deep change in the psyche. The reason is that as soon as kundalini descends again and takes its default position at the base chakra, the psyche reconfigures as before.

The only way to change the configuration of the psyche is to raise kundalini on a daily basis and that can only be done deliberately and for sure by pranayama practice.

Which pranayama?

That depends on the student. I feel that the student should try out several pranayama practices, until one is found which reliably causes kundalini to be aroused.

If the student can raise kundalini at least once per day, for some time, for years even, then eventually the *sushumna* central passage will remain free of obstructions, which means that kundalini will radiate its energy into the head continuously.

When kundalini is aroused by a pranayama practice, it does so with a gushing force. If one does this daily for some time, for years even, kundalini will continue ascending to the head by radiating its energy through *sushumna nadi* even after one finishes a daily session.

Once the student masters kundalini to the degree that the *sushumna* passage remains open, allowing kundalini's energy to radiate through it even after a breath infusion session, the student can study how the accumulated subtle energy causes the bliss force to arise.

At first a student has this idea that the bliss force is created by kundalini or that the bliss force is kundalini itself. This is similar to sex experience where after a first sexual intercourse experience, an individual gets this idea that the intercourse is the cause of sexual ecstasy. Since nature tied the ecstasy experience with the sexual sharing experience, one naturally concludes that sex sharing is an ecstasy in itself.

This nature-endowed conclusion suffocates a student yogi so that he/she does not advance beyond the stage of just raising kundalini through the spine into the brain. The student becomes obsessed with this just as after having sex experience, one cannot forget it and craves.

A student should move beyond the practice of merely raising kundalini daily. That practice should continue but with a difference in the motivation for doing it, with increased ability to hold kundalini and direct it instead of being directed by it to enjoy the bliss aspect. A student yogi should move from the enjoyer-consumer stage to the detached directive stage in relation to kundalini and any bliss aspect which is generated as a result of an effective breath infusion practice.

Here are three techniques for dealing with accumulated compressed infused energy which results from an effective pranayama practice:

- Infuse breath energy, but cause it to accumulate and force it through the frontal navel area, pass the groin area to the *muladhara* base chakra area.
- Infuse breath energy but cause it to accumulate wherever it will. Then push out this compressed energy through any other areas of the psyche. Show no special interest in making the energy fuse into kundalini.
- Infuse breath energy but cause it to accumulate wherever it will. Then when the bliss aspect begins, note where it is while you keep doing the breath infusion. When you stop the breathing, squeeze the accumulated energy inwards upon itself until it shatters into a million tiny pixels and then either explodes outwards and implodes upon itself even more.

Kundalini/Intellect – Alliance Broken

Practice this morning was great. During the breath infusion session everything went well with me complying with stipulations of yoga gurus.

I work on the aspect of forcing the infused energy to remain below the neck, directing it to seek out any heavy astral energy and blast that out. Previously, Yogesh and Pranayogi questioned as to why the kundalini when it is aroused, goes upwards through the spine and then into the head. Why does it not go downwards into the thighs, legs and feet? During practice this morning, I began to formulate an answer on the basis of some discoveries and observations.

The main reason is the kundalini is in alliance with the intellect. These adjuncts work in cooperation, with the kundalini being the predominant influence. In fact, the five sensual orbs even though these are linked to the intellect, are more attached to the kundalini than they are to the intellect? Due to this powerful attraction which is similar to sexual attraction, kundalini goes upwards to meet the intellect.

In sexual climax, if one could get some objectivity during those feelings, one may notice that the intellect abandons it default location in the head of the subtle body. It goes down to meet kundalini when kundalini arcs to the sexual organ chakra. Then there is a feeling of tremendous pleasure.

If the kundalini does not feel attracted to the sexual organ chakra, and if it is aroused, it will ascend to the head of the subtle body to meet its partner which is the intellect.

A yogi must break this alliance between the two adjuncts. When this happens, the kundalini will fire into the subtle body, even down through the thighs, legs and feet. Instead of fusing itself into the intellect when it is aroused into the brain, kundalini will locate the heavy astral energy in the psyche, and demolish it.

Kundalini is the lifeForce system in the psyche. Intellect is the psychic organ which does the analytical operations. It also monitors the five senses but these senses readily accept the influence of the kundalini and serve it directly.

Kundalini is the survival response system in the body. It has to get information from outside the body to properly calculate what it should do to protect the form, regarding how it should move the body, where it should locate the body, and how it should protect from biological, environmental and emotional danger.

For information about what happens inside the body, the kundalini uses the network of nerves which run in every part of the body, but for knowledge about what happens outside of the body, it relies on the news which it gets from the senses. If for instance, I use a body which is blind, then the kundalini will lack visual information. It will then cause the other senses, like the touch sense and the hearing sense, to be more acute. In addition, it will influence other bodies to suppliment information. For instance, you may see a blind man with a seeing-eye dog. In that case because the man's body is blind, the kundalini takes assistance from the visual sense of the dog. The dog is not the man, and still the eyes of the dog are made to serve the kundalini in the man's body by providing information about the visual scenes in the environment.

The design of the psyche is such that the intellect produces the five senses as its offshoot agents. The intellect divests some of its power into each of these senses so that they can discriminate before reporting whatever information they collect. Because the kundalini provides some power to operate the senses, it brings these senses under its influence. In that way the hold of the intellect over the senses is compromised.

You may understand this in the following example:

An intelligent man who was bed ridden had five daughters who were obedient to him. They had not met any other person. They lived in a remote forest with the father. They never knew the mother because she died in their infancy.

One daughter was named Smellie. She informed the father of odors. One other daughter was named Tastie. She gave details of various taste. One other daughter was named Touchie. She told the father about surfaces. Yet, another daughter was Lookie. She described shapes and colors. The last of these daughters was Listenie. She informed about sounds in the environment.

Once an attractive woman came to that part of the forest. Seeing the five women and their intelligent but crippled father, the attractive woman made a proposal to the five girls. She said this:

"Since the old man lost his wife early on, and since he is crippled, the six of us should live in harmony. I can provide leadership just as your mother would have. You girls are young. You do not know the ways of the forest. Suppose a huge serpent or even a jaguar attacks what could the old man do to protect either of you? He is crippled and cannot move from the bed.

As an experienced woman I could be of use to you. You could be useful to me. Let us join as a family.

After hearing the proposal, the five girls and their father agreed. Thereafter they lived together as a family with inter-related relationships but eventually the woman took control of the everyone, the five girls and even the father. In fact, as it worked out the man's analytical intelligence became subordinate to the woman and so did the sensual expertise of the daughters. The woman represents the kundalini. The man represents the intellect. The daughters represent the five senses.

Inner Focus Complete

Today breath infusion resulted in several charges, which when compressed resulted in bliss bricks, which when compressed resulted in splitting into tiny bliss pixels, which when compressed converted into spiritual knowing energy.

Bliss bricks are when there is an infusion of energy in a particular part of the subtle body. It molds into the form of a brick like a chunk of granite rock which is transparent and iridescent. One sees this as one looks down in the body during breath infusion practice.

It pays to be completely blindfolded during practice, otherwise due to the nature of the senses, especially the eyes, one's attention lingers outside the psyche. Because it damages the efficiency of the inner focus, that deters the rate of progress.

When the eyes are blindfolded, the inner focus is more intense. One can go on practicing yoga for millions of years, if one does not increase the inner focus and stop the tendency for the mind to wander outside the psyche, one will never reach an advanced stage. Somehow by some means, one should accomplish the complete inner focus because that is what it means to fulfill the fifth stage of ashtanga yoga which is *pratyahar* sensual energy withdrawal.

The kundalini is within the psyche but since it does not have a way to tell what happens outside the psyche, it urges the senses to get that information. During breath infusion and also during meditation practice, one should stop the kundalini from influencing the senses, so that the urge for seeing outside the subtle body is suspended.

There was a special shock effect in the arms, forearms and fingers, which is an area that is even harder to reach than the thighs, legs and feet.

Satya does mean truth but in the *Yoga Sutras* it means realism. Truth or honesty has to do with personal arrogance and has no place in higher yoga where one realizes that circumstantial untruth is a necessity in this social world.

Focus on realism, which means first of all to have insight into what occurs and secondly to plan in a way which is consistent with providence. Realism means knowing what will be true by the laws of nature and working as best as one can with that. Even though in elementary religion it is a great principle, personal honesty has no meaning in higher yoga.

Nature is not concerned with anyone's honesty. It may not reward someone in a good way for being honest. On occasion, for survival one must be dishonest.

Yama moral restraints and niyama approved behaviors are the bulwark of fundamentalist religion. If that is removed from a religion, it is finished. The two systems are the way to keep a religion intact. Still, yoga is not

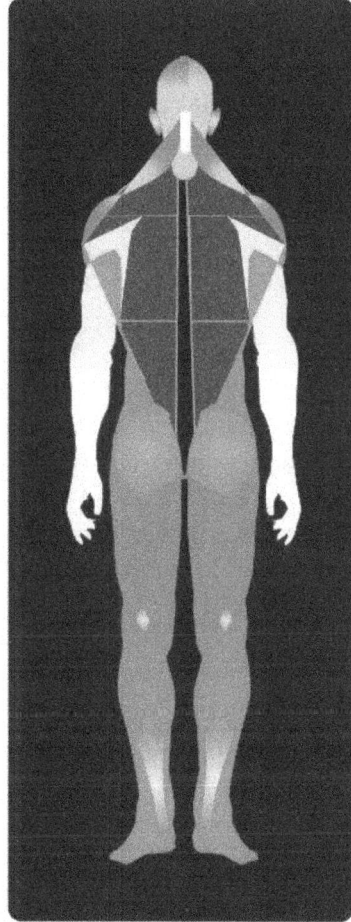

religion. Monitoring external behavior has nothing to do with higher yoga but it is everything in the beginning stages. Even in an ashram one is confronted with restrictions and permissions.

In higher yoga this is tackled from the inside, from the perspective of the urge which drive us to participate, which comes from the kundalini. From fundamentalist religions we get the clue of how to keep social order externally by forcing the psyche to strive for social approval. But when we get to a higher stage, we realize that external pressure was superficial. It only suppressed the urges for a time, while in fact they accumulated and did, or will in time, commandeer the psyche and cause it to do the prohibited acts while neglecting the recommendations.

It is then that a yogi thinks like this:

Since that is the case that when I monitor external behavior, the internal urges against that increase, the solution is to work with the inner energies directly. The student traces the need for these behaviors to the kundalini. But there arises a problem where it is a question of:

How can I, a wimp in the psyche, get a grasp on kundalini?

Special Flash Tunnel

Breath infusion practice this morning was efficient with focus into the trunk of the subtle body, into the thighs, knees and feet. There were several releases of charged energy in various parts of the shoulder and arms. Because of a reduction in the heavy astral energy, the charged force was electrified from the very beginning, so that I was alert from the moment I started the breathing. It threw darts, bundles and shimmers of bliss force which I compressed.

I did not see my astral gurus. I have not seen them for some days but there was a flash passage which linked to Yogesh. This is when during practice, one suddenly sees the face of the yoga guru way in the distance through a flash tunnel.

When this occurs during practice, it means that one reached a stage of infusement which connected with the level of existence the yoga guru resides in at that moment. This may also be taken to mean that one has the guru's approval.

During this practice, near the end of the session, there was a spike of energy in the center of the subtle body, from the neck down. This was in the center of the trunk. It was not the *sushumna nadi* central passage. When I noticed it, I focused on infusing more energy into it. I did so until it appeared to be like a white-hot piece of metal. It flashed and exploded through the subtle body, shattering as tiny chunks of bliss force.

After this I worked on infusing energy into various parts of the head because I remembered an instruction from Yogesh about doing at least a hundred numerical counts while infusing into the head of the subtle form, but doing this after the trunk of the form had no heavy astral energy.

Immediately after the session, I sat to meditate, assuming a tight reverse lotus, using a pillow to keep the lumbar area braced against a wall, and another pillow to support the knee which was uppermost.

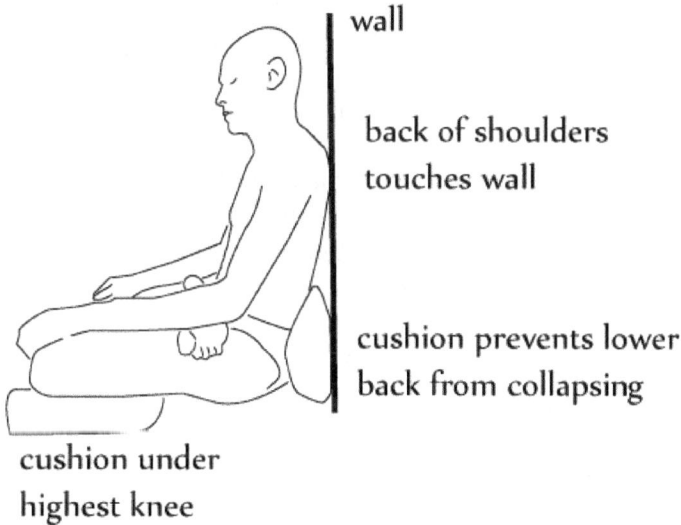

wall

back of shoulders touches wall

cushion prevents lower back from collapsing

cushion under highest knee

I found myself in a large chamber as if the inside of the subtle body was a tank. I was in the back corner of the tank looking down and forward. The intellect organ was present in the frontal part of the tank but it displayed nothing. It drifted about silently like a puff of cotton floating in the wind. Naad sound was present.

Infusing the Thighs

There are no locks when one infuses the thighs with breath energy. It is either a push down, pull up or a spread-out mystic action, where, as the yogi does the infusion, his attention is in the thigh(s) either pulling energy out, pushing energy in or spreading energy out.

If one finds that one has to apply locks, it means that one did not infuse enough energy into the trunk of the subtle body. That should be done thoroughly.

There are also special techniques relating to breaking the relationship between the thighs and the sexual organ. As it is genetically, by nature's grace, the thighs worship the sexual organs and serve as their most dutiful servants. A yogi should shatter this relationship, so that the thighs no longer dedicate their most prized production, which is bone marrow, to the genitals.

Of course, if one is to beget children, this function of the thighs is appropriate otherwise it is not required. The energy in the thighs must be pulled up and out through the trunk of the body. When that is done for some time, one can tackle the legs and feet.

Rebellious Attitude of Intellect Organ

Breath infusion in the lower part of the trunk of the body and in the thighs, legs and feet cause the intellect to totally abandon its thought-idea-image charade of activities, thus freeing the mind for real meditation in terms of *dhyana* effortless focus into higher planes of existence and *samadhi* lengthy stay in those higher realms.

It causes the attitude of the intellect to abandon its theatrical outlay which involved victimizing the coreSelf which for the most part had no authority on the lower planes of existence. Instead of staying on the lower levels and fighting with the mind, why not do the breath infusion practice, and jump to higher planets where the losing battle between the coreSelf and the psychic adjuncts do not take place.

Looking at this in detail, I found that the intellect totally abandons its rebellious attitude of conspiring with the kundalini energy to perpetrate acts of abandon for which the coreSelf is held responsible. Instead of hunting for enjoyment within and without the psyche, the intellect, once the lower parts of the subtle body are cleared of heavy astral force, wanders freely in the psyche attaching itself to naad sound and locating transcendental energy which is present. It does so without the compulsive attitude which it is infected with by association with a low-grade lust-impacted kundalini.

In this state, being freed from the compulsion of memories and images created by the intellect, the core jumps for joy, like a baboon which somehow escaped after its head was clamped in the mouth of lion.

Index

About the Author

Michael Beloved (Yogi *Madhvāchārya*) took his current body in 1951 in Guyana. In 1965, while living in Trinidad, he instinctively began doing yoga postures and tried to make sense of the supernatural side of life.

Later in 1970, in the Philippines, he approached a Martial Arts Master named Arthur Beverford. He explained to the teacher that he was seeking a yoga instructor. Mr. Beverford identified himself as an advanced disciple of *Śrī* Rishi Singh Gherwal, an Ashtanga Yoga master.

Beverford taught the traditional Ashtanga Yoga with stress on postures, attentive breathing and brow chakra centering meditation. In 1972, Michael entered the Denver, Colorado Ashram of *kundalini* yoga Master *Śrī* Harbhajan Singh. There he took instruction in bhastrika pranayama and its application to yoga postures. He was supervised mostly by Yogi Bhajan's disciple named Prem Kaur.

In 1979 Michael formally entered the disciplic succession of the Brahmā - Madhava-Gaudiya Sampradaya through *Swāmī* Kirtanananda, who was a prominent sannyasi disciple of the Great Vaishnava Authority *Śrī Swāmī* Bhaktivedanta Prabhupada, the exponent of devotion to Sri Krishna.

However, yoga has a mystic side to it, thus Michael took training and teaching empowerment from several spiritual masters of different aspects of spiritual development. This is consistent with *Śrī* Krishna's advice to Arjuna in the *Bhagavad Gītā*:

Most of the instructions Michael received were given in the astral world. On that side of existence, his most prominent teachers were *Śrī Swāmī* Shivananda of Rishikesh, Yogiraj *Swāmī* Vishnudevananda, *Śrī Bābāji Mahasaya* - the master of the masters of *Kriyā* Yoga, *Śrīla* Yogeshwarananda of Gangotri - the master of the masters of *Rāj* Yoga (spiritual clarity), and Siddha *Swāmī* Nityananda the Brahmā Yoga authority.

The course for kundalini yoga using pranayama breath-infusion was detailed by Michael in the book *Kundalini Hatha Yoga Pradipika*. This current book was composed from meditation and breath-infusion notes which were originally shared in staple bound booklets as Yoga Journals.

Michael's preliminary books relating to this topic are *Meditation Pictorial*, *Meditation Expertise*, and *Meditation ~ Sense Faculty* (co-author). Every technique (kriya) mentioned was tested by him during pranayama breath-infusion and *samyama* deep meditation practice.

This is a result of over forty years of meditation practice with astute subtle observations intending to share the methods and experiences. The information is published freely with no intention of forming an institution or hogtying anyone as a disciple.

Publications

English Series

Bhagavad Gita English

Anu Gita English

Markandeya Samasya English

Yoga Sutras English

Hatha Yoga Pradipika English

Uddhava Gita English

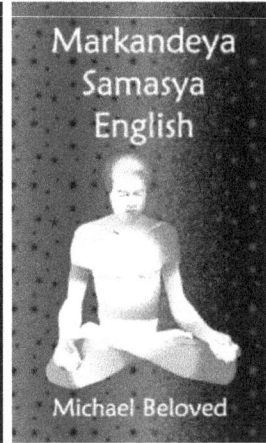

Yoga Sūtras English

Michael Beloved

Haṭha Yoga Pradīpikā English

Michael Beloved

Uddhava Gītā English

Michael Beloved / Madhvāchārya dās

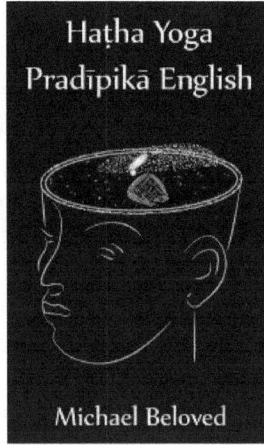

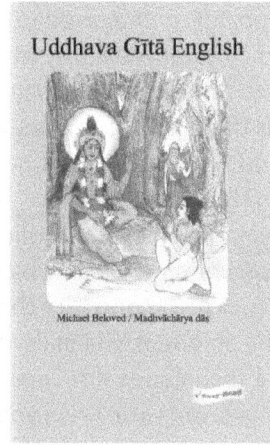

These are in 21st Century English, very precise and exacting. Many Sanskrit words which were considered untranslatable into a Western language are rendered in precise, expressive and modern English.

Three of these books are instructions from Krishna. **In Bhagavad Gita English** and **Anu Gita English**, the instructions were for Arjuna. In the **Uddhava Gita English,** it was for Uddhava. Bhagavad Gita and Anu Gita are extracted from the Mahabharata. Uddhava Gita was extracted from the 11th Canto of the Srimad Bhagavatam (Bhagavata Purana). One of these books, the **Markandeya Samasya English** is about Krishna, as described by Yogi Markandeya, who survived the cosmic collapse and reached a divine child in whose transcendental body, the collapsed world was existing.

Two of this series are the syllabus about yoga practice. The Yoga Sutras of Patañjali is elaboration about ashtanga yoga. Hatha Yoga Pradipika English, is the detailed information about asana postures, pranayama breath-infusion, energy compression, naad sound resonance and advanced meditation. The Sanskrit author is Swatmarama Mahayogin.

My suggestion is that you read **Bhagavad Gita English**, the **Anu Gita English, the Markandeya Samasya English,** the **Yoga Sutras English,** the **Hatha Yoga Pradipika** and lastly the **Uddhava Gita English**, which is complicated and detailed.

For each of these books we have at least one commentary, which is published separately. Thus one's particular interest can be researched further in the commentaries.

The smallest of these commentaries and perhaps the simplest is the one for the Anu Gita. We published its commentary as the Anu Gita Explained. The Bhagavad Gita explanations were published in three distinct targeted commentaries. The first is Bhagavad Gita Explained, which sheds lights on how people in the time of Krishna and Arjuna regarded the information and applied it. Bhagavad Gita is an exposition of the application of yoga practice to cultural activities, which is known in the Sanskrit language as karma yoga.

Interestingly, Bhagavad Gita was spoken on a battlefield just before one of the greatest battles in the ancient world. A warrior, Arjuna, lost his wits and had no idea that he could apply his training in yoga to political dealings. Krishna, his charioteer, lectured on the spur of the moment to give Arjuna the skill of using yoga proficiency in cultural dealings including how to deal with corrupt officials on a battlefield.

The second Gita commentary is the Kriya Yoga Bhagavad Gita. This clears the air about Krishna's information on the science of kriya yoga, showing that its techniques are clearly described for anyone who takes the time to read Bhagavad Gita. Kriya yoga concerns the battlefield which is the psyche of the living being. The internal war and the mental and emotional forces which are hostile to self-realization are dealt with in the kriya yoga practice.

The third commentary is the Brahma Yoga Bhagavad Gita. This shows what Krishna had to say outright and what he hinted about which concerns the brahma yoga practice, a mystic process for those who mastered kriya yoga.

There is one commentary for the **Markandeya Samasya English**. The title of that publication is Krishna Cosmic Body.

There are two commentaries to the Yoga Sutras. One is the Yoga Sutras of Patañjali and the other is the Meditation Expertise. These give detailed explanations of ashtanga Yoga.

The commentary of Hatha Yoga Pradipika is titled Kundalini Hatha Yoga Pradipika.

For the Uddhava Gita, we published the Uddhava Gita Explained. This is a large book and requires concentration and study for integration of the information. Of the books which deal with transcendental topics, my opinion is that the discourse between Krishna and Uddhava has the complete information about the realities in existence. This book is the one which removes massive existential ignorance.

Meditation Series

Meditation Pictorial

Meditation Expertise

CoreSelf Discovery

Meditation Sense Faculty

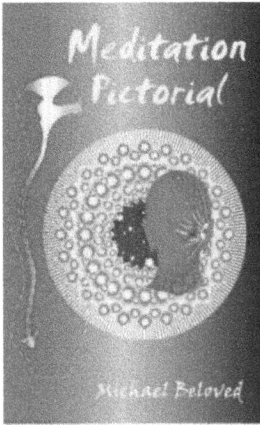

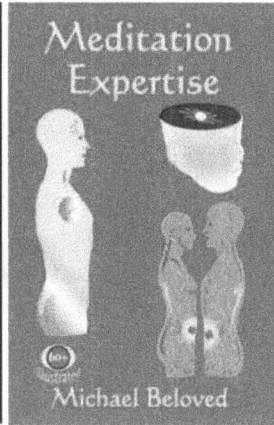

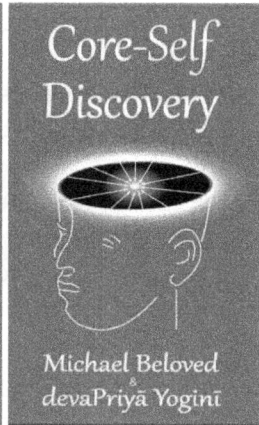

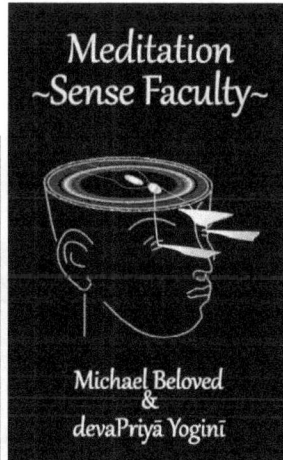

The specialty of these books is the mind diagrams which profusely illustrate what is written. This shows exactly what one has to do mentally to develop and then sustain a meditation practice.

In the **Meditation Pictorial**, one is shown how to develop psychic insight, a feature without which meditation is imagination and visualization, without any mystic experience per se.

In the **Meditation Expertise**, one is shown how to corral one's practice to bring it in line with the classic syllabus of yoga which Patañjali lays out as the ashtanga yoga eight-staged practice.

In **CoreSelf Discovery**, (co-authored with *devaPriya Yogini*) one is taken though the course of *pratyahar* sensual energy withdrawal which is the 5th stage of yoga in the Patañjali ashtanga eight-process complete system of yoga practice. These events lead to the discovery of a coreSelf which is surrounded by psychic organs in the head of the subtle body. This product has a DVD component.

Meditation ~ Sense Faculty (co-authored with *devaPriya Yogini*) is a detailed tutorial with profuse diagrams showing what actions to take in the subtle body to investigate the senses faculties. The meditator must first establish the location and function of the observing self. That self must be screened from the thoughts and ideas which usually hypnotize it.

These books are profusely illustrated with mind diagrams showing the components of psychic consciousness and the inner design of the subtle body.

Explained Series

Bhagavad Gita Explained

Uddhava Gita Explained

Anu Gita Explained

The specialty of these books is that they are free of missionary intentions, cult tactics and philosophical distortion. Instead of using these books to add credence to a philosophy, meditation process, belief or plea for followers, I spread the information out so that a reader can look through this literature and freely take or leave anything as desired.

When Krishna stressed himself as God, I stated that. When Krishna laid no claims for supremacy, I showed that. The reader is left to form an independent opinion about the validity of the information and the credibility of Krishna.

There is a difference in the discourse with Arjuna in the Bhagavad Gita and the one with Uddhava in the Uddhava Gita. In fact, these two books may appear to contradict each other. In the Bhagavad Gita, Krishna pressured Arjuna to complete social duties. In the Uddhava Gita, Krishna insisted that Uddhava should abandon the same.

The Anu Gita is not as popular as the Bhagavad Gita but it is the conclusion of that text. Anu means what is to follow, what proceeds. In this discourse, an anxious Arjuna request that Krishna should repeat the Bhagavad Gita and again show His supernatural and divine forms.

However, Krishna refuses to do so and chastises Arjuna for being a disappointment in forgetting what was revealed. Krishna then cited a celestial yogi, a near-perfected being, who explained the process of transmigration in vivid detail.

Commentaries

Yoga Sutras of Patañjali

Meditation Expertise

Krishna Cosmic Body

Anu Gita Explained

Bhagavad Gita Explained

Kriya Yoga Bhagavad Gita

Brahma Yoga Bhagavad Gita

Uddhava Gita Explained

Kundalini Hatha Yoga Pradipika

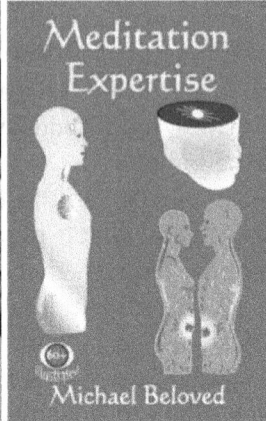

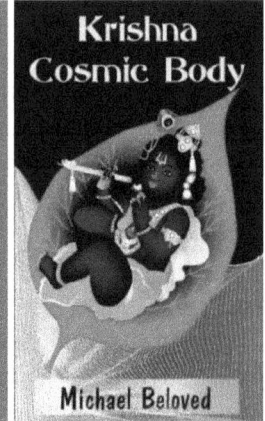

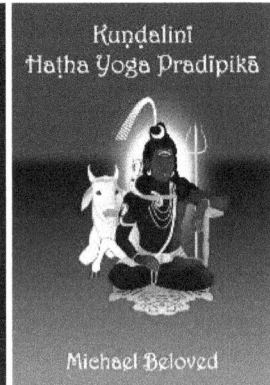

Yoga Sutras of Patañjali is the globally acclaimed text book of yoga. This has detailed expositions of yoga techniques. Many kriya techniques are vividly described in the commentary.

Meditation Expertise is an analysis and application of the Yoga Sutras. This book is loaded with illustrations and has detailed explanations of secretive advanced meditation techniques which are called kriyas in the Sanskrit language.

Krishna Cosmic Body is a narrative commentary on the Markandeya Samasya portion of the Aranyaka Parva of the Mahabharata. This is the detailed description of the dissolution of the world, as experienced by the great yogin Markandeya who transcended the cosmic deity, Brahma, and reached Brahma's source who is the divine infant, Krishna.

Anu Gita Explained is a detailed explanation of how we endure many material bodies in the course of transmigrating through various life-forms. This is a discourse between Krishna and Arjuna. Arjuna requested of Krishna a display of the Universal Form and a repeat narration of the Bhagavad Gita but Krishna declined and explained what a siddha perfected being told the Yadu family about the sequence of existences one endures and the systematic flow of those lives at the convenience of material nature.

Bhagavad Gita Explained shows what was said in the Gita without religious overtones and sectarian biases.

Kriya Yoga Bhagavad Gita shows the instructions for those who are doing kriya yoga.

Brahma Yoga Bhagavad Gita shows the instructions for those who are doing brahma yoga.

Uddhava Gita Explained shows the instructions to Uddhava which are more advanced than the ones given to Arjuna.

Bhagavad Gita is an instruction for applying the expertise of yoga in the cultural field. This is why the process taught to Arjuna is called karma yoga which means karma + yoga or cultural activities done with yogic insight.

Uddhava Gita is an instruction for apply the expertise of yoga to attaining spiritual status. This is why it explains jnana yoga and bhakti yoga in detail. Jnana yoga is using mystic skill for knowing the spiritual part of existence. Bhakti yoga is for developing affectionate relationships with divine beings.

Karma yoga is for negotiating the social concerns in the material world. It is inferior to bhakti yoga which concerns negotiating the social concerns in the spiritual world.

This world has a social environment. The spiritual world has one too.

Currently, Uddhava Gita is the most advanced and informative spiritual book on the planet. There is nothing anywhere which is superior to it or which goes into so much detail as it. It verified that historically Krishna is the most advanced human being to ever have left literary instructions on this planet.

Even Patañjali Yoga Sutras which I translated and gave an application for in my book, **Meditation Expertise**, does not go as far as the Uddhava Gita.

Some of the information of these two books is identical but while the Yoga Sutras are concerned with the personal spiritual emancipation (kaivalyam) of the individual spirits, the Uddhava Gita explains that and also explains the situations in the spiritual universes.

Bhagavad Gita is from the *Mahabharata* which is the history of the Pandavas. Arjuna, the student of the Gita, is one of the Pandavas brothers. He was in a social hassle and did not know how to apply yoga expertise to solve it. On the battlefield, Krishna gave him a crash-course on yogic social interactions.

Uddhava Gita is from the *Srimad Bhagavatam (Bhagavata Purana)*, which is a history of the incarnations of Krishna. Uddhava was a relative of Krishna. He was concerned about the situation of the deaths of many of his relatives but Krishna diverted Uddhava's attention to the practice of yoga for the purpose of successfully migrating to the spiritual environment.

Kundalini Hatha Yoga Pradipika is the commentary for the Hatha Yoga Pradipika of Swatmarama Mahayogin. This is the detailed process about asana posture, pranayama breath-infusion, complex compressions of energy, naad sound resonance intonement and advanced meditation practice.

This is the singular book with all the techniques of how to reform and redesign the subtle body so that it does not have the tendency for physical life forms and for it to attain the status of a siddha.

These books are based on the author's experiences in meditation, yoga practice and participation in spiritual groups:

Specialty

Spiritual Master

sex you!

Sleep Paralysis

Astral Projection

Masturbation Psychic Details

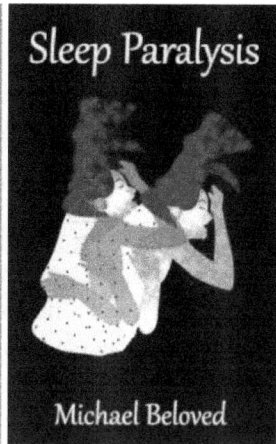

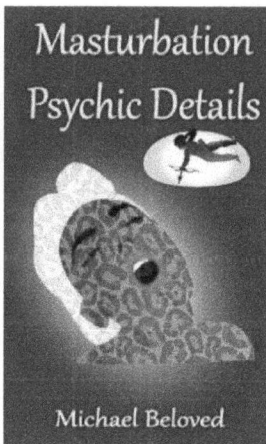

In **Spiritual Master**, Michael draws from experience with gurus or with their senior students. His contact with astral gurus is rated. He walks you through the avenue of gurus showing what you should do and what you should not do, so as to gain proficiency in whatever area of spirituality the guru has proficiency.

sex you! is a masterpiece about the adventures of an individual spirit's passage through the parents' psyches. The conversion of a departed soul into a sexual urge is described. The transit from the afterlife to residency in the emotions of the parents is detailed. This is about sex and you. Learn about how much of you comprises the romantic energy of one's would-be parents!

Sleep Paralysis clears misconceptions so that one can see what sleep paralysis is and what frightening astral experience occurs while the paralysis is being experienced. This disempowerment has great value in giving you confidence that you can and do exist even if one is unable to operate the physical body. The implication is that one can exist apart from and will survive the loss of the material form.

Astral Projection details experiences Michael had even in childhood, where he assumed incorrectly that everyone was astrally conversant. He discusses the lifeForce psychic mechanism which operates the sleep-wake cycle of the physical form, and which budgets energy into the separated astral form which determines if the individual will have dream recall or no objective awareness during the projections. Astral travel happens on every occasion when the physical body sleeps. What is missing in awareness is the observer status while the astral body is separated.

Masturbation Psychic Details is a surprise presentation which relates what happens on the psychic plane during a masturbation event. This does not tackle moral issues or even addictions but shows the involvement of memory and the sure but hidden subconscious mind which operates many features of the psyche irrespective of the desire or approval of the self-conscious personality.

inVision Series

Yoga inVision 1

Yoga inVision 2

Yoga inVision 3

Yoga inVision 4

Yoga inVision 5

Yoga inVision 6

Yoga inVision 7

Yoga inVision 8

Yoga inVision 9

Yoga inVision 1 | Yoga inVision 2 | Yoga inVision 3
Michael Beloved | Michael Beloved | Michael Beloved

Yoga inVision 4 | Yoga inVision 5 | Yoga inVision 6
Michael Beloved | Michael Beloved | Michael Beloved

Yoga inVision 7 | Yoga inVision 8 | Yoga inVision 9
Michael Beloved | Michael Beloved | Michael Beloved

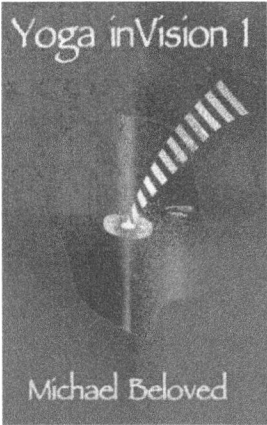

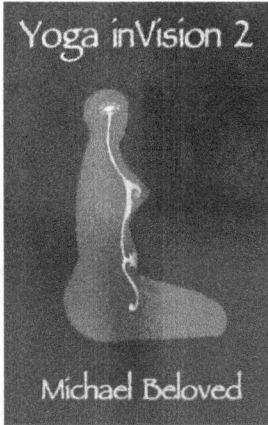

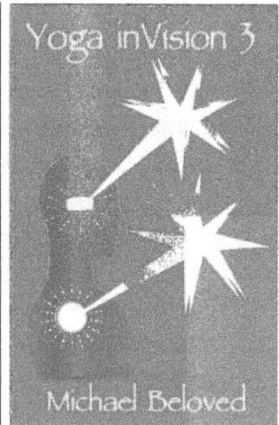

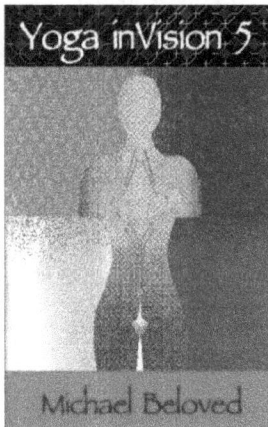

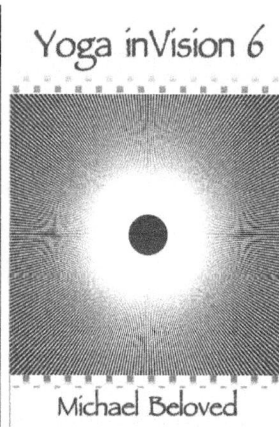

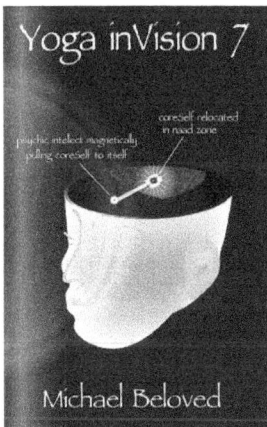

Yoga inVision 1, the first in this series, describes the breath-infusion and meditation practices during the years of 1998 and 1999. There are unique, once in a lifetime as well as recurring insights which are elaborated. inFocus during breath-infusion and the meditation which follows is an adventure for any yogi. This gives what happened to this particular ascetic.

Yoga inVision 2 reports on the author's experiences from 1999 to 2001. Each day the experience is unique, illustrating the vibrancy of practice. Many rare once-in-a-lifetime perceptions are described.

Yoga inVision 3 reports on the author's experiences from 2001 to 2003.
Yoga inVision 4 reports on the author's experiences from 2006 to 2009.
Yoga inVision 5 reports on the author's experiences from 2006 to 2008.
Yoga inVision 6 reports on the author's experiences in 2010.
Yoga inVision 7 reports on the author's experiences in 2011.
Yoga inVision 8 reports on the author's experiences in 2011.
Yoga inVision 9 reports on the author's experiences in 2012.

Online Resources

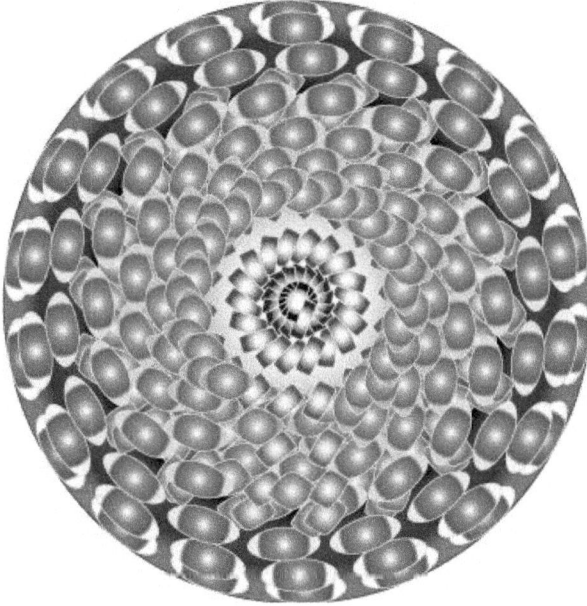

Email: michaelbelovedbooks@gmail.com
axisnexus@gmail.com

Website: michaelbeloved.com

Forum: inselfyoga.com

Posters: zazzle.com/inself